INSIGHT GUIDES *EATING IN*
LONDON

**Restaurants
Bars, Pubs
and Cafés**

ABOUT THIS BOOK

With somewhere in the region of 12,000 restaurants, London really spoils its diners for choice. Such choice can be overwhelming, particularly for visitors less familiar with the city and its constantly changing faces and fashions. To help you make an informed decision, we assembled a team of writers with a passion for food and asked them to give us a rundown of recommended restaurants for the neighbourhoods they live in, work in, relax in, and love to eat in.

We have divided the city up into 10 central areas, with an additional chapter covering the outer districts. Each chapter begins with an overview of the area and the type of restaurants you might find there, pinpointing any markets, food shops or other gastronomic landmarks worth a special mention. This introduction is followed by a list of around 40 recommended restaurants, each cross-referenced to a detailed area map, on which railway and tube stations are clearly marked. To help narrow your choice down even further, we give our top five recommendations for each area.

The Listings

The listings are organised by type of cuisine. Many restaurants and gastropubs fall under the 'Modern European' category, a catch-all term for the type of modern inventive cooking that fuses traditional staples with French, Italian, Mediterranean and ethnic influences introduced by Britain's immigrant cultures. There is often little to distinguish this and the term 'Modern British'; both are equally broad. We have therefore used 'British' as a category for both traditional and contemporary restaurants that use predominantly British ingredients and dishes. Restaurants which draw from a wider range of influences or feature more eclectic menus, using an exotic blend of ingredients from across the globe, fall under the 'International' category. Each restaurant is given a price code *(see opposite)* for an idea of how much you can expect to spend. The reviews are kept short and to the point; they aim to give an overall impression of the restaurant's food, style and ambience, and the level of service. On the whole they are positive recommendations, but any negative aspects, such as slow service, high noise levels, closely packed tables, are pointed out. The information is based on the experience of one person and should only be used as a guide. The restaurant reviews are supplemented by a short-list of recommended pubs, bars and cafés for each area.

The Contributors

The guide was compiled by Insight editor Cathy Muscat, with the help of Portia Colwell from *The Times*. Chapters and features were written by: Portia Colwell *(Kensington and Chelsea, Fulham to Hammersmith, Battersea and Clapham, Riverside Pubs)*, Liz Delliere *(Covent Garden and Holborn)*, Lisa Gerard-Sharp *(Afternoon Tea, Coffee Shops, Eating and Entertainment)*, Nick Hart *(Richmond and Kew)*, Jonathan Keane *(Soho and Chinatown, City and Clerkenwell, Hoxton and Shoreditch)*, Emma Mahoney *(Knightsbridge and Belgravia, Notting Hill and Bayswater, Eating with Children)*, Cathy Muscat *(Blackheath and Greenwich, Brixton and Dulwich)*, Sudi Piggott *(Mayfair, Piccadilly and St James's, Marylebone, Food Shops, Celebrity Chefs)*, Dorothy Stannard *(Islington)*, Vicky Thornton *(Camden to Hampstead)* and Robin Young *(Bloomsbury and Fitzrovia, Fish and Chips, The Chains)*. The guide was indexed by Sylvia Suddes and proofread by Emma Sangster.

How to use this guide

Each restaurant review contains the following information:

Address and telephone number: If calling from outside London, all numbers should be preceded with the London code **020**

Grid reference: this refers to the map that appears in the introduction to each area chapter, on which each restaurant is plotted. Train stations are also clearly marked.

Opening times: B=breakfast, Br=brunch, L=lunch, T=Tea, D=dinner. Specific opening times are not given, except where they are exceptional. Most restaurants close around 11–11.30pm, earlier on Sundays. Last orders are taken between half an hour and an hour before closing time.

Price codes: **£** = under £20 **££** = £20–30 **£££** = £30–45 **££££** = £45 + These prices are based on the cost of an average 3-course dinner per person including half a bottle of house wine, or the cheapest wine available, and any cover or service charge. Lunch is often cheaper. Where a cheaper set menu is available, this is specified.

Website: where the restaurant has its own website with up-to-date information on menus and prices, this has been given.

Editorial

Series Editor Cathy Muscat
Editorial Director Brian Bell
Art Director Klaus Geisler
Picture Manager Hilary Genin
Photography Britta Jaschinski
Production Linton Donaldson,
Sylvia George
Cartography Zoë Goodwin,
Laura Morris

Distribution

UK & Ireland
GeoCenter International Ltd
The Viables Centre, Harrow Way
Basingstoke, Hants RG22 4BJ
Fax: (44) 1256-817988

United States
Langenscheidt Publishers, Inc.
46–35 54th Road, Maspeth, NY
11378
Fax: (1)718 784-0640

Canada
Thomas Allen & Son Ltd
390 Steelcase Road East
Markham, Ontario L3R 1G2
Fax: (1) 905 475-6747

Worldwide
Apa Publications GmbH & Co.
Verlag KG (Singapore branch)
38 Joo Koon Road, Singapore 628990
Tel: (65) 6865-1600.
Fax: (65) 6861-6438

Printing

Insight Print Services (Pte) Ltd
38 Joo Koon Road, Singapore 628990
Tel: (65) 6865-1600.
Fax: (65) 6861-6438

©2004 Apa Publications GmbH & Co.
Verlag KG (Singapore branch)
All Rights Reserved

First Edition 2004

Maps reproduced by permission of
Geographers' A–Z Co. Ltd.
Licence No. B2432
© Crown Copyright 2003. All rights
reserved. Licence number 100017302

CONTACTING THE EDITORS
Although every effort is made to provide
accurate information, we live in a fast-
changing world and would appreciate it
if readers would call our attention to any
errors or outdated information that may
occur by writing to:

Insight Guides, P.O. Box 7910,
London SE1 1WE, England.
Fax: (44) 20-7403 0290.
insight@apaguide.co.uk

www.insightguides.com

Features

Directory

Maps

*For individual zone maps, see
area chapters*

Gordon Ramsay
68–9 Royal Hospital Rd, SW3 [page 99]
For an unbeatable gastronomic experience and the good-value set menu.

Locanda Locatelli
8 Seymour Street, W1 [page 80]
For startlingly good, ungreedily priced Italian cuisine.

Racine
239 Brompton Rd, SW3 [page 108]
For French flair and a relaxed atmosphere.

Hakkasan
8 Hanway Place, W1 [page 48]
For refined Chinese food and classy cocktails in sleek surroundings.

Moro
34–6 Exmouth Market, EC1 [page 139]
For an exotic blend of North African and Spanish cuisine.

The Anchor & Hope
36 The Cut, SE1 [page 150]
For meaty gastropub fare, friendly staff and buzzy atmosphere.

J Sheekey
28–32 St Martin's Court, WC2 [page 32]
For dedicated fish lovers and A-list celebrities.

Zaika
1 Kensington High St, W8 [page 96]
For exquisite Indian food, executed and presented to perfection.

Lindsay House
21 Romilly St, W1 [page 16]
For the best of British with a touch of the Irish.

Bleeding Heart
Bleeding Heart Yard, Greville St, EC1 [page 32]
For a romantic meal *à deux* or a leisurely lunch.

EATING OUT IN LONDON

The range of cosmopolitan cuisine and the advent of modern British cooking have transformed London into a gastronomic paradise

The London restaurant scene has never been so vibrant. Top restaurants are being showered with Michelin stars, high-flying chefs grab the headlines, and every week sees the opening of a new gastropub or gastrotemple. The fact that a record number of closures was announced in 2003 is clearly not indicative of a slump. Quite the reverse, in fact. We are spending more and more of our time and cash on eating out and, as a result, are demanding ever higher standards. It's a cut-throat business in which only the fittest survive, but this doesn't seem to deter budding restaurateurs. For every restaurant that closes, a new one is ready to take its place.

A significant factor in the growth of London's restaurants over the past decade is the re-evaluation of Britain's indigenous food. Its once scorned reputation of badly cooked, unimaginative, stodgy meals has been overturned by a new generation of innovative modern-minded British chefs. They have injected new life into traditional British recipes by combining them with French, Italian, Mediterranean and ethnic influences. They now take pride in making the best of top-quality and seasonal ingredients while also making meals lighter.

At the forefront of this revolution is the gastropub phenomenon that has taken the city by storm. Pub after pub is following the formula: having a stripped floorboard and stressed furniture makeover, drawing the punters in with a chalkboard menu of appetising 'modern European' dishes, and sounding the death knell for the plastic ploughman's lunch and limp sandwiches that were for all too long standard pub fare. The traditional English practices of a Sunday roast, carveries, and all-day 'greasy spoon' café breakfasts are, nevertheless, still very much part of the scene. However, choose carefully, as there is a huge difference between good and bad versions of these meals.

Opposite: Sketch, for dazzling and dizzily priced food

It's no secret that London is one of the most expensive cities in the world for eating out. At the top end of the scale, it's not at all uncommon to pay £100-plus for a meal for two. To eat at one of the most exclusive restaurants requires serious money, which a lot of people are obviously prepared to pay. Gastronomic temples such as Gordon Ramsay, Nobu and Locanda Locatelli, and fashionable hotspots like the Ivy, J Sheekey and, the latest see-and-be-seen venue, the Wolseley, must be booked weeks, in some cases months, in advance.

For those on a budget, London has a huge variety of ethnic restaurants – Chinese, Indian, Thai, Japanese, Malaysian – which offer some of the best value, while pubs (of the non-gastro variety) and wine bars often provide good inexpensive snacks in surroundings that are preferable to a fast food hamburger joint. And there's always good old fish and chips to take away.

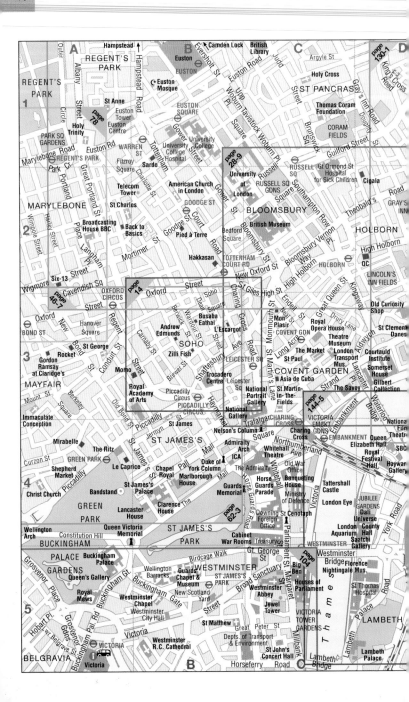

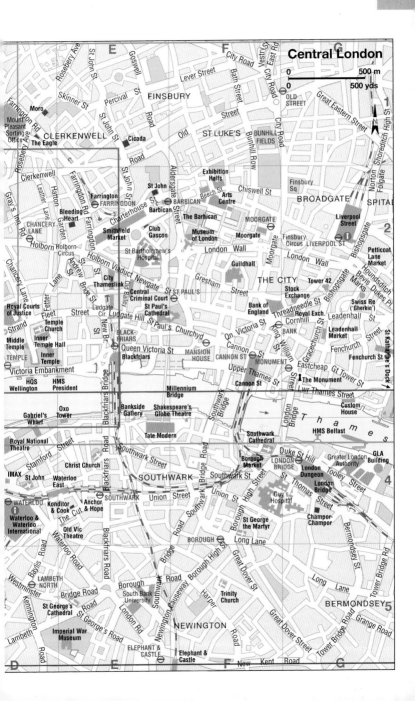

Central London

TODAY'S
SPECIAL

SPINACH & RICOTTA
RAVIOLI SERVED WITH
MIXED LEAF SALAD £7.95

APPLE CRUMBLE
W/VANILLA ICE CREAM
MADE W/ORGANIC APPLES
£3.90

NOW OPEN SAT & SUN
LUNCH 1-4 P.M

SOHO AND CHINATOWN

When it comes to eating out, this compact area, with its vibrant mix of restaurants, bars, cafés and clubs, offers the best choice in the capital

Soho is the vibrant, beating heart of London's West End, a dense, throbbing array of restaurants, cafés, clubs, theatres, peepshows and shops; a place where you are guaranteed a walk on the wild side day and night. Film stars, media types and musicians, clubbers and prostitutes, smalltown boys and uptown girls all flock here. It's difficult to imagine that things were ever different. Yet, just over 300 years ago, Soho was little more than a series of fields across which the aristocracy hunted wild game – it is in fact named after a popular hunting cry, 'So-Hoe'.

Food and eating have always played an important role in the life of the area. Remarkably, Greek Street's fine dining rooms – L'Escargot and Gay Hussar – stand on the same spot as a mid-16th-century banqueting hall where the mayor and aldermen of the city would retire to eat after hunting for hare. It was only after the Great Fire of London in 1666 that the need for property to house the rich and newly homeless gentry of the city precipitated the building of roads and houses in the area. To this day, Old Compton Street, Gerrard Street (the centre of present-day Chinatown), Greek Street and Frith Street are amazingly loyal to the original street plans. But all that is left of the original Soho Fields is the charming Soho Square and Golden Square to the west.

The Soho square mile

Modern-day Soho lies within the square mile roughly bordered by Oxford Street to the north, Regent Street to the west, Charing Cross Road to the east and Shaftesbury Avenue to the south. Dividing east and west Soho is Wardour Street. For foodies, a good place to start exploring is the intersection of Wardour Street and Old Compton Street. From this vantage point you can catch glimpses of Italian delis and French cafés, Japanese noodle bars and Chinese restaurants, gay bars and boutiques, the mix of which give Soho its unique flavour.

Opposite: cheap and cheerful Café Emm
Below: smart and modern Imperial China

Urban Soho has a long history as a refuge for foreigners. By 1688, 800 of the newly built houses were filled with Huguenots escaping persecution from France. The British nobility moved west to new and fashionable Mayfair, while the French transformed the ground floors of their houses into cheap cafés and restaurants and French food shops, echoes of which can be found today in Patisserie Valerie on Old Compton Street and Maison Bertaux on Greek Street *(see page 23)*. As late as 1844, Soho was described as 'a sort of petty France'. This free-thinking, exotic and very un-English environment has acted as a magnet to other émigrés, most notably from Italy and China, but also from Spain, Russia and Eastern Europe. The wide and eclectic range of restaurants crammed into this small area pay testament to this history and to the heady cocktail of cultures and tastes that emerged as a result.

After World War II, Soho's evolution into its modern-day incarnation began with the jazz scene, centred on the legendary Ronnie Scott's *(see page 41)*, still a great venue for world-class jazz acts. With it emerged a British youth subculture, in which coffee bars played a key role. According to Peter Ackroyd in his fascinating history of the metropolis, *London: The Biography*, the first coffee bar, Milka, opened on Frith Street in the early 1950s. Then Sandy's, the area's first sandwich bar, opened on Oxenden Street in 1953, starting a trend that would come to dominate food culture in Soho by the late 20th century. Many of these traditional, mostly Italian coffee shops have since been chased out of Soho by high rents and the encroaching sex industry. They have been replaced by a new generation of sleek, modern sandwich bars and brasseries, and American-style coffee houses assured a regular turnover from the dense population of workers and visitors. One or two survivors represent quaint Continental pockets of 'old Soho'. In the Italian corner is Bar Italia *(see page 25)*, while the aforementioned Patisserie Valerie and Maison Bertaux represent the classic face of French patisserie.

The 'coming out' of the Soho gay scene has also changed the face of the area. Always welcome in the most raffish of areas, gays, lesbians and their friends began to take advantage of the gay bar, restaurant and café culture that grew successfully during the 1980s and '90s around one of the oldest of Soho thoroughfares, Old Compton Street.

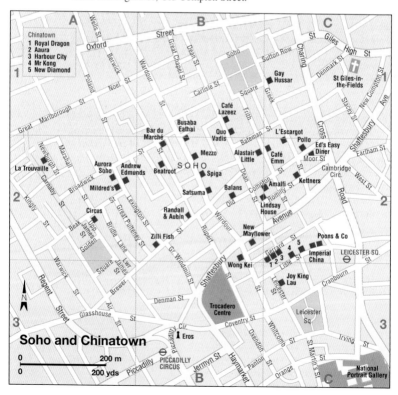

Soho and Chinatown

Chinatown
1 Royal Dragon
2 Aaura
3 Harbour City
4 Mr Kong
5 New Diamond

Maison Bertaux on Greek Street

Britain's awful reputation for food abroad was also largely dispelled during this time with major improvements in the quality and ambience of Soho restaurants. Michelin star chefs such as Marco Pierre White at Quo Vadis and L'Escargot, Alastair Little at his eponymous restaurant and Richard Corrigan of Lindsay House, along with Terence Conran's modern mega-restaurant Mezzo, have brought style and grandeur to contemporary Soho eating.

Chinatown

To the south of Wardour Street, in the area roughly bordered by Leicester Square and Shaftesbury Avenue, lies Chinatown, of which Gerrard Street is the main artery. Here the bustling mix of dim sum restaurants, Chinese food shops, barbers and stores all servicing London's Chinese community appears long established. But Soho's Chinatown is a relative newcomer.

Following the Blitz during World War II, the Chinese immigrants who lived in Limehouse, East London, were made homeless. Gerrard Street was then a shabby, rundown thoroughfare, and leases were cheap. So as soldiers returned from the war with a new taste for East Asian food, the dispossessed Chinese moved into the area and opened up restaurants to cater for the demand engendered by this newly acquired taste. At the same time, thousands of agricultural workers from Hong Kong, forced out of their traditional work because of a collapse in the rice market, arrived in London and found employment in the booming catering trade. Chinatown was born.

Most of the Cantonese restaurants in Chinatown serve food all day from noon until 11.30pm, often until midnight on weekends, which makes them a good option for pre- and post-theatre/cinema dining, or for anyone in need of a square meal between normal lunch and dinner sittings. A typical Cantonese meal is made up of several dishes including stir-fried vegetables, rice and noodles, hot and sour soups, duck, chicken and seafood dishes, and of course, dim sum – delicious filled dumplings, that are steamed or deep-fried, made by specially trained chefs and traditionally served in the daytime.

If you'd like to try your hand at Chinese cooking, Loon Fung Supermarket on Gerrard Street is the place to go for authentic ingredients. It's worth a visit just to see the weird and wonderful range of foodstuffs: spiky, fresh durian, the notoriously smelly fruit, are piled outside like abandoned hedgehogs, while inside, mounds of unfamiliar roots and plants lead you down an exotic path towards an excellent fish and meat counter where even the eel looks edible.

American retro at Ed's Easy Diner

American

Ed's Easy Diner

12 Moor St, W1 [C2]. Tel: 7439 1955. Open: daily, to midnight. £
Not so much a restaurant as an excuse to satiate salt and coke cravings, Ed's is London's premiere chip and burger experience. Beefburgers, veggie burgers, chicken burgers – you name it, they'll stick cheese on it – are dished up in 1950s Americana-style surroundings. You have to sit at the food bar to eat, which makes it impossible for groups but a great place for a mid-shop pit stop.

British

Lindsay House 🍴

21 Romilly St, W1 [B/C2]. Tel: 7439 0450. Open: L and D Mon–Sat. £££ (set menu), ££££ www.lindsayhouse.co.uk
In this carefully restored Georgian townhouse, Richard Corrigan delivers a Michelin-starred, expensive but exciting culinary experience, fusing modern British and traditional Irish cooking to produce such inventive dishes as his signature roast squab pigeon with peas and pancetta, or saddle of rabbit with black pudding. The puddings and wine list are exquisite. The elegant simplicity of the dining rooms

Did you know?
Chinese New Year takes place sometime between late January and mid-February when Gerrard Street becomes a bustling Chinese bazaar. In Leicester Square stage performances include dragon dances and martial arts displays. Be prepared for firecrackers!
www.chinatown-online.org.uk

makes for a comfortable ambience, although shouting from the kitchens can pepper your own mealtime conversation. For a money-is-no-object gourmet night out, this is a good choice. Booking essential.

Chinese

Aaura

38 Gerrard St, W1 [C2]. Tel: 7287 8033. Open: daily, all day. £ (set menu), ££
A noteworthy Chinatown newcomer. The interior is bright and cheerful and the standard of food is high, striking a good balance between unusual dishes and reassuringly traditional offerings. The lunchtime dim sum list offers plenty of choice.

Harbour City

46 Gerrard St, W1 [C2]. Tel: 7439 7859. Open: daily, all day. £ (set menu), ££
This is an excellent, reasonably priced restaurant in the middle of Chinatown. With its traditional wood-framed decor and great window table overlooking Gerrard Street, it feels civilised and welcoming. Dim sum (served Mon–Sat until 5pm) dominates the menu with some interesting variations to choose from.

Imperial China

White Bear Yard, 25a Lisle St, WC2 [C2]. Tel: 7734 3388. Open: daily, all day. £££
The decor of the majority of Chinatown restaurants veers between a (sometimes tacky) traditional look and brutal utility. So it's with some relief that you happen upon this new restaurant. It opens onto a falling wall of water over glass blocks that lead the eye to a pretty wooden bridge curving over an artificial stream and onto the open dining courtyard beyond.

It's an imaginative and very contemporary use of space; the food is less so, but dishes such as stewed Dover sole and common delicacies like chicken claws in chilli sauce are well presented and reasonably accessible.

Joy King Lau

3 Leicester St, WC2 [C2]. Tel: 7437 1133. Open: daily, all day. ££ (set menu), £££

A popular choice for those who know their Chinese food. You'll find some interesting set menus from around £28 where sizzling veal with black pepper sauce vies for attention alongside a good range of noodle dishes and the usual dim sum varieties.

Mr Kong

21 Lisle St, WC2 [C2]. Tel: 7437 7341/7437 9679. Open: daily, all day to 2.45am. £ (set menu), ££

With 100 seats ranging over three floors, Mr Kong is one of the more authentic (and claustrophobic) Chinese restaurants in the area. Dishes are off-putting or challenging, depending on your point of view and the subtleties of your palate, with such choices as Kon Chi baby squid with chilli sauce or sandstorm crab. There's a lively

vegetarian selection too, including fried mock pork with fresh mango.

New Diamond

23 Lisle St, WC2 [C2]. Tel: 7437 2517/7437 7221. Open: daily, all day to 3am. £ (set menu), ££

A stylish little venue with adventurous and polished meals on the specials menu such as venison with asparagus in XO sauce and an interesting line in quails – spicy, salted or chillied.

New Mayflower

68–70 Shaftesbury Avenue, W1 [B2]. Tel: 7734 9207. Open: D only, daily until 4am. £ (set menu), ££

Noisy Shaftesbury Avenue is not the ideal place for a calm, unhurried meal, but behind its smoked glass windows this popular restaurant serves up a tasty range of dishes, especially seafood, until the small hours. Reasonably priced set menus include starters such as shark's fin and crabmeat soup followed by fried oysters with ginger served on an iron plate. And there's plenty of eel – stewed, fried and steamed.

Poons & Co

27 Lisle St, WC2 [C2]. Tel: 7437 4549. Open: daily, all day. ££

TIP

Liberty (*214 Regent St*), the stylish department store on the western edge of Soho, has a discreet in-store café which serves a silky set afternoon tea of smoked salmon sandwich, lemon tart, champagne, tea or coffee.

Imperial China

TIP

Dim sum, steamed or fried dumplings with a variety of fillings, is traditionally eaten in the afternoon, and you won't find many authentic Cantonese restaurants serving it after 5pm. Some restaurants wheel their dim sum selection round on a trolley. Just point at whatever you like the look of.

A favourite in Chinatown, this little café is 30 years old and with its 1950s-style gingham table cloths, faded decor and meat hanging in its window kitchen this does not come as much of a surprise. Soups are good, as are hotpots, but there isn't enough space to dine with friends. So instead pop in for a quick lunchtime bite or simply for the experience.

Royal Dragon

30 Gerrard St, W1 [C2]. Tel: 7734 0935. Open: daily, all day to 3am. ££

Noisy, bustling and sizzling with quick-fire dishes that descend from on high. Set menus are reliable and filling with old familiars such as sweet and sour pork and beef in black bean sauce providing the kind of banquet that you would be happy taking a Western family who want to enjoy the atmosphere of a Chinese restaurant but don't want their taste buds overly challenged.

Wong Kei

41–43 Wardour St, W1 [B2]. Tel: 7437 8408/7437 3071. Open: daily, all day. £

Famous for its surly service and noisy canteen atmosphere, the ever-popular Wong Kei serves food to fill a hole rather than inspire gasps of delight. But this is quite edible Chinese fare and service is more brisk than aggressive. In short, a good place for a quick filling meal.

Fish

Randall & Aubin

16 Brewer St, W1 [B2]. Tel: 7287 4447. Open: L and D daily. £££ www.randallandaubin.co.uk

Named after the old delicatessen that inhabited this spot from 1904 to the late 1990s, Randall & Aubin has inherited a feeling of shopping bustle. Piles of lobster, crabs and oysters greet you as you enter and there's a good chance you'll end up sharing your catch with friendly strangers.

Zilli Fish

36–40 Brewer St, W1 [B2]. Tel: 7734 8649. Open: L and D daily. £££ www.zillialdo.com

Not cheap, but a great lunch venue. Zilli's fish is fantastic. Try the lobster spaghetti or the salmon stuffed with spinach, both fresh and delicate. Watch out for the banana spring rolls with chocolate sauce – they're divine. Buzzy but relaxed, and the staff are among the friendliest in London. The Covent Garden branch, Zilli Fish Too, is equally recommended *(see page 32)*. Booking advisable.

Zilli Fish: good fish, great desserts

French

L'Escargot
48 Greek St, W1 [C2]. Tel: 7437 2679. Open: L and D Mon–Sat. £££ (set menu) ££££
www.whitestarline.org.uk
The grand-père of French restaurants in London, L'Escargot is steeped in history with its 1920s Art Deco interior and priceless artworks that adorn the walls. Now safe in the sure culinary hands of Marco Pierre White, the restaurant offers a choice between the exciting hubbub of the sunny ground floor and the more intimate Picasso room upstairs, with à la carte and set menus (both of course with snails).

La Trouvaille ℗
12a Newburgh St, W1 [A2]. Tel: 7287 8488. Open: L and D Mon–Sat. ££ (set menu), £££
www.latrouvaille.co.uk
This is a small, intimate restaurant with a lovely atmosphere. Friendly and unobtrusive staff serve impeccably sourced and creatively conceived dishes, such as monkfish and mango, that are simple and delicious. The wine list is also quirky and exotic. Cleverly situated in West Soho, whose cobbled streets speak Huguenot France more than London, 'the discovery' is thoroughly recommended for a slow-paced romantic meal.

Gay Hussar

Hungarian

Gay Hussar
2 Greek St, W1 [C1]. Tel: 7437 0973. Open: L and D Mon–Sat. ££ (set menu), £££
A classic London restaurant just off Soho Square, the Gay Hussar has a long history of political intrigue and pays tribute to its Westminster village diners with a gallery of caricatures. In polished, gentleman's club surroundings (complete with smoke), you can treat yourself to a rib-lining mix of traditional hearty British and Hungarian dishes. Pork and potatoes are prominent.

Indian

Café Lazeez
21 Dean St, W1 [B1]. Tel: 7434 9393. Open: L and D Mon–Sat. £££ www.cafelazeez.com
A new pretender to the Soho scene, the Lazeez sits in the basement of the Soho Theatre beneath the Lazeez bar. Not the most welcoming of venues; it's more like walking into a bustling foyer than a restaurant. But take the plunge, as the modern Indian cooking is authentic, delicious and light, and the basement surprisingly peaceful.

International

Balans
60 Old Compton St, W1 [B2]. Tel: 7437 5212. Open: daily, all day (Mon–Thur 8am–5am; Fri–Sat 8am–6am; Sun 8am–2am). ££ www.balans.co.uk
Balans sets out to bring a little friendly buzz and glamour to gay eating in Old Compton Street with its range of New York brunch-style dishes – including an accom-

Did you know?
Soho has a number of private members' clubs, whose registers read like a Who's Who of writers, artists and film-makers. The most (in)famous is The Groucho Club on Dean Street, named after Groucho Marx who quipped 'I don't care to belong to any club that would accept me as a member.'

plished eggs benedict – club music, cute waiters and almost 24-hour opening. Despite changes in decor and seating plans to encourage more eating and less posing, the formula remains relentlessly successful. Where else can you be sure of getting tasty sausage and mash at 5am on a school night?

Café Emm 🍴

17 Frith St, W1 [C2]. Tel: 7437 0723. Open: L and D daily. £ www.cafeemm.com

Buzzy, intimate and exceptionally good value, Café Emm is packed out every night. Portions are always, sometimes off-puttingly, large, but well cooked, from fish dishes such as calamari and salmon fish cakes to lamb shank with ratatouille and creamy mash. Be prepared to queue and for boisterous birthday parties.

Italian

Amalfi

29–31 Old Compton St, W1 [C2]. Tel: 7437 7284. Open: L and D daily. ££

This popular stop-off point on Old Compton Street won't wow you with the quality of its service or its decor, which has resisted fashion for decades, but its appeal lies in the very fact that it's stuck in a time warp. The cooking is of the 1970s bistro variety, but pizzas, vegetable pastas and other Italian fare are tasty and filling and you'll always be sure of a good welcome, quick service and a table without reservation.

Kettners

29 Romilly St, W1 [C2]. Tel: 7734 6112. Open: daily, all day. ££ www.kettners.com

If you like a bit of fizz with your pizza then this sprawling, grand dame of a restaurant is a perfect

TIP

For a quick bite to eat on the move take a trip to the falafel shop on Old Compton Street or the fish and chip shop on Berwick Street. The market on Berwick Street is the place to go for cheap and fresh fruit and vegetables. If you arrive in the afternoon you can often get a large scoop of whatever's going for a pound.

Café Emm

choice. Fusing an extensive champagne list with a pizza menu is nothing if not original, but less surprising when you learn that Kettners is owned by the Pizza Express chain. However, don't let that put you off. Here, in these faded Edwardian surroundings, you'll find a touch more class, better cooking and a broader (albeit pricier) menu.

Pollo

20 Old Compton St, W1 [C2]. Tel: 7734 5456. Open daily, all day. £

Pollo's simple, cheap and stomach-lining pasta dishes draw students, tourists and anyone in the mood for a no-nonsense meal through its doors. Be prepared to lose your table as soon as your last plate is whisked away.

Spiga

84–86 Wardour St, W1 [B2]. Tel: 7734 3444. Open: L and D daily. £££

A contemporary Italian restaurant that has a cool and airy ambience conducive to chatting over a crisp pinot and tasty stone-fired pizza on a summer lunchtime or early evening. Be sure to ask for a booth when being seated as the free-standing tables jostle a little too closely for comfort. Reservations advisable, especially at weekends.

Japanese

Satsuma
56 Wardour St, W1 [B2]. Tel: 7437 8338. Open daily, all day. ££ www.osatsuma.com
Clean, bright and noisy. The clientele is a young, pre-clubbing crowd and the long beech tables don't allow for privacy or booking so be prepared to queue. This is fast food, but dishes are freshly cooked and well presented with some very tasty udon and ramen noodle dishes, plus sushi to suit even the most delicate stomach.

Modern European

Alastair Little
49 Frith St, W1 [B2]. Tel: 7734 5183. Open: L and D Mon–Fri, D only Sat. £££
Right in the heart of Soho, this small, calm and beautifully formed restaurant provides quality food made with seasonal ingredients. Its top chef namesake no longer mans the stoves, but the unfussy, flavour-packed dishes retain his stamp, and the service is as attentive as ever. Menus are fixed (and good value) so don't be surprised to discover courses without prices.

Andrew Edmunds
46 Lexington St, W1 [A2]. Tel: 7437 5708. Open: L and D daily. £££
A lack of signage out front gives an anonymous secretive feel to this romantic Soho hideaway. Inside, the soft candlelight and woodpanelled walls make it cosy and intimate. Dishes are simple but varied, ranging from rabbit to well-presented pasta. The staff are relaxed and friendly and the dining experience always colourful and enjoyable.

Aurora Soho
49 Lexington St, W1 [B2]. Tel: 7494 0514. Open: L and D Mon–Sat. £££
Aurora's courtyard garden is great for a chatty lunch or an intimate evening for two. There is a heavy accent on fresh fish such as the trout with roasted peppers and new potatoes that sit wonderfully

TIP
On a warm evening a good place to meet before moving on to a restaurant is Soho Square. You can sit and enjoy the sun, plus it's great for people watching.

Amalfi, an unpretentious slice of old Soho

alongside a very peasant-like bruschetta. Beautiful in summer.

Bar du Marché

19 Berwick St, W1 [B2]. Tel: 7734 4606. Open: all day, Mon–Sat. £ (set menu), ££
Tucked behind bustling Berwick Street Market, this is a surprisingly unpretentious Soho hangout. Bar-hugging regulars share the cosy eating space with couples, shoppers and small groups of friends enjoying a mix of French brasserie food, salads and seafood.

Circus

1 Upper James St, W1 [A2]. Tel: 7534 4000. Open: L and D Mon–Sat. ££ (set lunch), £££ www.cgami.co.uk
At the end of the 1990s, Circus mirrored the clean competency of media Soho with its black and white interior, basement members' bar and efficient, good-looking staff. Times move on, but the restaurant is ageing well. Its pan-fried risotto with smoked haddock and poached egg is still worth the visit and the set lunches and early dinners are competitively priced.

Mezzo

100 Wardour St, W1 [B2]. Tel: 7314 4000. Open: L and D daily (£5 music charge after 8.30pm Wed–Sat). ££ (set menus), £££ www.conran.com

Above: Busaba Eathai
Below: Alastair Little, Quo Vadis

Terence Conran's gastronomic monument to Soho's glamorous people can be both intimidating and exciting. For some the combination of stylish and sometimes diffident staff, brisk service and well-presented but expensive food is a good reason to avoid the restaurant. For others it is everything London should be. More style than substance.

Quo Vadis

26–29 Dean St, W1 [B1]. Tel: 7437 9585. Open: L and D Mon–Fri, D only Sat. £££ (set menu), ££££ www.whitestarline.org.uk
Marco Pierre White's Soho restaurant is a starched, professional establishment, and this goes for both its white linen as well as the service provided by informed and expert waiters. The Brit Art interior saves it from austerity. The menu is mainly (but not exclusively) modern Italian with dishes such as a delicious tortelloni of lobster with roast langoustine. A very expensive but laudable selection of French wines.

Thai

Busaba Eathai

106–110 Wardour St, W1 [B2]. Tel: 7255 8686. Open: L and D daily. ££

So popular is this trendy Thai eatery that queues regularly form on the pavement, but turnover is fast. The emphasis is on fragrant, communal eating around square tables, although if lucky you'll get a window seat that provides great people watching. Their pad kweito and sides such as maan prawn are all tasty and beautifully presented although flavours are toned down for the European palate.

Vegetarian

Beatroot

92 Berwick St, W1 [B2]. Tel: 7437 8591. Open: until 6.15pm Mon–Sat. £

Beatroot is a reminder of Berwick Street's fast-fading bohemian past. Veggie and vegan takeaway boxes are the norm, filled with hot tofu stir-fries and generous, tasty salads.

Mildred's

45 Lexington St, W1 [B2]. Tel: 7494 1634. Open: noon–11pm Mon–Sat. ££
www.mildreds.co.uk

With its jostling tables, vague 1950s decor and cheery staff, Mildred's is a real gem – the kind of friendly, laid-back vegetarian restaurant you wouldn't expect to find in the heart of London. Food is tasty and satisfying, with a surprising range from veggie burgers and chips to tofu stir-fries and a delicious ale pie, all accompanied by a flavoursome range of organic beer and soft drinks. You can't make a reservation and Mildred's is always full, but staff are skilled in estimating when a table will be ready.

PUBS, BARS AND CAFÉS

Soho probably has the highest concentration of watering holes in London. The choice may be staggering, but finding a seat in the evening is never easy, so be prepared to jostle with the crowds of shoppers, tourists, out-of-towners and after-work drinkers. The following selection is the tip of the iceberg.

If you're in search of a hip hang-out, head for west Soho and **Alphabet** *(61–63 Beak St)*. Arranged over two floors, the bar caters for a media in-crowd who flock here to wind down after work. For a touch of class, the grand **Atlantic Bar & Grill** *(20 Glasshouse St)* in the refurbished ballroom of the Regent Palace Hotel, is good for a champagne cocktail. For a taste of Soho history, visit **French House** *(49 Dean St)*. Its decadent and beautiful old bar was the centre of the French Resistance in London during World War II, and the regular haunt of Francis Bacon and Samuel Beckett to name just two. The upstairs restaurant *(tel: 7437 2477)* serves good French fare. **Bar Code** *(3–4 Archer St)* is a late-night, funky gay dance and cruise bar. Wine buffs in the vicinity of Oxford Street should seek out **Shampers** *(4 Kingly St; tel: 7437 1692)*, an Aladdin's cave of wine racks. Food is available, but it's best to book.

For those who like their ale from a barrel and not a bottle, Soho has plenty of classic Victorian pubs – the **Argyll Arms** *(18 Argyll St)*, the **Coach & Horses** *(29 Greek St)*, and the **Dog & Duck** *(18 Bateman St)* are just three.

If it's less beer and more a cup of tea or coffee and a spot of people-watching you want, the best cafés in Soho are found in and around Old Compton Street. **Bar Italia** *(22 Frith St)* is a Soho legend and serves great Italian coffee and snacks 24/7. The most wonderful, boho French café this side of the Channel is **Maison Bertaux** *(28 Greek St)*, where the surroundings look like they'll crumble to the touch, just like their exquisite cakes; and for a gentile French experience amid the bustle of gay Soho, **Pâtisserie Valerie** *(44 Old Compton St)* belongs to another age.

● *For more about London's tearooms and coffee bars, see pages 24 and 126.*

Coffee Culture

London's discerning coffee drinkers are abandoning the chains in favour of a new generation of individually run Continental-style cafés

At first glance, London seems to be dying of caffeine poisoning, with every street corner bristling with competing coffee bars. Those in search of a caffeine fix can choose from pseudo-Italian, fake-French or ersatz North American coffee shops. The competing chains have invaded most city quarters and all have their fans. Caffè Nero may claim the most genuine Italian-style coffee but Costa Coffee has the richest hot chocolate and Starbucks with its comfortable sofas has an air of American confidence and laid-back ease. Yet this coffee overload is hard to reconcile with the recent slump in the profits of the coffee chains in London, with shares in Caffè Nero falling from 531p to just 27p in 2003, and the Coffee Republic chain closing down. Although the picture may be somewhat bleak for the chains, it is proof that sophisticated city consumers are demanding better quality and more individual bars, preferably those with a Continental touch.

This cultural backlash against the supremacy of the chains is part of a trend to redress the balance in favour of authenticity and old-fashioned quality. To this end, the Italian government has even authorised inspectors to report on any dilution in authenticity of Italian coffee shops abroad. Meanwhile, smaller, more authentic Italian coffee shops and French patisseries have sprung up to satisfy sophisticated palates. Segafredo Zanetti, the Italian coffee barons, have just opened the first of many branches in London, and are hoping to woo customers with a mixture of superb coffee from their own Brazilian plantations, and a choice of alcoholic drinks, available at all times of day, just like a real Italian café.

Another shining example of the way forward is the Café Blanc group, founded by French master chef Raymond Blanc. These cafés offer fresh French patisserie produced on the premises and exude Continental cool, with style matched by substance. Although Blanc is no longer involved, the cafés thrive and maintain their distinctive appeal. As always, the presence of a Gaggia coffee-making machine on site is a promise of good coffee.

Bar Italia, open 24 hours a day

Coffee and cake stops

Bar Italia *(22 Frith St)*, with its Italian flags on the ceiling and neat displays of tin cans and fruit and vegetables, is a Soho institution. Reminiscent of 1950s Soho, it remains comfortingly impervious to fashion. The 24-hour bar shows all-Italian football matches on a screen at the back. Service is brisk, brusque and opinionated, with the atmosphere changing throughout the day: the mood embraces morning office workers and, in the wee small hours, welcomes refuelling ravers. The bar has spilled over into the next-door bar, which is now an extension of Bar Italia, with the same basic bar menu, from espresso to iced coffee. So, an unchanging institution – despite the fact that payment can now be made in euro.

The **Cinnamon Bar** *(One Aldwych; 7.30am–9pm)*. Set in the stylish One Aldwych hotel and restaurant complex *(see page 34)*, it is a contemporary classic, offering good, strong espresso and an updated version of afternoon tea, with a definite Continental touch. Yet as a cool fashion statement of a bar, designed along clean lines, it is light years away from the old-style Continental café. In keeping with this ethos, the broad range of food on offer should appeal to all tastes: muffins, cakes and cookies satisfy afternoon-tea grazers, while sandwiches and salads see to the lunch crowd and tapas and sangria make a good pre-theatre snack.

Small but engaging **Maison Blanc** *(7a Kensington Church St, W8; daily)* is a classic French boulangerie and patisserie combined, selling wonderful country bread and croissants, as well as chocolates, pastries, strawberry tarts and full-blown cakes for special occasions, all of which can be eaten in the tiny tearooms. The prominently displayed Gaggia machine is proof that the coffee will be worth waiting for. Other Maison Blanc café-bakeries can be found in Marylebone *(7 Thayer St, W1)*, Chelsea *(11 Elystan St, SW3)* and Fulham *(303 Fulham Rd, SW10)*.

Maison Bertaux *(28 Greek St; 9am-8pm daily)* claims to be the oldest patisserie in London, dating back to 1871, but the establishment is challenged on this score by its venerable neighbour, Patisserie Valerie. Even so, Maison Bertaux is often likened to a corner of Paris in the heart of Soho. 'Maison gateaux' would be more appropriate, given the profusion of pastries, from éclairs to tarts and almond cakes. Upstairs is a small tearoom where the manager, Johan, claims that his clients tend to be 'more arty-farty and sophisticated' than the younger, hipper patrons of Patisserie Valerie round the corner. Vive la difference!

Maison Bertaux, th oldest patisserie in London (1871)

Patisserie Valerie *(44 Old Compton St; Mon–Sat)* dates back to the 18th century when it was a book shop and tearoom for London's literati. This Soho institution is still renowned for its Continental breakfasts, French patisserie and classic teas. This is the founding member of the small and highly individualistic chain that now restricts itself to a handful of branches.

Segafredo Zanetti *(72 Baker St; daily)* is owned by the Zanetti Italian coffee barons who source the coffee from their own plantations in Brazil. Recently declared the best coffee in London by top Italian chefs, this café should be the first of a hundred planned for the UK over the next few years. Apart from challenging the dominance of the American-style coffee chains, now a fixture of every high street, Segafredo want to provide the classic Italian bar experience, where alcohol or coffee can be drunk at any time of day in a lively yet personable environment.

Area 2: Covent Garden and Holborn

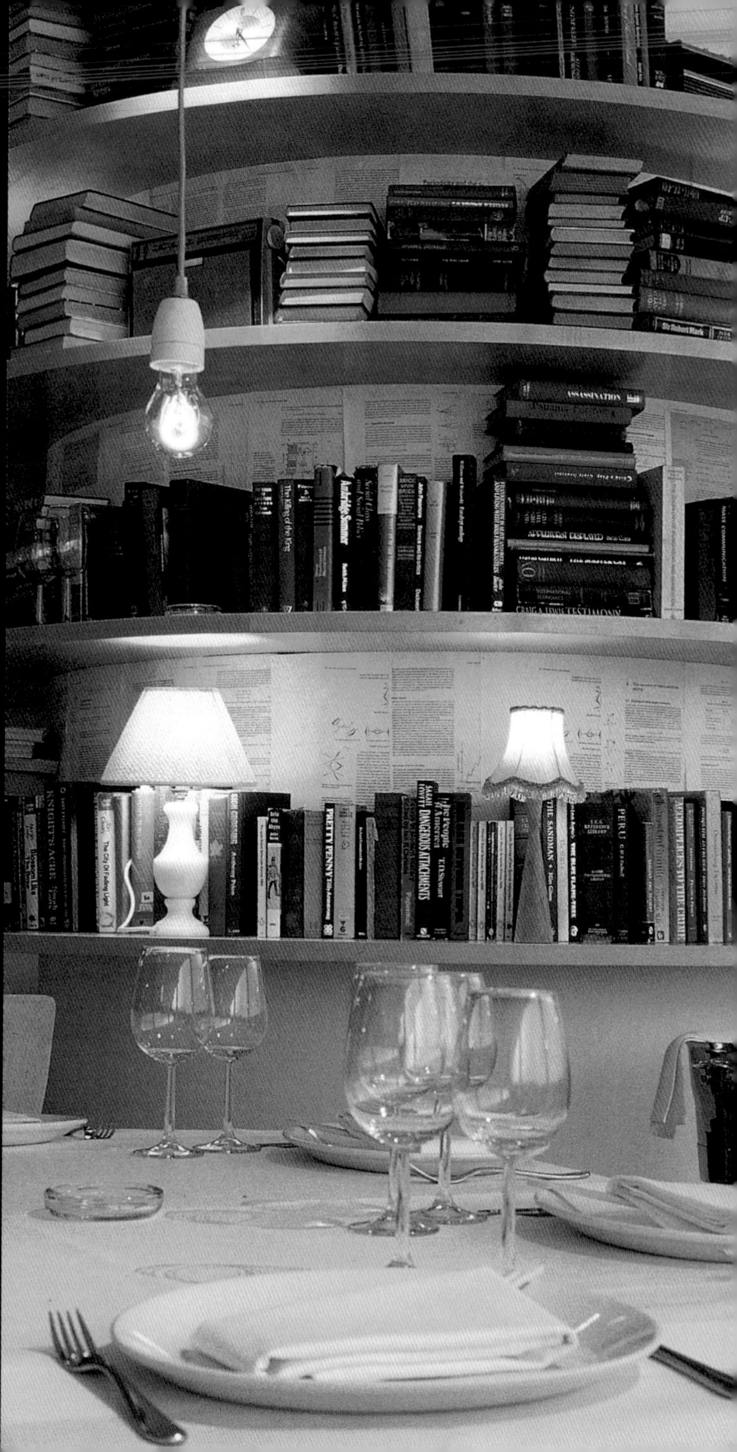

COVENT GARDEN AND HOLBORN

Covent Garden's many restaurants feed hungry hordes of theatregoers and clubbers. Holborn's gourmet hideaways offer refuge from the throng

One half of this area encompasses the sight-packed, entertainment epi-centre of Covent Garden, home to the Royal Opera House, the English National Opera and countless theatres; the other encompass-es the legal, press and financial institutions of Holborn. Fringed by Oxford Street and increasingly hip Clerkenwell to the north, Soho to the west, the City to the east and the Thames to the south, it's an eclectic mix – and one reflected in the incredible diversity of the restaurants that cater to it.

Covent Garden and the Strand

Named after a convent whose fields occuped the site, Covent Garden was for centuries the principal market in London for vegetables, fruit and flowers. After the market moved out in 1974, the area became a blueprint for turning old commercial buildings into a mall of designer boutiques, gift and special-ist shops and craft stalls. Numerous restaurants and cafés now occupy the old warehouses in the narrow streets and alleyways surrounding the market square. The Piazza itself was originally laid out in 1630 with colonnaded townhouses designed by Inigo Jones and is dominated by St Paul's church (known as the actor's church, it was used as a backdrop in the musical *My Fair Lady*). The pedestrianised square is still the hub of the area and is usual-ly occupied by street entertainers who draw the crowds.

Just north of the Piazza is the thoroughfare of Long Acre, much of which is given over to shops and coffee outlets, but there is the occasional individual restaurant worth seeking out. Nearby, the little alleys and cobbled streets that converge on Seven Dials are home to cosy restaurants. Indeed, often the best finds (such as The Ivy and Mon Plaisir) are tucked away down a side street.

West of the Piazza is the frenetic centre of Leicester Square – its overspill of visitors is clearly apparent around Garrick Lane, King Street and St Martin's Lane, with the first two almost entirely given over to food outlets. Among the ubiquitous Starbucks and All Bar Ones can be found the odd treat – including Asia de Cuba, Ian Schrager's wonderfully wacky St Martin's Lane hotel restaurant. From here, the National Portrait Gallery and the spires of St Martin's-in-the-Field are clearly visible, as well as Nelson atop his column, looking down over the newly pedestri-anised, fountain-filled Trafalgar Square.

Left: Asia de Cuba. Below: contemporary design at the Langley Bar

East of the Piazza, past the Theatre Museum, lies Drury Lane, traditional home of British theatre. Its principal venue is the Theatre Royal, but there are many theatres scattered around here and along the Strand, catered to by a wide selection of restaurants, many with special pre- and post-theatre offerings.

Although hard to believe today, the Strand once edged the Thames (the Victoria Embankment wasn't built until the 1860s), its south side lined with huge riverside mansions. Most of these have gone, replaced by streets named after their former owners, such as Buckingham and Villiers. Beyond, the Embankment Gardens offer a serene spot for a bench picnic, while down on the water, tourist boats offer river-view dining *(see page 37)*.

The Strand itself is a commercial thoroughfare, its shops and offices interspersed with the usual food chain and takeaway suspects. About half way down, Simpson's-in-the-Strand is a haven of British tradition. Next door, The Savoy Hotel (whose kitchens are being colonised by Gordon Ramsay and Marcus Wareing) also boasts river views. At the far end, the neoclassical Somerset House's terrace is ideal for a drink after perusing the Courtauld Institute collection of 20th-century European art. In winter, the courtyard is turned into a sparkling ice-rink, where after-work drinkers gather to sip chilly beer and wine and watch the skaters – or join in.

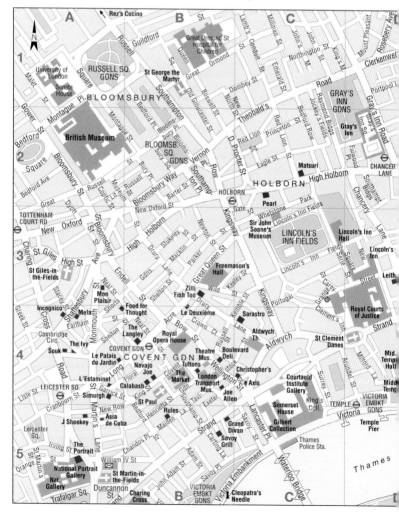

Holborn

Running north to south, Kingsway provides a neat division between the bright lights of Covent Garden to the west and Holborn to the east. The glorious neogothic facade of the Royal Courts of Justice heralds the start of more serious business. All around this area are the Inns of Court, home of London's legal profession. To the right are the narrow passageways of the Inner and Middle Temple Inns of Court, while ahead is Fleet Street – erstwhile home of Britain's national newspapers and now occupied by investment banks and multinationals. Fast-food chains and old-world taverns predominate.

North of here, in the heart of Holborn, modern office blocks rub shoulders with some outstanding historic buildings: the 15th- and 16th-century architecture and tree-lined squares of Lincoln's Inn and Gray's Inn. In these backstreets

there are ample refreshments if you know where to look, such as Leith's, tucked into the Law Society HQ, or the swanky new Pearl Restaurant, inside the Renaissance Chancery Court Hotel on High Holborn.

Heading east along High Holborn, past the distinctive 16th-century black and white facade of Staple Inn, the quiet streets just north of Holborn Circus encompass Hatton Garden – the centre of London's diamond trade – Leather Lane Market, a crowded street where market stalls sell fresh food and household goods, and the peaceful enclave of Bleeding Heart Yard, setting of much of the domestic action in Charles Dickens' *Little Dorrit* and home to a charming restaurant. And finally, the conjoining Farringdon Road and Clerkenwell Road together offer a surprising mix of international fare.

FIVE OF THE BEST

J Sheekey: tables are hot property at this excellent fish restaurant

Asia de Cuba: wacky restaurant with a creative 'fusion' menu, inside achingly hip St Martin's Lane hotel

Bleeding Heart: classic French gastronomy in a hidden courtyard – one of the City's best finds

Souk: candlelight, low seating, belly-dancing and good tagines. Exotic fun

The Portrait: for magical views of the West End skyline

African

Calabash

The Africa Centre, 38 King St, WC2 [B4]. Tel: 7836 1976. Open: L and D Mon–Fri, D only Sat. £

The food served in this relaxed basement eatery of the Africa Centre is good quality, hearty and surprisingly cheap (just £2.20 for some starters). An interesting menu exhibits a wide range of meat and vegetarian dishes along with their African countries of origin, such as chicken yassa from Senegal and fish/spinach egusi from Nigeria. Wines from South Africa.

American

Christopher's

18 Wellington St, WC2 [C4]. Tel: 7240 4222. Open: L and D Mon–Sat, Br Sat–Sun. ££ (set menus), ££££ www.christophersgrill.com

This beautifully renovated restaurant in a listed Victorian building offers a touch of class in this category. Dishes on the contemporary

Calabash, for cheap and hearty African specialities

American menu are imaginative and usually well prepared, though they don't always hit the mark, but the elegant dining rooms and sophisticated decor are the main attraction. Good-value pre- and post-theatre menus.

Joe Allen

13 Exeter St, WC2 [B4]. Tel: 7836 0651. Open: noon–midnight Mon–Sat, D only Sun. ££ (brunch, pre-theatre and late-supper menus), £££ www.joeallen.co.uk

Tucked away down an innocuous side street, below street level, there is something warmly welcoming about this relaxed diner, popular with the acting fraternity. The menu is predictable enough – salads, steaks, spare ribs, pecan pie – and the quality decidedly average, but the congenial atmosphere and the fact that diners can enjoy cocktails until 12.45am assure its popularity. Reservations advisable.

Navajo Joe

34 King St, WC2 [B4]. Tel: 7240 4008. Open: L and D daily. £££ www.navajojoe.co.uk

This big, bustling joint stocks 260+ varieties of tequila – apparently the largest collection outside Mexico. The huge bar meets most other alcoholic requests too, but the split-level restaurant also offers a relaxed place to go for 'comfort' fare. Choose from a selection of Tex-Mex dishes, salads, grills, and specials such as whole crab and nut-crusted sweet peppers. Live DJ bar downstairs Thur–Sat night.

British

Rules

35 Maiden Lane, WC2 [B5]. Tel: 7836 5314. Open: L and D daily. ££ (pre-theatre menu), ££££ www.rules.co.uk

Historic haunt of Charles Dickens and Dr Samuel Johnson

Being London's oldest restaurant (estab. 1798) is inevitably a draw in itself – Rules claims to serve 500 people a day – and the decor reflects its heritage: floor-to-ceiling prints, mounted horns, gently revolving fans, brass trimmings and red-velvet booths. The robust cuisine has also stood the test of time and the ingredients remain quintessentially English, with beef, lamb and a variety of game from Rules' own estate in the Pennines. Non-smoking throughout. Reservations advisable.

Simpson's-in-the-Strand, Grand Divan

100 The Strand, WC2 [B5]. Tel: 7836 9112. Open: L and D daily, plus B Mon–Fri. £ (breakfast menu), ££ (set menu), ££££ www.simpsons-in-the-strand.com
This bastion of Britishness retains all the grandeur of bygone days – high ceilings, gleaming chandeliers, oak-panelled 'booths' and tail-coated waiters – while also managing a surprisingly relaxed atmosphere. The menu remains traditional (beef fillet, calves liver, duck and Dover sole) but for many the famed roast beef, wheeled in on a silver-domed carving trolley, is the only choice. A good place to breakfast like a king. Reservations advisable.

El Vino

47 Fleet St, EC4 [D4]. Tel: 7353 6786. Open: L and D Mon–Fri. ££ www.elvino.co.uk
Licensed by the same family for over a century, El Vino has long been a favoured lunchtime haunt. The cellar restaurant, popular with journalists and politicians, remains hearteningly old-fashioned, bedecked with old prints and church pews for seats. British classics – steak and kidney pie, fish and chips, and smoked salmon – are assured, accompanied by fabulous wines (it doubles as a specialist wine shop). Reservations advisable.

Ye Olde Cheshire Cheese

145 Fleet St, EC4 [D3]. Tel: 7583 9656. Open: L and D Mon–Sat, L only Sun. ££ www.yeoldecheshirecheese.com
Easily dismissed as a tourist trap, the age and history of this ancient nooks-and-crannies pub are nonetheless impressive. As the sign states, it was 'the known haunt of Samuel Johnson, Charles Dickens and countless others'. The atmospheric restaurant, known as the Chop Room, has wood-panelling, sawdust on the floor and an open fire in winter and serves established English 'fayre', with daily specials.

Did you know?
Dr Samuel Johnson, who famously quipped 'a man who is tired of London is tired of life', lived near Fleet Street at 17 Gough Square from 1748 to 1759, where he compiled the first English dictionary. His house is now a museum dedicated to the great man of letters. Drinkers in the nearby Ye Olde Cheshire Cheese pub still raise a glass in his memory.

*The cobbled
courtyard
of Bleeding
Heart*

Fish

Le Palais du Jardin

*136 Long Acre, WC2 [A4]. Tel:
7379 5353. Open: L and D
daily. £££*

The oval bar, glossy wooden parti-
tions, and brass banisters of this
huge brasserie are reminiscent of a
ship's polished interior, while lush
greenery and large skylights give
the mezzanine an alfresco feel
(there is pavement seating in
summer). Fresh fish and seafood
platters are the focus, with supple-
mentary meat dishes. At £16.50,
the (whole) lobster thermidor is a
treat. No cheques.

J Sheekey ⑪

*28–32 St Martin's Court, WC2
[A5]. Tel: 7240 2565. Open: L
and D daily. ££ (weekend lunch
menu), ££££*

Sister restaurant to The Ivy and
Caprice, J Sheekey is a hot
favourite among critics. Set in a
series of panelled rooms hung with
black and white theatre prints, this
chic restaurant is a paradise for fish
lovers. Think chargrilled squid with
gorgonzola polenta, Cornish fish
stew and New England baby lobster, followed perhaps by rhubarb
pie or the famed Scandinavian iced
berries with white chocolate sauce.
The inventive menu is backed by
an impressive wine list.
Reservations necessary.

Zilli Fish Too

*8–18 Wild St, WC2 [B3]. Tel:
7240 0011. Open: L and D
Mon–Sat, L only Sun. ££ (set
menu), £££ www.zillialdo.com*

This pleasant brasserie is a good
pre-theatre choice, with some outside tables in summertime. At
night a youngish crowd fills the
upstairs, where the open-plan
kitchen produces fish-biased offerings, while downstairs alternates
between a weekday wine bar (with
separate menu) and a place for
kids to have their faces painted
and make their own pizzas on
Sundays. Set menu available,
reservations advisable late week.

French

Bleeding Heart ⑪

*Bleeding Heart Yard, Greville St,
EC1 [E2]. Tel: 7242 2056. Open:
L and D Mon–Fri. ££ (bistro),
£££ (set menu and à la carte)*

An absolute classic hidden away in
its own courtyard. Upstairs, lighter
fare is served in the breezy wine
bar or cobbled courtyard.
Downstairs is ideal for romance or
friends, in the low-ceilinged
'wine', 'library' and 'cellar'
rooms. Lobster millefeuille,
warm foie gras, roast Croisse
duckling, and steak are done to
perfection, with a well-stocked
cheese trolley and a superb wine

list, including offerings from its own vineyard in Trinity Hill, New Zealand. Reservations necessary.

L'Estaminet
14 Garrick St, WC2 [A4]. Tel: 7379 1432. Open: L and D Mon–Fri, D only Sat. ££ (pre-theatre menu), £££
There's an old-fashioned charm about this French restaurant: the pale yellow walls, barred and shuttered windows, and exposed brick-work of the main room have a gently Gallic feel, as does the menu, complete with hand-drawn illustrations. There are the requisite terrine, escargot and saucisson starters, followed by a good selection of classic meat dishes (not so good for vegetarians). Service not always as accomplished as it should be. Reservations advisable.

Incognico
117 Shaftesbury Ave, WC2 [A4]. Tel: 7836 8866. Open: L and D Mon–Sat. ££ (set menu), ££££
This oasis of calm amid the chaos of Shaftesbury Avenue is as well disguised as its name implies: the plain brown exterior and window blinds give little indication of the excellent restaurant within. The menu offers straightforward, beautifully executed brasserie dishes, and a French-biased but international wine list. Reservations advisable.

Mon Plaisir
19–21 Monmouth St, WC2 [A3]. Tel: 7836 7243. Open: L and D Mon–Fri, D only Sat. ££ (set menu), £££
www.monplaisir.co.uk
'A little piece of England that will remain forever France' – or so the publicity goes. It's true that this cosy and intimate restaurant couldn't be more French: from the owner and regulars to the posters, ornamental frogs and

accordians scattered around and, of course, the menu, which features escargots, coquilles St Jacques, veal, rabbit, foie gras and a mouthwatering selection of perfectly matured cheeses. Excellent pre-theatre menu. Reservations advisable.

Indian

Mela
152–156 Shaftesbury Ave, WC2 [A4]. Tel: 7836 8635. Open: L and D daily. ££
www.melarestaurant.co.uk
This large, brasserie-style Indian restaurant, with its yellow facade, wooden tables, and colourful wall-hangings, brings a fresh, modern approach to both decor and food. Creamy kormas are few and far between among the authentic

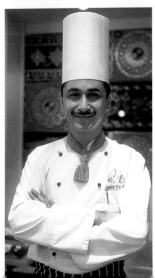

Mela's chefs create authentic dishes inspired by rural Indian recipes

regional dishes such as sula shaslik (skewered chargrilled duck), a variety of tawas (dishes cooked on a hotplate) and more exotic offerings like stir-fried peppered lobster, spicy rabbit in onion yogurt gravy, or sea bass in coconut, coriander and mint. There's a good vegetarian selection and numerous gluten and dairy-free options.

International

Asia de Cuba 🍽️

St Martin's Lane Hotel, 45 St Martin's Lane, WC2 [A5]. Tel: 7300 5500. Open: L and D daily. £££ (pre-theatre menu), ££££ www.asiadecuba-restaurant.com
Attached to one of London's hippest hotels, this restaurant is constantly buzzing. The decor is eccentric, with flowerpot-covered pillars, shelves stacked with old radios and books, all lit by low-slung naked light bulbs. The fusion menu is equally imaginative, and sharing is encouraged so that you get to sample more. Lobster

State-of-the-art venues Asia de Cuba (below) and Axis (opposite)

parcels, a flavour-packed pot-roast pork, and melt-in-your-mouth tuna are a few of the temptations on offer. Leave room for dessert. Reservations necessary.

Axis

One Aldwych, WC2 [C4]. Tel: 7300 0300. Open: L and D Mon–Fri, D only Sat. £££ (set menu), ££££ www.onealdwych.com
Aperitifs in One Aldwych's uber-trendy Lobby Bar are a must before heading to the double-height restaurant below. Under the striking New York skyline mural is served an intriguing melange of treats: perhaps smoked ham hock raviolo with vegetable remoulade, followed by wild Canadian halibut with artichoke barigoule, sweet pepper aioli and lobster dressing. The atmosphere is refined yet relaxed, and on Tues–Wed, an excellent set menu is accompanied by live jazz. Reservations advisable.

Pearl

Renaissance Chancery Court Hotel, 252 High Holborn, WC1 [C2]. Tel: 7829 7000. Open: L and D Mon–Fri, D only Sat. £££ (set menu), ££££ www.pearl-restaurant.com
As this book went to press, top designer Keith Hobbs (of Nobu and Metropolitan fame) was transforming the former QC restaurant into what promises to be a grand and opulent new venue. Happily, perfectionist chef, Jun Tanaka, will remain in the kitchen. His menu is select, but each dish is an inspired combination of seasonal ingredients. The choice might include smoked pigeon with baby beetroot, rocket salad and spring roll of confit leg; smoked red mullet with herb gnocchi, piquillo peppers, chorizo and paprika, ending with a caramel and honeycomb bombe.

Japanese

Matsuri

71 High Holborn, WC1 [C2]. Tel: 7430 1970. L and D Mon–Sat. ££–£££ (including set menus) www.matsuri-restaurant.com
Though the decor verges on the clinical, this relatively new Japanese has become a destination restaurant for aficionados of sushi, which is excellent here. There's a good selection of set menus for the uninitiated or those who simply can't make up their mind. The sister restaurant in St James's *(15 Bury St, SW1; tel: 7839 1101)* is more traditional, but comes equally recommended.

Yokoso Sushi

40 Whitefriars St, EC4 [E3]. Tel: 7583 9656. Open: Mon–Fri 11am–8pm. £
It's easy to miss this small restaurant just off Fleet Street. Inside it is a simple affair, with wooden floors and white-washed walls, but it is worth ducking into for a tasty, healthy meal. The central revolving belt transports a tempting array of all the usuals – nigiri, maki, sashimi, tempura – in colour-coded dishes, at reasonable prices.

Middle Eastern

Simurgh

17 Garrick St, WC2 [A4]. Tel: 7240 7811. Open: L and D Mon–Sat, D only Sun. ££ www.simurghrestaurant.com
Inside, the only indications of this restaurant's Persian leanings are a few silky ceiling drapes and cushions. However, the menu is pure Iranian, offering vine leaves, meatballs and reshteh soup followed by meat skewers and stews. Belly dancers enhance the mood

Italian

Cantina Augusto

91–95 Clerkenwell Rd, EC1 [D1]. Tel: 7242 3246. Open: L and D Mon–Fri. ££ www.cantinaaugusto.co.uk
This bustling Italian is very much a family affair, with various members offering a warm welcome. It's popular with locals, who come to enjoy the well-presented pasta dishes and generous pizzas (pick your toppings at the open kitchen), accompanied by a predominantly Italian wine list. A more formal area downstairs serves meat and fish dishes at lunchtime. Reservations advisable.

Rez's Cucina

17–21 Tavistock St, WC2 [A1]. Tel: 7379 9991. Open: L and D daily. £ (set menu) ££ www.rezs.co.uk
This big, airy Italian, run by enthusiastic staff, offers a choice of light and tasty dishes. Aside from the usual pasta and pizza selection, there's also a nice mix of fish and meat mains. Retractable doors allow tables to spill out onto the pavement in summer. It is popular with pre-theatre and weekend diners, attracted by its reasonable prices. Pre-theatre menu available.

on Saturdays; if it's busy, you get to eat in the tiny and rather more evocative room downstairs.

Modern European

Banquette

The Savoy, Strand, WC2 [B5]. Tel: 7420 2392. Open: noon–midnight Mon–Sat, until 10.30pm Sun £££ www.gordonramsay.com
The latest rabbit to be pulled out of the Ramsay/Wareing hat, is this cute 1950s American diner-style eatery, which brings a breath of fresh air to the stuffy Savoy. The menu, offering generous homely dishes such as shepherd's pie and steak and kidney pud, is a recipe for success. The same dynamic duo are also behind the revamped Savoy Grill *(see page 38)*.

Boulevard Deli

36 Wellington St, WC2 [B4]. Tel: 7836 6789. Open: Mon–Sat 9am–8pm, Sun 11am–8pm. £
For a light meal, this cool, high-class delicatessen just off the Strand is ideal. Sandwiches (made from bread freshly baked on-site), rotisserie chicken, delicious salads and snacks can be eaten at the small indoor or pavement tables. And while you're here, why not pick up some treats for supper or tomorrow's lunch from the gourmet deli.

Le Deuxième

65a Long Acre, WC2 [B3/B4]. Tel: 7379 0033. Open: L and D daily. ££ (set menu), £££
The stark white walls and crisp table linen interrupted with the occasional splash of floral colour, provide a cool contemporary setting for the refreshingly original menu. Perhaps a tian of crab and spinach for starters, followed by butternut squash ravioli tossed in sage and pine-nut butter, or pan-seared Arctic char on kedgeree with a light curry sauce. Good pre-opera venue. Reservations advisable.

Flâneur Food Hall

41 Farringdon Rd, EC1 [E1]. Tel: 7404 4422. Open: L and D Mon–Fri, Br (9–4pm) and D Sat, Br only Sun (closes 6pm). ££–£££
This Farringdon Road oasis will get your taste buds working overtime. The floor-to-ceiling shelves are stacked with top-quality gourmet treats from across Europe: chocolate, tea/coffee, olive oils, jams, sauces, biscotti, dairy products, fresh juices and cheese. The restaurant's offerings are both flavoursome and healthy, plus there is a separate takeaway menu of freshly prepared meat and vegetarian meals.

The Ivy

1 West St, WC2 [A4]. Tel: 7836 4751. Open: L and D daily. ££ (Sat–Sun lunch menu), ££££
It's one of London's most famous haunts, yet fame has not gone to its head, and it remains one of the most desirable. The downside is the difficulty in getting a table – you need to reserve weeks rather than

Flâneur Food Hall: gourmet food to eat in or take away

The Langley

days ahead. Given its popularity, the atmosphere is surprisingly unaffected. The menu is comfortingly familiar (British interjected with international favourites), the wine list strong and the surreptitious starspotting irresistible.

The Langley

5 Langley St, WC2 [B4]. Tel: 7836 5005. Open: D only Mon–Sat until 1am, Sun until 10.30pm. ££ (set menu), £££ www.thelangley.co.uk

Set in a series of underground cellars and decorated with angular sofas, cream leather booths and stripey walls, the Langley is an appealing blend of contemporary design and 1970s retro. The restaurant offers straightforward fare (crab/avocado salad, herb-crusted lamb) and is behind the cocktail bar/dance floor, so not good for a quiet bite to eat, but great if you're in the mood for funky music and a lively atmosphere. A good place to start or end the night. £7 entry charge after 10pm at weekends.

Leith's

113 Chancery Lane, WC2 [D3]. Tel: 7316 5580. Open: L only Mon–Fri (plus snack menu 5–9pm). ££

An offshoot of Leith's Cookery School, this relaxed corner of the Law Society's impressive HQ is ideal for a light, fresh lunch. Served in a contemporary, high-ceilinged room, its eclectic fish, meat, vegetarian and salad menu may include citrus-crusted lamb rump alongside spinach and blue cheese gnocchi, and seafood risotto – plus a signature dish taken from the famous cookery book. Set-price menu, daily specials. Reservations advisable.

The Portrait

National Portrait Gallery, St Martin's Place, WC2 [A5]. Tel: 7312 2490. Open: L only Sat–Wed, L and D Thur–Fri. £££ www.searcys.co.uk

When it comes to location, few can beat The Portrait on the top floor of the National Portrait Gallery. It offers wonderful views of Nelson's Column in the pedestrianised Trafalgar Square, Big Ben, and the Millennium Wheel revolving in the distance. And the food is above average by most gallery restaurant standards.

Sarastro

126 Drury Lane, WC2 [C4]. Tel: 7836 0101. Open: L and D daily. £ (set lunch menu), ££ www.sarastro-restaurant.com

TIP

Dining cruises on the Thames are offered by **Bateaux London** *(Embankment Pier; tel: 7925 2215; L and D Mon–Sat, L only Sun; ££–££££).* Choose between the elegant glass cruiser *Symphony* and the more traditional vessel *Naticia.* The international menu is more reliable than inspired, but it's pleasant to drift past the historic sights as you sip a glass of wine, particularly at night when they're all lit up. Live jazz on Sundays. Reservations advisable .

Above: Covent Garden rickshaw wallah.

Below: the vodka flows at Potemkin

'The show after the show' is this bizarrely over-the-top restaurant's slogan. It certainly makes for an unusual dining experience. The flamboyant decor is a stage set in itself with its velvet drapes, golden chairs, opera boxes and alcoves, chandeliers and theatrical props. The menu is more straightforward, offering basic fish, meat and vegetarian options. At £10, the two-course lunch/pre-matinee menu is very good value.

Savoy Grill
The Savoy, Strand, WC2 [B5]. Tel: 7592 1600. Open: L and D daily. £££ (set lunch), ££££ www.savoy-group.co.uk
The Savoy Grill, long synonymous with old-fashioned British gentility, has been restored to something of its former glory under the stewardship of Marcus Wareing of Michelin-starred Pétrus fame. Sophisticated creations like roast Anjou pigeon with sautéed cepes and pan-fried foie gras or prawn tortellini with lime and chervil, vegetable ribbons and white asparagus are as exquisite as you would expect from Gordon Ramsay's protégé and co-conspirator in the revitalisation of London's hotel dining. Marcus Wareing's magic touch, which has

brought him another Michelin star, also extends to the newly opened Banquette upstairs *(see page 36)*.

Tuttons
11–12 Russell St, WC2 [B4]. Tel: 7836 4141. Open: B, Br, L and D daily. ££ (set menu), £££
Tuttons is a Covent Garden landmark, particularly in fine weather when it unfurls the red awnings and tables spill out onto the piazza. Aside from the obvious merits of its position, it is a fun place for brunch or lunch, with some nice variations on the normal brasserie fare. For a tourist venue, it's surprisingly good.

Whites
1 New Street Square, EC4 [E3]. Tel: 7583 1313. Open: L and D Mon–Fri. £££ www.whitestarline.org.uk
Replacing Gary Rhode's sadly defunct City Rhodes, Marco Pierre White's Holborn restaurant (the eighth in the MPW London stable) has quickly established a reputation and is popular among city workers keen to impress clients over lunch. Simply furnished, it provides a neutral backdrop for the sort of accomplished fare you would expect. The accent, of course, is Gallic. Reservations advisable.

Moroccan

Souk
27 Litchfield St, WC2 [A4]. Tel: 7240 1796. Open: L and D daily. ££ www.soukrestaurant.net

A narrow side corridor leads down to small candlelit rooms below, where low seats and cushions are set around brass tables, with two tiny 'caves' offering more intimate dining. Cramped but decidedly atmospheric, it's the perfect setting for a Moroccan feast. The menu offers the usual mezze for starters, with a selection of couscous and tagine dishes for the main. Belly-dancing on most nights. Good fun. Reservations advisable.

Russian

Potemkin
144 Clerkenwell Rd [D1]. Tel: 7278 6661. Open: D only Sat–Wed, L and D Thur–Fri. £ (set lunch), £££ www.potemkin.co.uk

The huge success of this Russian restaurant is largely down to the 140+ types of vodka it serves in the compact bar upstairs (live music Weds). The downstairs restaurant has an interesting menu of Russian offerings: cossack lamb casserole, golubtsy (stuffed cabbage), pelmeni (siberian dumplings), perepeulka (quail) and of course caviar.

Vegetarian

Food for Thought
31 Neal St, WC2 [A4]. Tel: 7836 9072. Open: Br, L and D Mon–Sat, L only Sun. £

This small, pleasant eatery offers an imaginative selection of generous and affordable dishes, with a daily changing menu. Tom yam soup might be followed by gnocchi gorgonzola with garlic roasted chestnuts and oyster mushrooms, while a BYOB policy (no corkage) means it can be enjoyed with your favourite tipple. No credit cards, no smoking and no reservations.

PUBS, BARS AND CAFÉS

As expected, cafés, wine bars and pubs are ten a penny in the Covent Garden area – ideal for a relaxed lunch or a night on the town, with happy hours/late closing hours commonplace. For sheer location, it's hard to beat **The Portrait Bar** overlooking Trafalgar Square or **The Opera Terrace Bar** above the Piazza. Old favourites, such as the **Cork & Bottle** (44–46 Cranbourn St), still pull in the crowds thanks to their comfort factor and excellent wine lists, while venues like **Blend** (1a Shorts Gardens), **Browns** (4 Great Queen St) and **Denim** (4a Upper St Martin's Lane) appeal to trendy urbanites. If beer is your thing, try the **Freedom Brewing Company** (41 Earlham St), with huge copper tanks in situ, or the **Lowlander** (36 Drury Lane), boasting an impressive lager and ale list.

The American bar and grill **Smollensky's** *(see page 42)* stages live jazz, while the quieter streets along Embankment shelter more traditional English pubs.

Alternatively, some of the best bars are found in hotels, from classics like the **American Bar** *(Savoy Hotel, Strand)* to the ultra-fashionable **Lobby Bar** at One Aldwych.

The historic taverns around Fleet Street and Holborn are as popular as ever with tourists and local workers alike. Try **Ye Olde Cheshire Cheese** *(see page 31)*, **The Punch Tavern** *(99 Fleet St)* or **Cittie of Yorke** *(22 High Holborn)*. And wine bars such as **Holborn Colony** *(33 Brook St)*, **Tooks** *(17–18 Tooks Crt, Cursitor St)* and the romantic **Bleeding Heart Tavern** *(Greville St)* introduce a more modern touch.

Eating and Entertainment

For good food and great fun, consider choosing an establishment that combines both, such as a Soho jazz club or a Latin dance bar

A supper cruise on the Thames, with live music or a disco? Dinner in a Soho jazz club? A salsa class followed by a Tex-Mex supper? Or Sunday brunch in Indigo, One Aldwych, followed by a private viewing in the hotel's plush cinema? Whatever your mood and preferences, London has a vast array of interesting places where you can eat and be entertained at the same time.

The prices below are per person for a three-course meal (dinner) with half a bottle of house wine: **£** less than 20; **££** 20–30; **£££** 30–45; **££££** 45+. Bear in mind that there is also often a music charge, which is indicated below.

Music and dining clubs

These predominantly West End clubs represent some of the best places of entertainment in London. To find out what's on, pick up the *Jazz in London* leaflet from the main music venues or look at www.jazz-live.info. For other music venues, consult the weekly listings supplements in the weekend editions of the quality national newspapers or pick up the listings magazine that appears with the *Evening Standard* newspaper every Thursday.

Dover Street *(10 Dover St, W1; tel: 7629 9813; Mon–Fri noon–3pm, Mon–Thur 5.30pm–3am, Fri–Sat 7pm–3am, main act performs from 10.30pm; **££–£££** plus music charge of £6–15)*. This smart, well-established Mayfair club provides a tried and trusted French-inspired menu worthy of an upmarket restaurant. Asparagus hollandaise could be followed by sea bass or steak and matched by well-chosen French wines. The musical repertoire embraces jazz, rhythm and blues, Motown, funk and sassy dinner-jazz vocalists and bluesy singers such as Dana Gillespie. The house band, the Dover Street Jazz Trio, provides a sophisticated background to an early dinner, but when the big guest bands take over at 10.30pm the club really comes alive.

London's premier jazz club promises a great night out

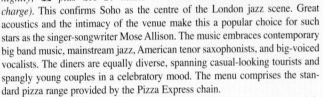

Jazz Café *(5 Parkway, NW1; tel: 7916 6060; 7pm–late; ££–£££ plus music charge of £17–30).* This self-consciously cool Camden Town venue attracts both big-name artists, such as Wynton Marsalis, and up-coming stars. The trendy vibe is reflected by cutting-edge sounds, from contemporary jazz to funk, soul jazz and Latin jazz, often with vocalists to the fore. The food often errs on the side of style over content but the clients seem not to mind.

Pizza Express Jazz Club *(10 Dean St, W1; tel: 7439 8722; nightly; ££ plus £15–20 music charge).* This confirms Soho as the centre of the London jazz scene. Great acoustics and the intimacy of the venue make this a popular choice for such stars as the singer-songwriter Mose Allison. The music embraces contemporary big band music, mainstream jazz, American tenor saxophonists, and big-voiced vocalists. The diners are equally diverse, spanning casual-looking tourists and spangly young couples in a celebratory mood. The menu comprises the standard pizza range provided by the Pizza Express chain.

In full swing at Ronnie Scott's

Pizza on the Park *(11–13 Knightsbridge, SW1; tel: 7235 5273; nightly from 7.30pm; ££ plus music charge of £10–18).* This music and dining venue specialises in showcasing mainstream live entertainment in a relaxed yet sophisticated setting, overlooking the park. The artists include cabaret singers, big-voiced blues and dinner-jazz vocalists, with vocals usually to the fore even in powerful jazz combos. The pizza-dominated menu is fine but unlikely to be as memorable as the music and sparkling atmosphere.

Ronnie Scott's *(47 Frith St, W1; tel: 7439 0747; Mon–Sat 8.30pm–3am, live music from 9.30pm; ££ plus music charge of £15–25).* This venerable Soho institution still manages to remain cool, despite its advanced age. As the premier jazz club in town, it attracts all the big names. The restaurant menu offers reasonably priced but uninspired nightclub food, ranging from pasta and salads to steak and chips. **Upstairs at Ronnie Scott's** is a popular night-club (Fri–Sat), which specialises in Latino music and hip-hop, with informal free salsa classes at 10pm on some nights.

606 *(90 Lots Rd, SW10; tel: 7352 5953; nightly from 8pm; ££ plus music charge of £6–8).* Tucked away behind the King's Road, this unobtrusive basement jazz restaurant is always buzzing with a good choice of traditional and contemporary bands, from piano trios to vocalists singing jazz standards. Freshly prepared dishes include lamb curry and swordfish.

Shino's *(Riverside Building, County Hall, SE1; tel: 7401 6514; daily 11am–1am, until 2am Fri–Sat, music from 8.45pm; ££ plus music charge of £6–10).* Run by Mr Shino, the eccentric and ever-present Japanese jazz aficionado, the venue is far more serious about its jazz credentials than its cuisine, which is vaguely Italian. The long, glass-fronted room exploits its lovely riverside location, overlooked by the London Eye, to draw in a languid, late-night 30-something crowd.

Smollensky's on the Strand *(The Strand, WC2; tel: 7497 2101; daily noon–11pm or midnight, live music from 7.30pm; ££ plus £5 music charge).* This popular venue offers sassy Latin jazz, including ingenious crossovers of salsa, merengue, rap and Afro-Cuban jazz. Billed as an American grill, it specialises in steaks, burgers and beef chilli, with good-value 'jazz menus' (£20).

Fun venues with live music

The Africa Centre *(38 King St, WC2; tel: 7836 1973, Calabash restaurant tel: 7836 1976; daily until 11pm; £ plus £7 music charge).* This is the starting point for all things African in London, from food and entertainment to crafts and culture. African cuisine is available in **Calabash**, the inexpensive basement restaurant where the homely ethnic mood is miles away from Covent Garden cool. **Club Limpopo** on the ground floor is the place for live entertainment on Friday and Saturday nights.

Bar Salsa *(96 Charing Cross Rd, WC2; tel: 7379 3277; £ plus music charge of £5–9).* A mecca for all those devoted to Latin American culture. Food is vaguely Tex-Mex, with fajitas and tapas to the fore. The vibrant Latin spirit embraces all ages, nationalities and body types, particularly during the free Salsa classes on Sunday and Wednesday.

Cubana *(36 Southwick St, W2; tel: 7402 7539; open nightly until late, live music Thur–Sat; £–££, no music charge).* This Cuban-themed cocktail bar and restaurant is the place for dancing of every Latin persuasion (includes late-night salsa lessons). The menu offers filling Cuban and Mexican dishes. It has a sister restaurant in Waterloo *(Lower Marsh Street, SE1. Tel: 7928 8778).*

Jazz After Dark *(9 Greek St, W1; tel: 7734 0545; Mon–Sat from 10.30pm; ££ plus £10 music charge).* Specialises in Latin-tinged jazz, blues, funk and soul in a scruffy but fun Soho club that is casual and cool. Serves tapas and Tex-Mex staples and cocktails.

La Rueda *(102 Wigmore St, W1; tel: 7486 1718; daily noon–11pm, flamenco dancing on Sat night, best to book; ££ but no music charge).* This well-established Spanish bar and restaurant prides itself on excellent food and service. It does all the staples well, from paella to fish, and is the antithesis of the 'feed them and fleece them' tourist menus so common in London.

Smollensky's on the Strand

Unusual venues

Axis *(One Aldwych, WC2; tel: 7300 0300; L except Sat & Sun, D except Sun; ££. Live jazz Tues and Wed evenings).* Set on the lower ground floor of the hotel, Axis provides a high-ceilinged, contemporary space in which to sample sophisticated cuisine. The jazz ranges from '20s classics to Latin jazz. Alternatively, take in a movie and a meal or enjoy Sunday brunch followed by a private screening *(see Indigo entry below).*

Bateaux London *(Embankment Pier, WC2; tel: 7925 2215; dinner, music and cruise packages £63–95; £££–££££).* French-run and as serious about food as they are about fun, Bateaux London is the best of the dinner-cruise companies. Its cruise includes a '360 degrees turn' at Tower Bridge, usually accompanied by a James Bond 007 theme tune.

Elysium *(68 Regent St, W1; tel: 7439 7770; Wed–Sat 10pm–late; £££–££££).* Set within the Café Royal, this nightclub, restaurant and cocktail bar has received plenty of celebrity endorsement from soap stars, pop stars and premiership footballers. The hot nightspot covers two floors, with a chill-out lounge bar area, and a would-be den of iniquity down below. Wednesday night is 'deep R&B' (that's American hip-hop, house and rap). The restaurant is designed in kitsch Moroccan style and features a pricey but eclectic set menu.

Festival Square, National Theatre Square *(Belvedere Rd, South Bank, SE1; tel: 7928 2228; Mon–Fri 7.30am–11pm, Sat 11am–11pm, Sun 11am–10pm. L noon–3pm, D 5–10pm; £; booking recommended for alfresco dining and at weekends).* This new café, bar, deli and brasserie represents the first phase in the redevelopment of the classical music complex. The buzzy brasserie serves modern European food from weekend brunch to quick bites, afternoon teas and full meals, including pre-concert menus.

Indigo *(One Aldwych, WC2; tel: 7300 0400; B, L and D daily; in-house movie and a meal option £35; ££).* This relaxed restaurant specialises in creative modern European cuisine (with 'healthy' and organic options) and overlooks the Lobby Bar, the stunning centrepiece of this contemporary hotel. On Friday to Sunday evenings it offers 'Give Me Movies' – dinner followed by a private screening in the hotel's cinema. Equally appealing is Sunday brunch followed by a Bloody Mary (or Bellini) and a movie. (These options are also available at Axis *(see above).*

Yatra *(34 Dover St, W1; tel: 7493 0200; daily, nightclub Thur–Sat evenings; ££).* Both a beguiling Eastern fantasy and a clever marketing exercise. Inspired by Planet Hollywood, Yatra's personable Indian owner plunges diners into the depths of Bollywood. The **Yatra Lounge** is a bohemian, faintly Arabian affair, which is a welcoming place for cocktails, beer or inexpensive but filling tapas. Beyond is the Indian-inspired **Yatra Restaurant**, divided between normal seating and floor-level seating with low tables. The menu features updated versions on Indian classics, with some creative twists. In the basement is the club known as **Café Bollywood** *(Tel: 7408 2001. Thur–Sat evenings. Diners at Yatra receive a 50 percent discount on the £8–£10 entry charge)* offering a blend of Indian and Western music.

Above: Eastern promise at Yatra's Café Bollywood

BLOOMSBURY AND FITZROVIA

Charlotte Street, the hub of media-savvy Fitzrovia, is a showcase of world food. For a taste of Bloomsbury elegance, head for Lamb's Conduit Street

Bloomsbury and Fitzrovia are cultural kingpins among the cluster of villages that make up London. Bloomsbury, the smarter and grander of the two areas, bounded by Gray's Inn Road to the east and Tottenham Court Road to the west, is dominated by the British Museum to the south and London University and its associated hospitals in the north. The area's name is still internationally identified with the Bloomsbury Group – artists and writers centred on Virginia Woolf, her sister Vanessa Bell, their husbands Leonard Woolf and Clive Bell, and their friends Roger Fry, Maynard Keynes, Duncan Grant, Lytton Strachey, Mark Gertler and Dora Carrington. For years Bloomsbury was the traditional home of London's book publishers and its name is still proudly carried by the leading house, which publishes many prestigious authors and bestselling titles, including the phenomenally successful Harry Potter books.

However, now that many of the publishers have moved away their place has been partly taken by other media, IT and television companies, and advertising and PR agencies. Literary and artistic associations, though, are still plentiful. Charles Dickens lived in Doughty Street, where his house is now a museum, and blue plaques commemorate the residence of very many other famous writers, as well as artists, down the years. The Pre-Raphaelite Brotherhood was founded in a house in Gower Street in Bloomsbury, while Dante Gabriel Rossetti and Holman Hunt shared a studio in Cleveland Street, Fitzrovia.

Georgian squares and Bohemian backstreets

Antiquarian bookshops and art galleries still cluster before the British Museum, and the Bloomsbury area is well served with hotels, the smartest close to the museum or overlooking green squares, the cheapest concentrated to the north, close to the three mainline railway termini of Euston, St Pancras and King's Cross. Many of the smarter hotels have restaurants of their own, some open also to non-residents, but in general they tend to be pricey and a little disappointing in comparison with the livelier dining rooms situated in the surrounding streets. Bloomsbury is also characterised by its Georgian streets and its squares, which give it prestige, architectural distinction and more green space than most parts of the capital enjoy. Bloomsbury Square, indeed, was the very first of London's squares to be so named, having originally been the Earl of Southampton's garden, while Bedford Square is the only complete Georgian square surviving in London.

Fitzrovia, west of Tottenham Court Road, is more modest, more tawdry, more cosmopolitan and more bohemian than its Bloomsbury neighbour. The area was developed in the 18th century by the Stuart earls of Southampton whose family name was Fitzroy (lit. 'son of the king', because they

Opposite: Villandry Below: palate refreshers at Rasa Samudra

were descended from an illegitimate son of Charles II and the Duchess of Cleveland) in competition with the neighbouring more richly endowed Bedford and Newcastle (later Portland and Howard de Walden) estates, which were the origins of Bloomsbury and Marylebone respectively. It was a competition in which Fitzrovia almost inevitably finished a poor third, its buildings soon carved up into lodging houses and workshops, cheap enough to attract immigrant communities plus artists and writers who either could not afford a smarter address or did not want one.

The name Fitzrovia was coined by literati in honour of their haunt the Fitzroy Tavern, on the corner of Charlotte and Windmill streets, which attracted a notoriously motley gaggle of louche characters in the period between the two world wars. Regulars included the ostentatiously bohemian artist Augustus John, the polemical Wyndham Lewis, the contrasting Etonians George Orwell and Anthony Powell *(A Dance to the Music of Time)*, and the prodigiously gifted alcoholics Dylan Thomas *(Under Milk Wood)* and Malcolm Lowry *(Under the Volcano)*. Most recent upholders of Fitzrovia's artistic traditions have included the artists Francis Bacon and Lucien Freud.

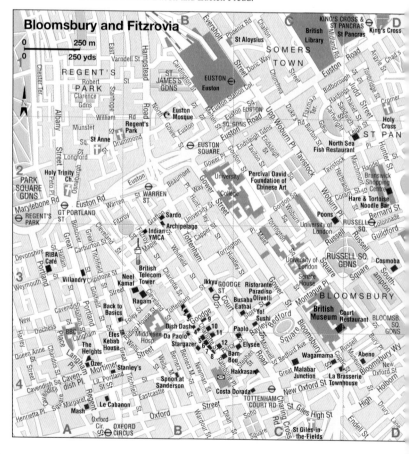

World food

Eating out has always been a defining feature of both areas. Indeed, butchers, bakers, confectioners, greengrocers and even delicatessens are almost entirely absent (I Fratelli Camisa at 53 Charlotte Street was the solitary exception until Villandry migrated from Marylebone to Great Portland Street a few years ago). There are supermarkets along Tottenham

Court Road and in Brunswick Square, but no food market. By contrast with that seeming poverty of provision, there is a proliferation of cheap sandwich bars and cafés, and Fitzrovia's principal food street, Charlotte Street, is a living atlas of the world's cuisines. Even so, it is rivalled in its eclecticism by the more modest and often unpreposessing premises along Cleveland Street,

Charlotte Street
1 Giardinetto
2 Navarro's
3 Pescatori
4 Fino
5 Bertorelli
6 Oscar
7 La Perla
8 Rasa Samudra
9 Pied à Terre
10 Elena's l'Etoile
11 Passione
12 Josephine's

where cheap eats and bargain meals for those, such as students, nurses and backpacking tourists, who are on a tight budget, abound.

Other concentrations of good restaurants are found around Lamb's Conduit Street in the heart of Bloomsbury and in the pleasingly village-like atmosphere centred on Foley Street in the south of Fitzrovia. To the southwest, where the area abuts the West End shopping meccas of Oxford and Regent streets, it is the rag trade (wholesale fashions) that traditionally predominates, but here too the side roads and alleyways provide opportunities for tired shoppers and office workers to slip away for affordable meals in a catholic variety of cuisines.

In pretty Queen Square, tucked away behind the large hotels along Southampton Row, there is still a notice, attached to a pub adjacent to the Italianate church, commemorating the wise words of Robert Louis Stevenson about the area. Observing that it was dominated by seats of learning, art galleries, publishing houses, libraries, hospitals and children's homes, he wrote that it seemed 'set aside for the humanities of life and the alleviation of all hard miseries'. The words are as true today as when he wrote them.

British

Court Restaurant

The British Museum Great Court, Great Russell St, W1 [C3]. Tel: 7323 8990. Open: L and T daily, D Thur–Sat. ££ (set lunch), £££ www.digbytrout.co.uk
Overlooking the Reading Room and bathed in light from the elegant glass and steel roof, this underappreciated, often quiet catering facility offers dishes such as Welsh cockle and sea trout stew, Gloucester Old Spot pork with pink peppercorns, and broad bean and lemon risotto. Recommended whether or not you happen to be visiting the museum.

Oscar

Charlotte Street Hotel, 15 Charlotte St, W1 [B4]. Tel: 7806 2000. Open: L and D Mon–Sat, D only Sun. ££££ www.firmdalehotels.com
Cavernous wooden-floored restaurant in a sleekly chic hotel converted from Victorian factory premises. The open kitchen adds to the air of business, and tables and chairs spill out in front of the large ground-floor windows in summer. The eclectic 'modern British' menu includes luxuries (caviar, oysters, truffle risotto), exotica (char-grilled halloumi, seared Thai marinated beef, mozzarella di bufala) and classics (roast rib of beef, grilled Dover sole) in roughly equal numbers. Sunday night is movie night, when a three-course dinner and a classic or popular movie costs £30 per person excluding drinks and service.

Stanley's

6 Little Portland St, W1 [A4]. Tel: 7462 0099. Open: L and D Mon–Sat. ££
Big and bustling beer and sausage restaurant offering an imaginative range of own-made sausages (from pure pork and Welsh lamb to Caribbean jerk and stuffed squid), which are all preservative-free, and a good choice of ales and beer. Fish and vegetarian alternatives available. The bar also does cocktails, and sausages are sold at £8.50 to £10.25 a kilo to cook at home.

Chinese

Hakkasan 🍷

8 Hanway Place, W1 [C4]. Tel: 7907 1888. Open: L and D Mon–Sat, D only Sun. Bar open until 2am Thur–Sat. ££££
Glamorous, hip designer basement restaurant surprisingly concealed down a hell-hole alley at the back of Sainsbury's, Tottenham Court Road. Exquisite dim sum (at lunch only), exotic and classily executed fish and meat dishes, and even the puddings are delicious (unusual in a Chinese restaurant). Prices, though, are punishing. Booking advisable.

Poons

50 Woburn Place, WC1 [C2]. Tel: 7580 1188. Open: L and D daily. £££
Well-sited for tourists from nearby large hotels, if nobody else, this most Westernised of Poons (related only loosely by family ownership to other restaurants sharing the name around London) plays safe with mild, bland dishes that will not alarm anybody.

Sheng's Tea House

68 Millman St, WC1 [E2]. Tel: 7405 3697. Open: L and D Mon–Fri, D only Sat. £
Freshly made stock and no MSG are welcome undertakings at this cheerful Chinese noodle shop behind Coram Fields. There is a menu for vegetarians and a handful of outdoor tables in summer.

Back to Basics, the neighbourhood favourite for fresh fish

Fitzrovian gastro-temple, Pied à Terre

Fish

Back to Basics
21a Foley St, W1 [A3]. Tel: 7436 2181. Open: L and D Mon–Sat. £££ www.backtobasics.uk.com
A blackboard menu of a dozen or so fish dishes is the centrepiece of this excellent neighbourhood restaurant, so beloved by its regulars that it is best to book or arrive early. The unpretentious room is usually crowded, but dining extends onto the pavement in summer.

North Sea Fish Restaurant
7–8 Leigh St, WC1 [D2]. Tel: 7387 5892. Open: L and D Mon–Sat. £–££
Veteran chippie serving big portions of straightforwardly cooked fish and chips. The menu is filled out with starters, such as smoked mackerel, and a selection of pre-fabricated desserts. *(For more about fish and chips, see page 84.)*

French

La Brasserie Townhouse
24 Coptic St, WC1 [C4]. Tel: 7636 2731. Open: L and D Mon–Sat, D only Sun. £££ www.townhousebrasserie.co.uk
Changes of name (earlier no 'La', or 'New Brasserie Townhouse') suggest a crisis of identity not reflected in the well-conceived short French menu, which is properly executed. Friendly staff and very convenient for the British Museum. Bed and breakfast rooms are available upstairs.

Le Cabanon
35 Great Portland St, W1 [A4]. Tel: 7436 8846. Open: L and D Mon–Fri, D only Sat. ££–£££ www.trpplc.com
Good standard French cuisine, with some Italian touches, in a setting designed to evoke rural Provence. Service is not always as attentive as it claims to be.

Elena's l'Etoile
30 Charlotte St, W1 [B3]. Tel: 7636 7189. Open: L and D Mon–Fri, D only Sat. £££ www.trpplc.com
A time-warp haven of old-fashioned virtues, still presided over by one of London's most popular restaurant personalities, veteran hostess Elena Salvoni. The food is deeply traditional bistro fare, reliably prepared, professionally presented and satisfyingly substantial.

Pied à Terre
34 Charlotte St, W1 [B3]. Tel: 7636 1178. Open: L and D Mon–Fri, D only Sat. ££££ www.pied.a.terre.co.uk
Fitzrovia's most prestigious restaurant was lucky to have New

TIP

Russell Square, the biggest of Bloomsbury's squares, originally laid out in 1800 by Humphrey Repton and recently refurbished, is the only Bloomsbury square that has a café.

*Archipelago,
an exotic
menu for the
adventurous*

TIP

For a taste of the Bloomsbury Group's work, visit the Bloomsbury Workshop *(5 Pied Bull Court, WC1; admission by intercom, Tues–Thur 10am–5.30pm),* London's only gallery specialising in the work of the Bloomsbury Group artists.

Zealander Shane Osborn on hand to take over and bring his magic touch, after (in)famous predecessors Richard Neat and Tom Aikens quit. Having regained its second Michelin star, the place now runs on a more even keel than ever before and at last actually deserves its rating among London's best. The two-course lunch is reasonably priced at £19.50, but if you want to sample it all, the eight-course tasting menu will set you back £59.50.

Greek

Elysée

13 Percy St, W1 [C4]. Tel: 7636 4804. Open: L and D Mon–Fri, D only Sat. ££–£££

This Greek taverna has hardly changed since the owners opened it in 1960. Live music and cabarets with belly dancer accompany the prawn cocktails, kleftico, taramasalata and steak Diane. A roof terrace is open in summer. Note that Zorba-like plate breaking is chargeable.

Indian

Hason Raja

84 Southampton Row, WC1 [D3]. Tel: 7242 3377/48888. Open: L and D daily. £

Smart new enterprise opened by a serially successful restaurateur, Rafu Miah. Hason Raja is named in honour of a mystical poet, but there is not so much mystery about the appeal of a 12-dish buffet lunch including tea or coffee at £9.95.

Indian YMCA

41 Fitzroy Square, W1 [B3]. Tel: 7387 0411. Open: L (noon–2pm Mon–Fri, 12.30–1.30 Sat–Sun) and D (7–8pm only) daily. £

You do not have to be young, you do not have to be a man, you do not have to be Christian and you do not have to be Indian to enjoy Indian college-type meals dispensed from the service hatch in this canteen. Curries, rice, vegetables, bread and raita for £5 cannot be bad.

Malabar Junction

107 Great Russell St, WC1 [C4]. Open: L and D daily. £££

Much classier than its unprepossessing frontage suggests, this internally elegant restaurant specialises in spicy and nutty Keralan cuisine, with religiously separated vegetarian and nonvegetarian kitchens supplying delicious dishes to the glass-roofed dining room.

Neel Kamal

160 New Cavendish St, W1 [B3]. Tel: 7580 6125. Open: L and D daily. ££

'The one and only' Neel Kamal (formerly of Percy Street) has been around since 1970, offering authentic North Indian tandoori and vegetarian dishes, with chips if required.

Ragam

57 Cleveland St, W1 [B3]. Tel: 7636 9098. Open: L and D daily. £

South Indian and Keralan restaurant, neither smart nor spacious but secure in its enduring popularity for good, homely cooking at very reasonable prices. Vegetarian menu available.

Rasa Samudra

5 Charlotte St, W1 [B4]. Tel: 7637 0222. Open: L and D Mon–Sat, D only Sun. £££
www.rasarestaurants.com
London's first Indian seafood restaurant, offering high-quality, spicy Keralan seafood and vegetarian dishes in a rambling series of highly decorated town-house rooms.

International

Archipelago

110 Whitfield St, W1 [B2]. Tel: 7383 3346. Open: L and D Mon–Fri, D only Sat. ££ (set lunch), ££££
Voodoo decor on the blood-red walls and a menu of weird exotica such as croc steaks, marinated emu, peacock satay, wok-seared frog, peppered kangaroo and locusts. A fun night out if you're not too squeamish (and have a well-lined wallet).

Italian

Bertorelli

19–23 Charlotte St, W1 [B4]. Tel: 7636 4174. Open: L and D Mon–Fri, D only Sat. £££
www.santeonline.co.uk
A long-established name in the neighbourhood (founded 1913), this original but much remodelled branch now heads a small chain (of three) and is in group ownership, yet remains a popular venue for its hospitable bar and not over-fussy Italianate and bistro food.

Cosmoba

9 Cosmo Place, off Southampton Row, WC1 [D3]. Tel: 7837 0904. Open: L and D Mon–Sat. ££
A hidden gem in an alley connecting Southampton Row and Queen Square. Plain, family run and specialising in homely and satisfying Italian food.

Da Paolo

3 Charlotte Place, W1 [B4]. Tel: 7580 0021. Open: L and D Mon–Fri, D only Sat–Sun. ££
www.paolorestaurants.com
Another find is this easily overlooked little Italian restaurant tucked away in a mews off

Bertorelli, a popular Charlotte Street hang-out

Goodge Street; Italian village atmosphere in the heart of London. Friendly and more old-fashioned than its nearby sibling *(see below)*.

Giardinetto

69 Charlotte St, W1 [B3]. Tel: 7637 4907. Open: L and D Mon–Fri, D only Sat. £££
This honest family-run restaurant is strong on well-prepared specialities of Genoa, the home town of the chef proprietor Signor Vilona, such as farinata, ravioli and pesto. Some dishes are offered for customers to cook themselves on a heated stone brought to the table. The reasonably priced wine selection is an added bonus. However, the scruffy decor and the fact that it's in a rather dingy basement is a big downside so if you're sensitive to your surroundings, go elsewhere.

Goodfellas

50 Lamb's Conduit St, WC1 [E3]. Tel: 7405 7088. Open: B, L and T Mon–Sat. £
Italo-American café offering indulgent breakfasts, a plate-loading lunchtime buffet, build-your-own sandwiches, and salads. Tables in the basement and on the pavement. Unlicensed.

Paolo

16 Percy St, W1 [C4]. Tel: 7637 9900. Open: L and D Mon–Sat. £££ www.paolorestaurants.com
Sleek, light and modern restaurant with clean-lined blond wood interior and an unusually ambitious menu prepared by chef Maurizio Morelli, including stewed baby octopus or pan-fried foie gras as starters, duck ragout and tuna bottarga among the pastas, and choices of four each of fish and meat courses. Same ownership as Da Paolo *(see above)*.

Passione

10 Charlotte St, W1 [B4]. Tel: 7636 2833. Open: L and D Mon–Fri, D only Sat. £££ www.passione.co.uk
Delectable modern Italian in two small but well-patronised rooms, featuring light and rustic southern Italian fare, often enhanced with unusual herbs and fungi, which illustrious chef Gennaro Contaldo (one of Jamie Oliver's mentors) goes out and gathers himself. Attentive service.

Pescatori

57 Charlotte St, W1 [B3]. Tel: 7580 3289. Open: L and D Mon–Sat. £££
At this address for more than 40 years, Pescatori guarantees a good variety of simple, pleasing seafood dishes in the Italian manner, though service can be gruff and portions not as generous as they might be.

Ristorante Paradiso Olivelli

34 Store St, WC1/3 Great Titchfield St [C3]. Tel: 7255 2554/7436 0111. Open: L and D daily (Gt Titchfield St), L and D Mon–Sat (Store St). ££ www.ristoranteparadiso.co.uk
The local branches of a small chain founded in 1934, specialising in popular pizzas (London's best according to one American critic) and simple grills. Children under 14 eat free (one per accompanying adult) at weekends until 7pm in Great Titchfield St.

Sardo ⑨

45 Grafton Way, W1 [B2]. Tel: 7387 2521. Open: L and D Mon–Fri, D only Sat. £££ www.sardo-restaurant.com
Sardinian specialities, including crunchy dried flatbreads, swordfish, fregola with frutti di mare, honey-drizzled cheese sebada and mirto honey and myrtle liqueur, served with panache and pride by sassy waitresses in a popular, coolly contemporary environment. Daily specials.

TIP

Alfresco dining is possible at the **Blue Door Bistro** in the sunny conservatory and garden at the back of the Montague on the Gardens Hotel *(15 Montague St, WC1; tel: 7637 1001; L and D daily; ££ lunch menu, £££)* beside the British Museum. Suggested barbecue grills include red mullet, Dover sole, lamb steak, duck breast or entrecôte.

Japanese

Abeno
47 Museum St, WC1 [D4]. Tel: 7405 3211. Open: L and D daily. ££ www.abeno.co.uk
Oriental pancake house specialising in okonomi-yaki (tasty, if messy, omelettes and pancakes crammed with chopped meat, vegetables or fish) in a score of varieties, cooked on a hotplate at the table and supplemented with noodles. Staff are helpful. Starters include Japanese fish salad, squid with garlic and soy, or tofu and avocado gyoza. Finish with tropical fruit salad. Set menus and takeaway also available.

Hare & Tortoise Noodle Bar
15–17 Brunswick Centre, WC1 [D2]. Tel: 7278 4945. Open: L and D daily. £
Unlike most Japanese noodle bars, the repertoire here extends beyond ramen soup noodles to include Chinese, Korean and Malaysian dishes. Sushi, stir-fries and takeaways are all good value.

Ikkyu
67a Tottenham Court Rd, W1 [B3]. Tel: 7636 9280. Open: L and D Mon–Fri, D only Sun. ££
Popular and long-established, though now slightly shabby, bargain basement for sushi and robatayaki, speedily prepared and cheerily served. Grilled chicken skin on skewers is a speciality. Set menus at lunch.

Wagamama
4a Streatham St, WC1 [C4]. Tel: 7736 2333. Open: L and D daily. £ www.wagamama.com
Bloomsbury's was the original of a chain which, at last count, is 13 strong. Canteen-like basement with communal tables and bench seating, where willing young staff dish up orders of wholesome budget noodles and garnishes such as dumplings, salads, soups and juices. It still attracts queues of students in term time.

Wagamama, the flagship restaurant of the noodle-bar empire

RIBA Café, architects' lunchtime HQ

Yo! Sushi

myhotel, 11–13 Bayley St, WC1 [C3]. Tel: 7636 0076. Open: L and D daily. ££
www.yosushi.co.uk

Some 180 different dishes delivered by conveyor belt on colour-coded plates. The chain also supplies Sainsbury's (branch on Tottenham Court Road), but the hotel surroundings here are smarter than eating in the street or neighbouring Bedford Square. Across the lobby, the hotel bar is an elegant and relaxed venue for cocktails.

Mexican

La Perla Bar & Grill

11 Charlotte St, W1 [B4]. Tel: 7436 1744. Open: L and D Mon–Sat. ££

Third in a small chain of cheap and cheerful Mexican places around London. Bars on two floors for margaritas, tequilas and beers; separate dining room serves 'classic and modern' Mexican tapas.

Middle Eastern

Dish Dash

57–59 Goodge St, W1 [B3]. Tel: 7637 7474. Open: L and D Mon–Fri, D only Sat. £££

Modern Persian restaurant, one half concrete with communal tables, wooden chairs and kitchen open to view, the other half chrome, silk and leather, with large bar area. Starters include plates of mazzaz, muhammura dip and sorkeh panir (deep-fried halloumi cheese), with kebabs or 'mish mash' selections to follow. Crowded with partying cocktail drinkers towards the end of the week.

Efes Kebab House

80 Great Titchfield St, W1 [A4]. Tel: 7636 1953. Open: L and D Mon–Sat. ££

These twin Turkish restaurants have been dispensing meze and kebabs for nearly 30 years and are relied upon by regulars for consistent value and quality. Prices are slightly lower upstairs. Belly dancing is laid on at Efes II (*175 Great Portland St, tel: 7436 0600*).

Özer

5 Langham Place, W1 [A4]. Tel: 7323 0505. Open: L and D daily. ££

Stylish, welcoming restaurant with bold decor and eclectic Middle Eastern and Mediterranean menus produced to a consistently reliable and flavourful standard that translates as very good value for money. Takeaway available.

Modern European

The Heights
St George's Hotel, Langham Place, W1 [A4]. Tel: 7580 0111. Open: B, L and D daily. £££
Elevated views over the West End add appeal at this newly refurbished 15th-floor restaurant frequented by BBC execs from Broadcasting House opposite. Prices start from £17.50 for two courses and £22.50 for three.

Mash
19–21 Great Portland St, W1 [A4]. Tel: 7637 5555. Open: B daily and Br Sat downstairs, L and D upstairs Mon–Fri. ££
Extensive ground-floor bar/deli and roomy first-floor restaurant using wood-fired oven and grill to turn out trendy food with which you can drink its own micro-brewery's beers. Breakfast (downstairs) £10, two courses £12, three £15.

Perseverance
63 Lamb's Conduit St, WC1 [E3]. Tel: 7405 8278. Open: L and D Mon–Sat, L only Sun. £££
Popular gastropub on the corner with Great Ormond Street, offering light, inventive, tasty and well-presented dishes in its often crowded bar or the more secluded first-floor dining room. Some pavement tables outside, too, in summer.

RIBA Café
66 Portland Place, W1 [A3]. Tel: 7631 0467. Open: B, L and T Mon–Sat. ££
Tasty breakfasts and boldly colourful lunches in an appropriately beautiful space provided by the Royal Institute of British Architects. Terrace open in fine weather.

Spoon at Sanderson
50 Berners St, W1 [B4]. Tel: 7300 1444. Open: L, T and D daily. £££–££££
Super-chef Alain Ducasse's Parisian mix-and-match innovation, where guests make up their own dishes by picking numbers, translated to London with modern minimalist style, lofty attitudes among the staff, and prices elevated to match.

Stargazer
11 Rathbone St, W1 [B4]. Tel: 7636 1057. Open: L and D Mon–Fri. ££
Bright and cheery little place, using quality ingredients in sometimes imaginative combinations, offering very fair value for money.

Mash restaurant and micro-brewery

Villandry

170–176 Great Portland St, W1 [A3]. Tel: 7631 3131 Open: L and D Mon–Sat, Br Sat and Sun. £££

A charcuterie bar has been added to this large complex, which already included a grocery, deli-catessen, restaurant, café-bar and flower shop. Interesting but unfussy treatments of fresh ingredients ensure that the minimally decorated (non-smoking) restaurant's severely hard chairs are always well occupied. Their take-away hampers are a real treat for a special summer picnic.

Philippine

Josephine's

4 Charlotte St, W1 [B4]. Tel: 7580 6551. Open: L and D Mon–Sat, D only Sun. £

Philippine cuisine uses excellent, mild palm vinegar and toffeeish palm sugar. It also involves a new set of strange names for formulations reminiscent of Chinese (spring rolls), Malay (satay), Thai or Vietnamese dishes. But Josephine's Philippine cuisine beats a lot of the Oriental rivals for quality and pleasure. Vegetarian menu also available.

Did you know?

The witty and notoriously promiscuous parliamentarian Tom Driberg (1905–76) claimed the credit for having coined the name Fitzrovia by which the area centred on Charlotte Street and the Fitzroy Tavern became known in the 1930s. Nowadays the hip – some say pretentious – new name for the area is 'Noho' (an abbreviation of 'northern Soho').

Spanish

Cigala 🍴

54 Lamb's Conduit St, WC1 [E3]. Tel: 7405 1717. Open: L and D Mon–Sat, lunch only Sun. £££

Owner-chef Jake Hodges (ex-Moro; *see page 139*) wins accolades in Spartan surroundings for simple but immaculately executed seafood, succulent meats and well-chosen wines. The menu changes daily.

Costa Dorada

47–55 Hanway St, W1 [C4]. Open: D only Mon–Sat. ££ (tapas), £££ (restaurant)

An imitation Spanish hacienda secreted off Oxford Street, catering largely to office groups, tourist parties and rowdy hen nights and offering flamenco shows and Spanish staples such as paella and tapas, washed down with jugs of sangria.

Fino

33 Charlotte St, W1 (entrance on Rathbone St) [B3]. Tel: 7813 8010. Open: L and D Mon–Fri, D only Sat. £££

Smart and lively restaurant and tapas bar, the first venture of Sam and Eddie Hart, sons of provincial hotelier, Tim (Hambleton Hall hotel and Hart's Nottingham). The emphasis is on fresh ingredients, simply cooked by chef Jean-

Villandry, high-class foodstore and dining room

Thai

Busaba Eathai

22 Store St, W1 [C3]. Tel: 7255 8686. Open: L and D daily. ££
Sleek and rather quieter replica of the Soho original, serving fresh and well-prepared (mostly) Thai dishes with plenty of original vegetarian options. Very reasonable prices for such chic surroundings. No smoking and no bookings taken.

Vietnamese

Bam-Bou

1 Percy St, W1 [B4]. Tel: 7323 9130. Open: L and D Mon–Fri, D only Sat. £££
This Fitzrovia townhouse, once London's top Greek restaurant, now evokes colonial Hanoi with decorative Vietnamese cuisine (roast duck with green papaya, marinated squid with bitter lemon, chocolate spring rolls with kumquat) served by staff with more attitude than skill.

Philippe Patruno (ex-Chez Nico), much of it *a la plancha* (griddled). The eating bar overlooks the kitchen and the cocktail bar overlooks the restaurant.

Navarro's

67 Charlotte St, W1 [B3]. Tel: 7637 7713. Open: L and D Mon–Fri, D only Sat. ££
The bright blue frontage and cheerily colourful interior decor provide an appropriate setting for a choice of some 50 tapas selections, in which seafood dishes generally excel.

PUBS, BARS AND CAFÉS

Who knows how many of tomorrow's famous writers and artists now people the pubs and bars of Bloomsbury and Fitzrovia? Their likeliest haunts are the pleasantly civilised **Museum Tavern** on the corner of Museum and Great Russell streets, opposite the entrance to the British Museum; among the uniquely Victorian fittings of **The Lamb** *(94 Lamb's Conduit St)*; at **The Fitzroy Tavern** *(16 Charlotte St)* where they still display George Orwell's journalists' union card; at **The Newman Arms** *(23 Rathbone St)*, a small pub famed for its pies served in the pie room upstairs; or **The Jeremy Bentham** *(31 University St)* where attractions include a wax cast of the philosopher's embalmed head.

Bars range from the modish celebrity hang-outs **Ling Ling** at Hakkasan *(see page 48)* and the **Long Bar** in the Sanderson Hotel *(50 Berners St)* to the cultish basement **Jerusalem** *(33–34 Rathbone Place)*, the conspiratorial **Bradley's Spanish Bar** *(42–44 Hanway St)* and the heaving **Social** *(5 Little Portland St)* owned by Heavenly Records.

Among the area's legion cafés and sandwich bars **Alicia** *(23 Warren St)*, run by the author of a book of original Lebanese recipes, is worth seeking out. The **Table Café** in the basement of Habitat *(196 Tottenham Court Rd)* has a daily changing menu of homely accomplished Italian dishes alongside staple café fare, with communal seating for lone lunchers.

Restaurant Chains

Most chain restaurants are mediocre at best, but a select few provide good, innovative food at affordable prices

Increasing numbers of London restaurants, cafés, bars and pubs belong to chains. In general, these have been excluded from this guide because the chief advantage of chain ownership is also its greatest weakness: predictability. This is an advantage when the customer is in unfamiliar territory and in search of something that will at least be satisfactory, if not exciting. It is a disadvantage when the formula is replicated *ad nauseam* all over town or, in some instances, all over the world.

In the late 1990s commercial restaurant groups (Conran, Belgo, Marco Pierre White, A–Z Restaurants, Harvey Nichols, Groupe Chez Gérard and, more recently, Gordon Ramsay) even came to dominate the top end of the London restaurant scene. Such group-owned high-quality restaurants mostly qualify for separate entries in this guide because they have individual names and don't reproduce the same menu in every venue.

At a more modestly priced and less gastronomically ambitious level, the ubiquitous chains range from time-warped leftovers (Aberdeen Steak House) and tourist traps (Garfunkels, Ponti's) to the big US fast food imports (KFC, McDonald's, Burger King, Starbucks) to useful standbys (Pizza Express, IT'S and Ask for pizzas; Prêt à Manger and Benjys for sandwiches).

Some have been around a long time (Spaghetti House started in the 1950s, Bertorelli's in the 1930s), some have quickly become household names (Prêt-à-Manger, All Bar One), while others are regarded as recent, up-to-the-minute and exciting innovations, likely to be welcomed wherever they choose to open (Sofra, Carluccio's, Strada, Wagamama).

However, some have over-extended and collapsed, leaving only scattered remnants behind (most notably Pierre Victoire and fish!), while others have sadly passed their best (the stylish and still-expanding Pizza Express seeming the most recent backslider).

Ed's Easy Diner, a good choice for burgers, shakes and beers

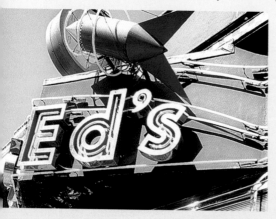

There are popular chains of varying lengths and reach dealing in particular cuisines: American (Smollensky's, Ed's Easy Diner, T.G.I. Friday's and Tootsies, as well as the burger bars); Mexican (La Perla) and Argentinian (El Gaucho, Gaucho Grill); pan-Asian (Singapura, Tiger Lil's, Yellow River Café), via Chinese (the excellent Royal Chinas), Indian (Café Lazeez, Mobeen, Rasa), Japanese (Moshi Moshi Sushi, Yo! Sushi and Wagamama) and Thai (Thai Square); Middle Eastern (Fairuz, Maroush); Spanish (The Finca, La Rueda) and Italian, which is particularly well represented, with Calzone, Getti, Strada

Bertorelli's, in business since the 1930s

and Spiga smaller and more authentic than the tired Pizza Huts and other conglomerate-owned pizza and pasta places.

Less well represented among the chains are French cuisine (Café Rouge is particularly disappointing, though Chez Gérard has successfully weathered changes of ownership and management) and Mediterranean (Café Med does not live up to its name).

There is at least one chain specialising in traditional British fare (Browns) and commendable chains concentrating on fresh, expertly prepared fish (Livebait, Loch Fyne Restaurants) and soups (Soup Opera) or catering for vegetarians (The Gate, Ravi Shankar). Among wine bars, Davy's deserves a mention, and among pubs JD Wetherspoon, Young's, and Fuller's Ale and Pie Houses rank among the best.

Choosing a chain

There are some handy rules of thumb that will help customers feel their way around the chains. First, the more branches there are, the lower the common denominator. Secondly, longevity is generally a good sign (survival of the fittest), though more excitement and publicity attaches to novelty. Thirdly, the more outlets the company has under its direct management, as distinct from franchises run by subcontracted operators, the more consistent and reliable the standards.

There is no shame in eating in a chain restaurant. Indeed, as already mentioned, some of London's finest eateries belong to chains. But as a general rule it is probably wise to regard chains as a useful reserve to fall back upon when no suitable independent and freestanding establishment is available sufficiently close to hand.

Tea and Cakes

Patisserie

Parlour

MAYFAIR, PICCADILLY AND ST JAMES'S

Mayfair, the heart of aristocratic London, is also the capital's epicentre of haute cuisine, with more than its fair share of luxury restaurants

Mayfair has long been established as one of London's most aristocratic and exclusive areas. Its social cachet is rooted in its proximity to St James's Palace and the royal parks. Many of the buildings – brick and stucco terraces feeding into grand, formal squares with mews and stables – were built in the 17th century on six aristocratic estates, including those of the Grosvenors and the Berkeleys. Burlington House, now the Royal Academy, was typical of the dozens of great noblemen's mansions of the area.

Luxury hotels and gastronomic temples

Mayfair denotes a large area bounded to the north by Oxford Street, to the east by Regent Street, to the south by Piccadilly and to the west by Park Lane. Grand hotels abound. Curiously, several of these were built by former servants. The oldest, Brown's Hotel on Dover Street, famous for its civilised afternoon teas, was opened in 1837 by former manservant James Brown. Not long after, former butler William Claridge opened his hotel (in 1855). Claridge's was extensively redesigned in the 1930s to become one of London's most dazzling Art Deco gems, now home to one of superstar chef Gordon Ramsay's restaurants. Further north on Carlos Place, the fabulously aristocratic Connaught has had something of a facelift since Ramsay protégé Angela Hartnett took over the kitchen introducing an Italian influence and, more radically, an outdoor dining terrace.

On the whole, Mayfair's monied residents are spoilt for choice of top-end restaurants, from Albert Roux's stately Le Gavroche to Philip Howard's stylishly modern The Square, and see-and-be-seen-in haunt Le Caprice.

Food shops are less in evidence. Almost opposite the Connaught is the venerable butcher Allen & Co (established over 150 years) with its wonderful old butcher's blocks, mosaic floors and window displays of game in full plumage. Deli/restaurant Truc Vert on North Audley Street has a great choice of cheeses and charcuterie – good for impromptu picnics in one of the grand squares. Victorian shopping mall, the Royal Arcade, with its tall arched bays and elegant glass roof, first opened so that wealthy guests at Brown's Hotel could have a sheltered and suitably elegant approach to the shops on Bond Street. Chocoholics should make a beeline for Charbonnel & Walker within the arcade, established as Britain's master chocolatiers since 1875.

Opposite: entrance to extravagantly designed and priced Sketch Below: menu of the more down-to-earth Thai Pot

St James's

The epitome of gentility, St James's is an enclave between The Mall and Piccadilly (so-named from the ruffs or pickadills worn by dandies who used to promenade here in the late 17th century), home to many a gentleman's club. Pall Mall (which gets its bizarre name from the game of 'paglio a maglio', literally ball and mallet) was one of London's first gas-lit streets, and within the Sofitel Hotel, with its gorgeous pink lounge boasting an excellent champagne list, is Albert Roux's reassuringly afford-able Roux Brasserie.

Piccadilly and Bond Street

On Piccadilly proper stands The Ritz, a byword for decadence since it first wowed Edwardian society in 1906. Book well ahead for afternoon tea in the Palm Lounge *(see page 127)* or sip cocktails in the beautifully restored Rivoli Bar. Neighbouring food emporium Fortnum & Mason, purveyors to the Royal Family, was founded by Charles Fortnum, one of George III's former footmen in 1770 who had intimate knowledge of the royal household, together with his partner Hugh Mason from the now defunct St James's Market. They bow to each other on the hour beside the clock over the main entrance.

St James's is home to an eccentric collection of quintessentially English food shops for the traditional connoisseur, from the impeccable Paxton & Whitfield cheese shop on Jermyn Street to Davidoff, which celebrates the cigar as a status symbol, and the superlative cellars of Berry Brothers on St James's Street. For sheer indulgence, Caviar House on Piccadilly has an amaz-ing choice of caviar and extravagant accessories.

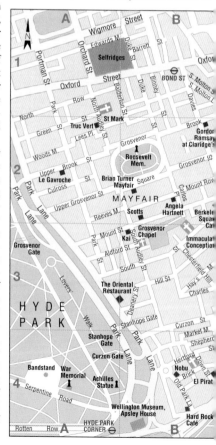

Shoppers heading for Bond Street should take note that Nicole Fahri has a chic restaurant serving breakfast, lunch and after-noon tea. A more funky alternative is the bar in Donna Karan, good for all-day brunch. Fenwick's, an excellent fashion depart-ment store, has a branch of the estimable Carluccio's for a restorative coffee and pastry or signature mush-room risotto. Otherwise, the area is well served for cafés, with the original branch of Richoux on Piccadilly and plenty of small, quirky cafés tucked around the art galleries of Cork and Dover streets.

Shepherd's Market is a highly appealing area of contemporary galleries and jewellers, housed in Georgian buildings jostling for position with plenty of pavement dining possiblities, from the ever-bustling Lebanese Al Hamra to quintessentially French Le Boudin Blanc and L'Artiste Musclé wine bar. The curious might try L'Autre in Mayfair's oldest wine lodge, serving a bizarre but not unhappy mixture of Polish and Mexican food. Originally, the infamous May Fair took place in Shepherd's Market until it was suppressed in the mid-18th century because of 'drunkenness, fornication, gaming and lewdness,' but reputedly it remains a haunt for high-class prostitutes as well as discerning diners.

FIVE OF THE BEST

Le Caprice: this glamorous brasserie is still one of the hottest addresses in town

Gordon Ramsay at Claridge's: exceptional haute cuisine in a chic Art Deco setting

Mirabelle: a Mayfair classic reinvented by Marco Pierre White

Momo: stylish and authentic Moroccan restaurant with a party atmosphere

Rocket: tasty wood-fired pizzas in a Mayfair mews – a bargain for the area

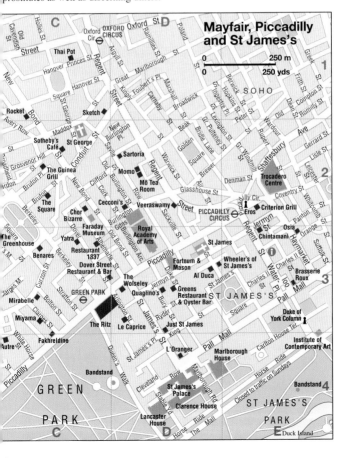

Mayfair, Piccadilly and St James's

American

Hard Rock Café

*150 Old Park Lane, W1 [B4].
Tel: 7629 0382. Open: L and D
daily. ££ www.hardrock.com*
Be prepared to queue to pay
homage to rock'n'roll memorabilia at this landmark almost as
famous for the wait as the huge
portions of food served to the
rhythm of thumping music.
Nachos, chicken wings, sundaes,
and hamburgers with every conceivable trimming more than
exceed expectations. Visit its
'vaults museum' next door for
guitars belonging to rock legends
Hendrix, Presley et al.

Australian

Osia

*11 Haymarket, SW1 [E3]. Tel:
7976 1313. Open: L and D
Mon–Fri, D only Sat. ££££
www.osiarestaurant.com*
Chic modern restaurant showcasing
the innovative cooking of Aussie
super-chef Scott Webster. Good for
dedicated foodies, and handy post-
theatre. Try the crab or scallop
ceviche served in a cocktail glass
to start and sign off with hot
chocolate soup with vanilla pepper
ice cream. The sleek bar serves
well-made cocktails too.

British

Brian Turner Mayfair

*Millennium Hotel, 44 Grosvenor
Square, W1 [B2]. Tel: 7596
3444. Open: L and D Mon–Fri,
D only Sat. £££*
Posh British food impeccably
sourced courtesy of Brian Turner,
one of Britain's best-loved TV
chefs, who works the elegant modern dining room. Treats include
smoked eel, bacon and potato salad,
definitive steak and kidney pie with
oysters or Dover sole, and nostalgic
desserts such as treacle sponge with
clotted cream, or trifle.

The Guinea Grill

*30 Bruton Place, W1 [C2]. Tel:
7499 1210. Open: L and D
Mon–Fri, D only Sat. £££*
Old-world, wood-panelled pub
restaurant in a cobbled mews with
many fans who flock here for its
ace steak and kidney pie, grills and
oysters and its good choice of
ports, beers and wines. Often
packed with fervently loyal
besuited locals.

Chinese

Kai

*South Audley St, W1 [B3]. Tel:
7493 8988. Open: daily, all day.
££££ www.kaimayfair.co.uk*
Opulent Chinese whose cool marble interior with elegant tropical
fish tanks is pitched at a wealthy
clientele. The menu focuses on luxury, exotic ingredients: specialities
include braised shark's fin with
beansprouts, dried abalone with
oyster sauce, and pork cooked in

The ultimate
English chocolatier,
Charbonnel &
Walker *(1 The
Royal Arcade, 28
Old Bond St)*, has
been supplying
aristocratic draw-
ing rooms with
beautifully pack-
aged boxes of
violet creams and
buttermints since
1875.

The Guinea Grill

The Dorchester Hotel's Oriental Restaurant

champagne sauce served flaming in Chinese rice wine. Smart wine list and polished service to match.

The Oriental Restaurant

The Dorchester, 53 Park Lane, W1 [A/B3]. Tel: 7629 888. Open: L and D Mon–Fri, D only Sat. ££ (set lunch), ££££ www.dorchesterhotel.com

Lavishly decorated with antique silks and objets d'art, The Oriental's Cantonese menu knocks spots off most of its competition. Wonderfully inventive dishes include deep-fried eel with cinnamon blossom sauce, and the extravagant beggar's chicken stuffed with dried red dates and mushrooms baked in lotus leaves and clay for five hours. Dinner prices veer towards the astronomical but the superb lunchtime dim sum menu is a steal for the location.

Fish

Greens Restaurant & Oyster Bar

36 Duke St, SW1 [D3]. Tel: 7930 4566. Open: L and D daily. ££££ www.greens.org.uk

Clubby Mayfair stalwart owned by Simon Parker-Bowles (brother of Camilla, Prince Charles's constant escort) and a favourite of the impeccably mannered old school. Expect fabulous traditional dishes, from potted shrimps to lemon sole

with perfect hollandaise to treacle tart. Cheeseboard is supplied by nearby Paxton & Whitfield. Picnics, hampers and gourmet gifts can be bought through the website.

Scotts

20 Mount St, W1 [B2]. Tel: 7629 5248. Open: L and D daily. £££ www.scottsrestaurant.co.uk

This treasured culinary institution, more than 150 years old, went through a rocky patch, but since the recent management takeover it seems to be back on track, serving impeccable fish dishes (exemplary fish pie, scallops, and Dover sole among them), created by the resident Australian chef, in grand surroundings. Old-fashioned puddings are given a modern twist. The mint-green basement bar is a discreet venue for a glass of champagne or more.

Wheeler's of St James's

12a Duke of York St, SW1 [D3]. Tel: 7930 2460. Open: L and D Mon–Sat. £££

Yet another success story for Marco Pierre White, who's revived the fortunes of this St James's classic, with racy new decor, whilst retaining the canoodling banquettes and cosy ambience. Food is stunningly presented, from sensational scallops with girolles to grilled sole of melting perfection to tart red-berry jelly.

TIP

Enjoy great views over Mayfair's rooftops from the sofas of the Studio Lounge, the cocktail bar/café on the fifth floor of **Waterstone's** *(203–206 Piccadilly; tel: 7851 2433; L and D Mon–Sat; ££),* Europe's largest bookstore. Accompanying the tempting cocktail list is a short menu of fishcakes, pasta, salads and pastries. The downstairs Red Room doesn't have the view, but it's a classy alternative if you want the whole three-course works.

French

Right:
Benares,
for
creative
Indian
cuisine

Brasserie Roux

Sofitel St James, 8 Pall Mall, SW1 [E3]. Tel: 7968 2900. Open: L and D Mon–Fri. £££
www.sofitel.com

Definitive brasserie conceived by the celebrated Albert Roux of Le Gavroche fame *(see below)* serving impeccable Gallic classics, from escargots à la bourguignonne to duck confit to exquisite lemon tart. Unpretentious pricing coupled with stunning interior ensure it's constantly busy. The luscious pink hotel bar/lounge offers an excellent choice of champagne and whiskies.

Criterion Grill

224 Piccadilly, W1 [E2]. Tel: 7930 0488. Open: L and D Mon–Sat. ££ (set menu), £££
www.whitestarline.co.uk

Another prizewinner in the Marco Pierre White stable, the newly revamped Criterion on Piccadilly Circus has a simple please-all menu of flavoursome French classics, all excellently prepared. But the real draw of this place, apart from its location, remains the opulent neo-Byzantine interior.

Le Gavroche

43 Upper Brook St, W1 [A2]. Tel: 7499 1826. Open: L and D Mon–Fri, D only Sat. £££ (set lunch), ££££
www.le-gavroche.co.uk

This legendary restaurant, which opened more than 35 years ago, is still of the highest order, with Michel Roux Jnr inheriting the mantle from Albert Roux *(see above left)*. Elegantly balanced French haute cuisine is given a lighter touch with hints of Asian influence. The soufflés are masterly. A chic, civilised operation with polished, welcoming service.

Mirabelle ⑪

56 Curzon St, W1 [C3]. Tel: 7499 7071. Open: L and D daily. £££ (set lunch), ££££
www.whitestarline.org.uk

A classic restaurant, re-invented by gourmet entrepreneur Marco Pierre White, that remains one of Mayfair's hottest addresses, with a stunning Art Deco-inspired interior, magnificent flowers and a divine menu brimming with luxury ingredients – foie gras terrine with Sauternes jelly, and gratinee of cod with champagne sabayon exemplify the treat factor. Beware steep mark-ups on the wine list. Lovely terrace open lunch and early dinner.

L'Oranger

5 St James's St, SW1 [D4]. Tel: 7839 3774. Open: L and D Mon–Fri, D only Sat. ££££

One of Mayfair's prettiest dining rooms, decorated in pistachio tones, with a huge skylight and the added bonus of a secluded courtyard for alfresco meals. First-class cooking takes its inspiration and ingredients from the South of France, with the accent on fresh fish. Try the signature starter of salty-sweet sautéed scallops with lettuce velouté and Iberico ham or be guided by seasonal specialities such as wild sea bass with truffle vinaigrette or wild strawberries with Muscat granita. Food arrives slowly, but the attentive service compensates.

The Square

6–10 Bruton St, W1 [C2]. Tel: 7495 7100. Open: L and D Mon–Fri, D only Sat–Sun. £££ *(lunch menu),* ££££ *www.squarerestaurant.com*
Gastronomic sparks fly at Philip Howard's much-lauded restaurant. The menu is firmly rooted in French classical cuisine, but with striking modern twists. Seared loin of venison, for example, is paired with deep-fried quails' egg and salad of beetroot and apple. The wine list is strong on Burgundies. Among the petits fours is a delectable home-made nougat.

Truc Vert

42 North Audley St, W1 [A2]. Tel: 7491 9988. Open: Mon–Fri 7.30am–9pm, L only Sat–Sun. £££
Informal, buzzy restaurant in a wonderful deli. 'From the shop' choose exceptional salads, pâtés, quiches and pastries plus charcuterie/cheese plates made to order from an epic array. The enticing 'from the kitchen' menu changes daily, and vegetarians are always well catered for. Wines are shop price plus reasonable corkage. Booking essential.

Indian

Benares

12 Berkeley House, Berkeley Square, W1 [C3]. Tel: 7629 8886. Open: L and D Mon–Fri, D only Sat–Sun. ££ *(set lunch),* £££ *www.benaresrestaurant.com*
Benares' swish interior provides a suitably sophisticated backdrop to Atul Kochhar's distinctly spiced Indian cooking. Hits include salad of scallops, prawns and pomegranate in a mint and ginger dressing, crab simmered in coconut and chilli, and chilli-infused grilled pineapple with coconut ice cream. But not every dish delivers and portions are modest.

Chor Bizarre

16 Albemarle St, W1 [C2]. Tel: 7629 9802. Open: L and D daily. £££
www.chorbizarrerestaurant.com
Combine your meal with a shopping spree: all furnishings and decorations, from the Indian wedding bed to the ornamental jewellery, are for sale at this bizarre bazaar of a restaurant. The far-reaching menu offers authentic dishes from

L'Oranger, offers a connoisseur's choice

*Slick and
sophisticated
Cecconi's*

TIP

The well turned
out restaurant
Nicole's *(158
New Bond St,
W1; tel: 7499
8408; L and D
Mon–Fri, L only
Sat; £££)*, within
Nicole Fahri's
Mayfair boutique,
offers seasonal,
simple and fash-
ionable food, as
perfectly acces-
sorised as you
would expect.
Breakfast and tea
served too.

across the subcontinent. The inde-
cisive should try the maharaja
thali. For £24 you get a large platter with a selection of dishes
served in small bowls. Vegetarians
well catered for.

Veeraswamy

*99–101 Regent St, W1 [D2]. Tel:
7734 1401. Open: L and D daily.
££ (set menu), £££
www.realindianfood.com*
London's oldest Indian restaurant
has been brought bang up to date
with an elegant, spacious decor
and an adventurous menu combining north and south Indian cooking
ranging from Barbary duck cooked
with spices and apricot to aromatic
pineapple curry with coconut.

Yatra

*34 Dover St, W1 [C3]. Tel: 7493
0200. Open: L and D Mon–Fri, D
only Sat–Sun. ££ (set menu),
£££ www.yatra.co.uk*
Sleek but cosy contemporary
Indian offering familiar favourites
like rogan josh and more adventurous modern dishes such as salmon
with chilli, coriander and coconut
paste baked in banana leaf. Strong
on vegetarian dishes. Weekly
Thursday yoga plus lunch is a
draw, as is live music and dancing
at the hip Bar Bollywood *(see page
43)* in the basement. Kick off with
an exotic cocktail at the ground-
floor lounge bar.

Italian

Al Duca

*4–5 Duke of York St, SW1 [D3].
Tel: 7839 3090. Open: L and D
Mon–Sat. £££
www.alduca-restaurant.co.uk*
Lively, modern Italian restaurant
with simple decor and no-nonsense set menus, including
smoked swordfish salad, home-
made pasta, char-grilled fish, and
memorable tiramisu.

Angela Hartnett at
The Connaught

*16 Carlos Place, W1 [B2]. Tel:
7499 7070. Open: L and D daily.
£££ (lunch menu), ££££
www.savoy-group.co.uk*
The arrival of Gordon Ramsay's
protégé Angela Hartnett sent
shivers of disapproval through the
Establishment but even her harshest
critics agree that her lighter Italian-
inspired menu is a revelation: especially her pumpkin ravioli with
butter and sage, and superlative
desserts. The mahogany-panelled
room remains as awe-inspiring as
ever, and service is very proper.

Cecconi's

*5a Burlington Gardens, W1 [D2].
Tel: 7434 1500. Open: L and D
Mon–Sat, D only Sun. ££££* ·
Sophisticated Italian, with an allur-
ing menu of classic regional gems,
which attracts an impeccably

dressed, lively crowd. Talented chef Stephen Terry's specialities include salt duck breast with raisins, pine nuts and sweet and sour pumpkin. The sommelier will guide you through the formidable wine list.

Rocket 🍴

4–5 Lancashire Court, W1 [C1]. Tel: 7629 2889. Open: L and D Mon–Fri, D only Sat. ££ www.rocketrestaurant.co.uk
Lively, simply decorated modern Italian with a menu of 12-inch wood-fired pizzas, pasta and salad in a pretty enclave just off New Bond Street. Arrive early for a seat outside, as these can't be reserved.

Sartoria

20 Savile Row, W1 [D2]. Tel: 7534 7000. Open: L and D Mon–Sat, D only Sun. £££ (set menu), ££££ www.conran.co.uk
Ever-popular Conran restaurant where authentic rustic meets refined Milanese, with an inventive twist. Dishes such as grilled lobster with rosemary butter and porcini, and baked peaches with amaretto and almonds, put authentic Italian ingredients to excellent use, but the menu also incorporates quality British produce. The bespoke decor is a witty reference to the restaurant's location on Savile Row, the home of English tailoring.

Japanese

Miyama

38 Clarges St, W1 [C3]. Tel: 7493 3807. Open: L and D Mon–Fri, D only Sat–Sun. ££ (set menu), £££
Find top sashimi and more unusual dishes, such as soft-shell crab deep-fried with ponzu sauce, at this unassuming Japanese, incongruously housed within a distinctly English town house. Sweet service by calm, kimono-clad waitresses.

Nobu

Metropolitan Hotel, 19 Old Park Lane, W1 [B4]. Tel: 7447 4747. Open: L and D Mon–Fri, D only Sat–Sun. ££££ www.noburestaurants.com
Haunt of A-list celebrities and jet-setters and notoriously hard to book, Nobu continues to cash in on its reputation for sensational Japanese food with a Peruvian twist, from sublime sushi and perfect tempura to the famous black cod in miso. Only too-close tables and two-hour time limits may sour expectations.

Middle Eastern

Chintamani

122 Jermyn St, SW1 [E3]. Tel: 7839 2020. Open: L and D Mon–Sat. ££ (set lunch), £££ www.chintamanilondon.co.uk
This stunning restaurant, with its Ottoman antiques and jewel-like decoration, is good for beautiful-people-watching. Excellent choice of mezze to share, including plenty for vegetarians, and interesting fish dishes, though the overpriced

Upmarket Turkish restaurant, Chintamani

*Berkeley
Square
Café*

kebabs are more lacklustre. Good-value set lunches, but the atmosphere really hots up at night.

Fakhreldine

85 Piccadilly, W1 [C4]. Tel: 7493 3424. Open: L and D daily (until midnight Mon–Sat), Br Sun. £££ www.fakhreldine.co.uk

This long-established restaurant has been given a sleek and stylish makeover. The Parisian-born Lebanese chef gives a modern interpretation to traditional dishes, from tabouleh to tender slow-cooked lamb with pistachio rice. Try the platter of assorted kibbeh, including pumpkin and orange blossom-scented strawberry soup. Lebanese brunch menu on Sundays.

Modern European

Berkeley Square Café

7 Davies St, W1 [B2]. Tel: 7629 6993. Open: L and D Mon–Fri, D only Sat. £££ www.berkeleysquarecafe.com

Café is a misnomer for Stephen Black's contemporary glass-fronted restaurant with pavement terrace. The highly original menu includes signature seared scallop, foie gras, cepes, salsify and parsnip purée, grilled fillet of Cornish sea bass with a vinaigrette of sherry and mustard, and greengage crumble with clotted cream ice cream. Gourmet children's menu too. Instead of Muzak, the loos have a tape of actor Timothy West reading *Animal Farm*.

Le Caprice ⓨ

Arlington House, Arlington St, SW1 [D3]. Tel: 7629 2239. Open: L and D Mon–Sat, D only Sun. £££

Chic, buzzy bistro with vaguely Art Deco decor and fabulous celebrity photographs on the walls. Like its sibling, The Ivy, Le Caprice's tables remain among the hottest in town, so booking well ahead is essential. The food – sophisticated salads, excellent seafood and a long list of creamy desserts with wine list to match – is more for picking over than wolfing down. Last-minute seating at the bar sometimes an option.

Dover Street Restaurant and Jazz Bar

8–10 Dover St, W1 [C3]. Tel: 7629 9813. Open: L and D Mon–Sat until 3am. £ (lunch menu), £££ www.doverst.co.uk

Smart and furiously busy, Dover Street is a Mayfair institution. It attracts an affluent post-work crowd who come here to unwind over drinks and the live jazz, soul and Latin sounds. The modern European brasserie-style menu is unadventurous but reliable. Good-value lunchtime deals. Music charge after 10pm (9pm on Monday). No jeans or trainers. *(see also page 40)*.

Gordon Ramsay at Claridge's ⑪

Claridge's Hotel, Brook St, W1 [B2]. Tel: 7499 0099. Open: L and D daily. £££ (set lunch), ££££ www.gordonramsay.com
Gordon Ramsay is London's most feted chef/restaurateur and tables are hard to come by in this gorgeous, unashamedly romantic dining room. Working under Ramsay's supervision, head chef Mark Sargeant cooks dreamy rich, intricate dishes. Exquisite extra mini courses, a superb wine list and pampering service all add up to a memorable culinary experience. Set lunch is a relative bargain. Booking essential.

The Greenhouse

27a Hay's Mews, W1 [B3]. Tel: 7499 3331. Open: L and D Mon–Fri, D only Sat. £££ (set lunch), ££££ www.greenhouserestaurant.co.uk
Secreted away in a Mayfair mews, this newly spruced-up restaurant is a romantic hideaway worth seeking out. The success of Paul Merrett's highly original cooking lies in his imaginative use of spices – try the signature pan-fried sea bass on sag-aloo with onion bhajee and tomato pickle – and exotic sweet combinations. A first-rate sommelier is on hand to help make an informed choice from the bewildering wine list.

Just St James

12 St James's St, SW1 [D3]. Tel: 7976 2222. Open: L and D Mon–Sat, L only Sun. £££ www.juststjames.com
The ambience in this former Edwardian banking hall is pleasingly relaxed. Acres of marble fill the palatial interior, at the centre of which a glass elevator whisks diners up to the galleries. The inspiring, eclectic menu runs from white gazpacho to sea bass with spinach and irresistible orange-scented crème caramel. Good for dining in larger groups.

Quaglino's

16 Bury St, SW1 [D3]. Tel: 7930 6767. Open: L and D daily. £££ www.conran.com
This Conran brasserie attracts a lively, young crowd. The dramatic, sweeping staircase and highly decorated columns, inspired by La Coupole in Paris, make for a glamorous dining experience. The reliable menu has a strong Oriental slant and memorable desserts. Live music on Fridays and Saturdays adds to the atmosphere, but expect a steepish bill.

Below left:
Berkeley Square
Below: Just
St James

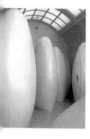

The Ritz

150 Piccadilly, W1 [C3]. Tel: 7493 8181. Open: L and D daily, dinner dance Fri–Sat. ££££ www.theritzlondon.com

One of London's grandest dining rooms – a boudoiresque confection of pink and green marble, gold leaf and dazzling chandeliers – has a terrace resplendant with box hedging and views over Green Park. Flawless cooking caters for every whim: wild smoked salmon carved at the table; Caesar salad assembled at a trolley beside you; and poached Dover Sole garnished with truffles. *(For tea at The Ritz, see page 127).*

Sketch

9 Conduit St, W1 [C1]. Tel: 0870 777 44 88. Open: Lecture Room L and D Mon–Sat, Gallery D only Mon–Sat. ££££ www.sketch.uk.com

Sketch opened in 2003 to a barrage of publicity for its outrageously decadent and witty interior and dazzling yet dizzily priced food by Parisian super-chef Pierre Gagnaire. Choose between the gastronomic Lecture Room and the more modestly priced Gallery (all things being relative – set lunch is £48), which serves mezze and desserts on designer trolleys. Visit the late-night lounge bar and Parlour for irresistible patisserie, including shot-glass multilayered mousses.

Above: Sketch
Below right: Momo

Sotheby's Café

34–35 New Bond St. W1 [C2]. Tel: 7293 5077. Open: B, L and T Mon–Fri. ££

Within the famous auction galleries, this smart wood-panelled room offers a short Italianish menu. Dishes might include wild mushrooms with grilled polenta or rocket and ricotta ravioli. Very civilised afternoon teas too. Booking advisable; ask for a place 'indoors' to avoid getting seated in the corridor.

The Wolseley

160 Piccadilly, W1 [D3]. Tel: 7499 6996. Open: 7am–midnight Mon–Sat, 9am–midnight Sun. £££

Erstwhile owners of The Ivy and Le Caprice, Jeremy King and Christopher Corbin, are the masterminds behind this, one of London's hottest new restaurants. Housed in a stunning 1920s listed building which started life as a Wolseley car showroom, the concept is a Viennese-style grand café, where you can breakfast on coffee and cake or feast on a blow-out meal at midnight. Its current A-list status means getting a table at short notice is nigh-on impossible. Time will tell if it manages to live up to the hype.

Moroccan

Momo 🍴

25 Heddon St, W1 [D2]. Tel: 7434 4040. Open: L and D Mon–Sat, D only Sun. ££ (set lunch), £££ www.momoresto.com

Momo's wonderfully theatrical decor and authentic Moroccan cuisine is a hit with tourists and locals alike. It has a real party feel in the evening, when candles are lit and the music is upbeat. Share pastilla, couscous or tagines and linger over many cups of mint tea. Fabulous cocktails too.

Mô Tea Room

23 Heddon St, W1 [D2]. Tel: 7434 4040. Open: L and D Mon–Sat. £

Low tables and leather pouffes spill out onto the street at this relaxed, bazaar-like offshoot of neighbouring Momo, hung with Moroccan artefacts and jewellery, all for sale. Drink cocktails, fresh fruit juices or mint tea and graze on salads, spicy sausages, scented pastries or crepes.

Polish

L'Autre

5b Shepherd St, W1 [C4]. Tel: 7499 4680. Open: L and D Mon–Fri, D only Sat–Sun. ££

In the heart of Shepherd's Market, this quaint, tiny, half-timbered restaurant offers a bizarre combination of Polish and Mexican food, which works surprisingly well. Friendly service and romantic, candlelit atmosphere.

Spanish

El Pirata

5–6 Down St, W1 [B4]. Tel: 7491 3810. Open: L and D Mon–Fri, D only Sat. ££

Unpretentious, bustling bar/restaurant serving reliable tapas, including authentic tortilla, garlicky prawns and a decent paella. Invariably packed with local after-workers. Not a place for a quiet tête-à-tête.

Thai

Thai Pot

5 Princess St, Hanover Square, W1 [C1]. Tel: 7499 3333. Open: L and D daily. £ www.thaipot.co.uk

Buzzy, friendly, canteen-style dining immensely popular with a younger crowd. Great for a quick refuel on satay sticks, green or red curries and noodles at shared tables.

PUBS, BARS AND CAFÉS

Mayfair drinkers frequent some of London's grandest hotel bars where the scale of the complimentary nibbles can offset the steep drinks prices. Try the stately **American Bar at the Connaught** *(Carlos Place)*, the mirrored piano **Dorchester Bar** *(53 Park Lane)*, the fashionabledeco **Claridge's Bar** *(55 Brook St)* serving immaculate Martinis in crystal glass, or the **Rivoli Bar** at The Ritz *(150 Piccadilly)*.

Old-fashioned boozers are thin on the ground, but there are a few gems. The posh, high Victoriana **Audley** *(41 Mount St)* attracts the Mayfair rich. More cosy is timber-framed **Coach & Horses** *(5 Bruton St)* and most lively is **Ye Grapes** *(16 Shepherd Mkt)* frequented by a mix of Mayfair grandees and lost tourists.

Chic Café *(Shepherd St)* serves good pastries, Godiva chocolates and iced coffee, with tables spilling on to the street. **La Madeleine** *(5 Vigo St)* off Regent Street has passable snacks, puddings and cakes.

Among the trendy late-night hotspots to be seen are **Aura** *(48–49 St James's St)*, a deeply fashionable cocktail bar with leather sofas and hydraulic tables which change height from dining to lounging level, and **Havana** *(17 Hanover Square)*, a funky Latino bar where the zebra-skin banquettes are almost as loud as the music. The **Met Bar** *(Metropolitan Hotel, 19 Old Park Lane)* is no longer *the* fashionable celeb venue, but its sleek interior and creative cocktails still attract beautifully dressed drinkers.

Eating Out with Children

*Dining out with young children can be a discouraging experience,
but a few London restaurants pull out all the stops to please*

There are rules to eating out with children in London, and the smaller the children the more firmly they apply. Forget the spontaneity of Southern Europe, where restaurateurs squeeze children's cheeks and scoop up babies into their arms. Forget even the benign tolerance of Northern Europe, where Dutch and Danish children appear at the bar alongside mother and father. Britain's restaurant culture is totalitarian. Apart from some chains, often Italian such as Pizza Express, Est Est Est or ASK, London restaurants are wary of kids. Generally, the more upmarket the restaurant, the more hostile it will be.

The most important rule is to prepare for a restaurant trip with as much care as a military strike. Phone ahead to book highchairs or seating in booths and check on buggy access and nappy-changing facilities if your child needs them.

Unless your children are into inventive cuisine, it may be best to stick to what they know and head for American-style diners or themed restaurants. In general, you'll find it takes an American to dress up as Rocky the Guitar and wander around offering free face painting, as they do at the Hard Rock Café.

Other safe bets include park cafés. The café at the Princess Diana Memorial Playground in Kensington Gardens *(Bayswater Rd entrance)*, for example, serves good lamb chops with salad and new potatoes, from a wooden hut that promises nothing more than an ice cream. Also noteworthy are the café by the round pond in Battersea Park, serving hot dishes such as spaghetti Bolognese and soup, and the café in Holland Park, serving salads and smoothies.

Face painting and fun are on the menu at Sticky Fingers at weekends

Parents who want to steer clear of nuggets and burgers and eat well themselves should look out for restaurants and gastropubs that serve child portions. Also good are **Carluccio's Caffès** (assorted branches) where the children's menu includes chicken Milanese with potatoes, foccacia sandwiches, and ravioli. At the Belgian *moules-et-frites* specialists **Belgo** *(Camden, Notting Hill, Islington)* up to two children per adult choosing from the à la carte menu can eat free, choosing from sausage and mash, mussels, chicken, or sole goujons.

Children's choice

The **Rainforest Café** (*20 Shaftesbury Ave; tel: 7434 3111*) wows children of all ages with its canopy foliage, thunder and lightning displays, and life-like animals. Queuing can take up to 1½ hours so it is best to arrive early, get your 'Rainforest passport' stamped and browse around the shops while you wait. The American-style food includes set menus for tinies at £8.50 (the Ozzie) up to £30 (the Maya) for adults.

Also on a wild animal theme, the **Giraffe** chain of restaurants (*Battersea, Chiswick, Hampstead, Islington, Kensington, Marylebone and Richmond; tel: 8457 2776 for details*) offers bright, funky interiors with 'world music and global food'. Its children's menu at £4.95 includes standard fare such as chicken and chips, plus fresh fruit smoothies. Children get to take away a balloon and a swizzle stick.

Fast food tends to be favourite when it comes to eating out with kids

Hard Rock Café (*150 Old Park Lane, W1; tel: 7629 0382; daily 11.30am–12.30am*) displays a vast collection of pop-music memorabilia, from Madonna's pink bustier to Jimi Hendrix's guitar. It serves great burgers (children's menu only £4.25). It doesn't take bookings, so just turn up and queue.

Planet Harrods (*Harrods, Knightsbridge, SW1; tel: 7730 1234; Mon–Sat 11am–6.30pm*), off the toy department, has a futuristic theme, with video screens showing nonstop cartoons. The children's menu is predictable, with chicken goujons, burgers and lasagne at £5.75, but the quality is good.

Planet Hollywood (*Trocadero, Piccadilly, W1; tel: 7287 1000; daily 11.30am–1am*) isn't for parents with a headache, but the loud music and film memorabilia ensures that even the most truculent teenager will be kept busy exploring the Horror Room, the Alien Grotto and the James Bond Suite. The children's menu is expensive at £7.95, but the quality is excellent.

Sticky Fingers (*1a Phillimore Gardens, W8; tel: 7938 5338; daily noon–late*), owned by Rolling Stone Bill Wyman and full of rock memorabilia, welcomes children, particularly at weekends, when they are treated to colouring books, face painting and a special menu (burgers, pasta) at £7.25.

Smollensky's Balloon (*105 The Strand, WC2; tel: 7497 2101; L and D daily, children's entertainment noon–5pm weekends*). At weekends kids can enjoy old favourites, such as bangers and mash at £4.95, between watching magic shows or playing video games in the supervised play area, while adults eat large steaks and sip wine.

Texas Embassy Cantina (*1 Cockspur St, SW1; tel: 7925 0077; daily noon–late*). Huge portions of Tex-Mex fare. The unflappable staff are quick to provide puzzles and highchairs. The children's menu is £4.75.

Zilli Fish Too (*8–18 Wild St, WC2; tel: 7437 4867*). Children are always welcome here and at Zilli Fish on Brewer Street, but on Sunday this branch makes a special effort to entertain them with face painting, lessons in pizza making, and a special menu. Parents can eat sophisticated fish and pasta dishes in peace upstairs.

MARYLEBONE

This residential pocket of Georgian streets and squares is well provided for with specialist food shops and gourmet restaurants

To the north of Oxford Street lies Marylebone (pronounced *mar-luh-bun*), once the outlying village of St Mary-by-the-Bourne and now very much on the map as a gastronomic and shopping destination, with highly desirable housing too. Samual Pepys recorded walking through open country to reach its pleasure gardens in 1668, where all manner of food and drink was served alongside entertainment, and declared it a 'pretty place'. During the course of the next century the gardens, which became increasingly disreputable, were closed and the village swallowed up as its main landowners – chief among them the Portlands and the Portmans – laid out elegant Georgian streets and squares, many of which remain little changed. One of London's best and most fashionable restaurants, Locanda Locatelli, is discreetly hidden just off Portman Square. The club Home House, which attracts a glamorous celebrity crowd, is here too; beg or charm your way inside to admire the glorious, over-the-top restoration of the ornate building, which once housed the Courtauld Institute.

Marylebone has long been famous as the home of the fictitious detective Sherlock Holmes whose stomping ground was around Baker Street. It is also home to Madame Tussaud's with its perennial queue, the London Planetarium and London's hub of private health care clinics, Harley Street. The area is bounded by Regent's Park (north), Oxford Street (south), Great Portland Street (east) and Edgware Road (west), with a large concentration of lively, late-night Lebanese restaurants where belly-dancing is standard with the mezze.

The opening of the chic Orrery, serving Michelin-starred food on the top floor of London's second-largest Conran Shop, was instrumental in raising the culinary profile of Marylebone and encouraging other restaurants to the area. The Orrery Epicerie next door sells highlights from the menu, including the peerless foie gras terrine and an impressive range of cheeses. Sit at high stools for a post-shopping snack or take an impromptu picnic into the gardens of St Marylebone Church opposite. Amble down Marylebone High Street, which still has a pleasing village feel despite the arrival of many of the smartest fashion chains interspersed with an increasing choice of restaurants. Relax over brunch at the Tapa Room, the informal, no-reservations café of fusion star Peter Gordon's hip Providores restaurant. More off the beaten track is the glass-roofed Café Bagatelle at The Wallace Collection of 18th-century French paintings and decorative arts. Among the many other cafés, Patisserie Valerie at Sagne is the best for cakes and people-watching.

Opposite: fusion star Peter Gordon's Providores restaurant and Tapa Room. Below: Patisserie Valerie's cakes are works of art, almost too beautiful to eat

Gourmet shopping

Foodies will thrill at the number of specialist food shops in the area. Biggles *(66 Marylebone Lane)*, sausage-maker extraordinaire, captures the flavour of almost every sausage-producing country in the world. Find superb breads, including organic sourdough, at Dan Schickentanz' De Gustibus *(53 Blandford St)*, who supply some of the finest restaurants in the country with their breads. There's a small pavement café too. La Fromagerie (*2–4 Moxon St*), tucked away in a converted dairy in a mews, has an astonishing selection of cheese temptingly arranged in a dedicated climate-controlled cheese room besides all manner of cheese-related gifts, from wonderful knives to cheeseboards, plus exceptional deli goodies, cakes and wines. The large communal table in

FIVE OF THE BEST

Locanda Locatelli: outstanding Italian food in a glamorous setting

Orrery: for its exceptional tasting menu, cheeseboard and roof terrace

The Providores: unusual ingredients to excite the most jaded tastebuds

La Porte des Indes: extraordinary lush interior and exotic menu

Six-13: gourmet Jewish cuisine and the best chicken soup

the middle of the shop acts as an all-day café. Just off Edgware Road, drink in the mesmerising Belgian chocolate aroma at the bizzarely named Choccywoccydoodah (*47 Harrowby St*). Besides chocolates, there are fantastical wedding cakes. At open-all-hours Green Valley (*36 Upper Berkeley St*) there's a stunning array of Middle Eastern food, from fresh olives to pastries and all manner of unusual ingredients such as pomegranate molasses and dried limes for Iranian cooking plus takeaway dishes including tabbouleh and falafel.

Little known, except among locals, on Fridays and Saturdays there can be more than 200 stalls at the lively Church Street food market, just off Edgware Road. Old Church Street has an excellent antique market too.

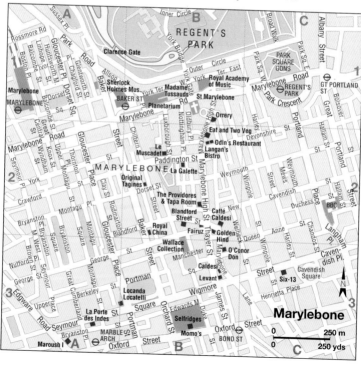

British

Langan's Bistro

26 Devonshire St, W1 [B2]. Tel: 7935 4531. Open: L and D Mon–Fri, D only Sat. ££ www.langansrestaurants.co.uk
Old-timer serving simple, old-fashioned bistro fare with considerable aplomb and waiters who treat allcomers like VIPs. No culinary fireworks in the kitchen but good for more sedate romantic occasions.

Chinese

Royal China

40 Baker St, W1 [B2]. Tel: 7487 4688. Open: L and D daily. £££ www.royalchinagroup.co.uk
The Marylebone branch of a small chain of quality Oriental restaurants. It is invariably packed and extremely lively at weekend lunchtimes as it's no secret that the dim sum is regarded among the best in town. Plenty of Chinese dining en famille confirms their reputation. The trick is to put your name on the waiting list as soon as you cross the threshold. Crabmeat dumpling in soup is the delicious house special.

Fish

Golden Hind

73 Marylebone Lane, W1 [B2]. Tel: 7486 3644. Open: L and D Mon–Fri, D only Sat. £
Vintage chippie dating back to 1914, still boasting a magnificent 1930s fryer now purely decorative. Fabulous, glisteningly fresh fish in crispy, golden batter and grilled/steamed options too, plus expertly cooked chips. Try spotted dick and custard for 'afters'. BYOB. No corkage.

Vintage chippie, Golden Hind

French

La Galette

56 Paddington St, W1 [B2]. Tel: 7935 1554. Open: daily. £ www.lagalette.com
Bright, minimalist, perennially packed, modern creperie serving savoury galettes – try the ham, cheese and egg for a complete 'all-day breakfast' – decent salads and flambéed sweet crepes. Perfect washed down with crisp Breton cider from an earthenware tankard. Bookings taken only for tables of six or more.

Le Muscadet

25 Paddington St, W1 [B2]. Tel: 7935 2883. Open: L Mon–Fri, D only Sat. ££
Unpretentious French brasserie of long vintage offering simple classics, including snails in garlic butter and chicken in a cep cream sauce. Good cheeseboard.

Indian

La Porte des Indes ⑪

32 Bryanston St, W1 [A3]. Tel: 7224 0055. Open: L and D Mon–Fri, D only Sat, L only Sun. ££ www.pilondon.com
Show-stopping, opulent decor, with lush greenery, cascading

Did you know?

Baker Street, Marylebone High Street and Portland Place all lead to Regent's Park, an elegant 470-acre (190-hectare) space surrounded by John Nash's handsome Regency terraces. It's the perfect place to spend a lazy sunny day with a picnic. The boating lake is a tranquil spot and Queen Mary's Garden is noted for its roses. The nearby Open Air Theatre puts on Shakespeare plays in summer, but the main attraction is London Zoo, which has more than 8,000 animals.

waterfalls and a sweeping staircase, adds to the culinary experience, which draws extensively on the Indo-French connection of Pondicherry, a former colony of south India. Good seafood dishes, but the food sometimes struggles to match the exotic surroundings. Popular with families at weekends.

International

The Providores and Tapa Room 🍴

109 Marylebone High St, W1 [B2]. Tel: 7935 6175. Open: L and D daily. ££ Tapa Room (no reservations), £££ Providores www.theprovidores.co.uk

A favourite among foodies who delight in the refreshingly different ingredients that the inimitable fusion food master Peter Gordon and fellow New Zealander Anna Hansen use in cunningly balanced combinations. The downstairs Tapa Room (named after the ceremonial aboriginal cloak that hangs on the wall) is more informal, with banquette seating and a communal high bar. The grazing menu offers more unexpected and delightful taste combinations. Well worth queuing for weekend brunch. Don't leave without sampling the chocolate, raisin and sherry brownie.

Irish

O'Conor Don

88 Marylebone Lane, W1 [B3]. Tel: 7935 9311. Open: L and D Mon–Fri. ££ www.oconordon.com

Elegant yet homely dining room over a pub, offering modern Irish menu including exemplary oysters and beef in Guinness casserole, plus a sophisticated take on Irish stew. Modest, well-considered wine list, and sweet service.

TIP

Whether or not you're taking in the Wallace Collection (which is definitely worth making time for), the gallery's **Café Bagatelle** *(Hertford House, Manchester Square, W1; tel: 7563 9505; Mon–Sat 10am–4.30pm, Sun noon–4.30pm)* is a relaxing place for a civilised lunch, coffee or tea break. Diners sit in a vast pink-walled courtyard surrounded by palm trees, sheltered under a glass roof.

Italian

Caldesi

15–17 Marylebone Lane, W1 [B3]. Tel: 7935 9226. Open: L and D Mon–Fri, D only Sat. £££ www.caldesi.com

With a facade re-creating a Tuscan townhouse complete with flowers and shutters and handpainted Florentine murals in the candle-lit dining room, this is a relatively undiscovered gem. Dishes such as monkfish with prawns, tomato, wild fennel and basil transport, and warm, friendly service add to the Mediterranean ambience.

Caffè Caldesi

118 Marylebone Lane, W1 [B2]. Tel: 7935 1144. Open: daily. ££ Buzzy, contemporary younger sibling to Caldesi *(see above)*, serving sunny, simple Italian food. The char-grilled squid starter with lemon and chilli is exemplary, as is the all-Italian wine list. Great value for lunch.

Locanda Locatelli 🍴

Churchill InterContinental, 8 Seymour St, W1 [B3]. Tel: 7935 9088. Open: L and D Mon–Sat. £££ www.locandalocatelli.com

Right: Six-13, sophisticated kosher cuisine

Locanda Locatelli, Italian elegance and refinement at its best

Both Madonna and Tony Blair are fans of Giorgio Locatelli's startlingly good and ungreedily priced north Italian food, making great persistence necessary to secure a reservation among the see-and-be-seen crowd. Try elegantly presented dishes of own-made ravioli with pork ragout and lemon cream, the signature duck with spelt, and a *degustazioni* of Amedei chocolate desserts. Take care not to fill up too much on the wonderful bread basket featuring metre-long home-made cheese grissini. The comfortable room by top designer David Collins is fashionably retroelegant.

Jewish

Six-13 🍽

19 Wigmore St, W1 [C3]. Tel: 7629 6133. Open: L and D Sun–Thur, L only Fri, D only Sat. ££ (set lunch), ££££
www.six13.com

One of a kind. A smart kosher restaurant serving modern reinterpretations of classic Jewish cuisine and Mediterranean fish dishes in Art Deco-style surroundings. The name refers to the 613 Jewish rules for living. All wines are kosher. The basement New York-style diner serving pastrami sandwiches and the like is cheaper.

Middle Eastern

Fairuz

3 Blandford St, W1 [B2]. Tel: 7486 8108. Open: daily. ££
For new initiates into Lebanese cooking, the set mezze, plenty for a light lunch or supper, is the way to order: the herby tabbouleh, stuffed vine leaves, and spicy lamb sausages are all excellent. The charcoal grills are generous and cooked to perfection, and the coffee and pastries authentic. Helpful staff, who are happy to advise, and warm decor are the icing on the cake. Pavement seating in summer.

Levant

Jason Court, 76 Wigmore St, W1 [B3]. Tel: 7224 1111. Open: L and D daily, Fri/Sat until midnight. ££ www.levantrestaurant.com

TIP

For ultra-healthy, stylish refreshment check out totally organic **Quiet Revolution** within the Aveda health and beauty store *(28 Marylebone High St)*. Great juices, salads and crepes.

Seasonal dishes in a stylish setting at Blandford Street

TIP

Kitchenware emporium **Divertimenti** *(33–34 Marylebone High St)* has a fabulous café serving delectable soups, salads and pastries. Arrive early to grab a pew at the large communal table. Plenty of foodie magazines to read for solo diners.

Enter via a lantern-lit staircase into the exotic low-seating and low-lighting interior. Noise levels are high, and when it comes to ordering from the epic mezze menu you have to compete with souk music and belly dancers. There's a good choice of set menus if you have trouble choosing and the own-made breads and inventive puddings such as pistachio and honey brûlée are very moreish. Suited to large and lively groups.

Maroush I

21 Edgware Rd, W2 [A3]. Tel: 7723 0773. Open: daily noon–2am. £££ www.maroush.com
For midnight munchies the mezze, charcoal grills and kebabs at Maroush I are hard to beat. The steepish cover charge includes belly-dancing and live music. There are seven restaurants in the Lebanese chain, the nearby Maroush Gardens *(1–3 Connaught St)*, the latest addition, offers good-value set menus while Ranoush Juice *(43 Edgware Rd)* does a mean kebab and stays open until 3am.

Modern European

Blandford Street

5–7 Blandford St, W1 [B2]. Tel: 7486 9696. Open: L and D Mon–Fri, D only Sat. £££ www.blandford-street.co.uk
Stylish minimalist restaurant with a laid-back ambience, serving a thoroughly enjoyable eclectic menu. Favourites include the mixed fish grill with aioli and real chips, and a superb rib-eye steak, partnered by a bottle of wine from a well-rounded list. Round your meal off with a homemade ice or parfait.

Odin's Restaurant

27 Devonshire St, W1 [B2]. Tel: 7935 7296. Open: L and D Mon–Fri. £££ www.langansrestaurants.co.uk
Grand, antique-filled dining room of long-standing that's good for a confidential business lunch or intimate dinner as each table is hidden behind an old-fashioned screen. Nostalgic dishes include crab bisque, and grilled Dover sole.

Orrery Ⓨ

55 Marylebone High St, W1 [B1]. Tel: 7616 8000. Open: L and D daily. £££ (set menu), ££££ www.orrery.com

Dinner in this elegant Conran dining room is a romantic gastro-experience. Barbary duck with pain d'epice, foie gras tarte tartin and banyuls jus are typical of the intensely flavoured dishes. Prize-winning cheese trolley, memorable soufflés and a definitive wine list.

Moroccan

Momo's

Second Floor, Selfridges, 400 Oxford St, W1 [B3]. Tel: 7318 3620. Open: Mon–Sat 10.30am–8pm, Sun noon–6pm. ££–£££ www.selfridges.co.uk

Selfridges has an incredible 22 in-store eateries to choose from, ranging from quick-snack juice and espresso bars to buzzy wine bars, a pizza parlour, an oyster bar and a branch of Japanese conveyor-belt restaurant Yo! Sushi. Cream of the crop is the newly opened Momo, sibling to the glitzy Mayfair Momo *(see page 72)*. It offers foot-sore shoppers a light mezze menu in relaxed surroundings. Or you can stop off for a refreshing mint tea in the luxurious tearoom.

Original Tagines

7a Dorset St, W1 [B2]. Tel: 7935 1545. Open: L and D Mon–Fri, D only Sat. £ (set lunch), ££ www.originaltagines.com

Buzzy little restaurant specialising in delicately spiced Moroccan tagines such as lamb in black pepper sauce with caramelised pepper, and chicken in saffron, ginger and fresh herbs. Laid-back atmosphere.

Vegetarian

Eat and Two Veg

50 Marylebone High St, W1 [B2]. Tel: 7258 8595. Open: daily, all day. ££ www.eatandtwoveg.com

A welcome newcomer to the Marylebone scene, this formica and leatherette diner serves creative vegetarian concoctions.

PUBS, BARS AND CAFÉS

Marylebone has a wide choice of characterful pubs and bars. For sheer indulgence visit the imperial **Tsar's Bar** at Langham Hilton *(1 Portland Place)* and choose from the 100+ vodkas to go with your caviar. Or soak up the dark, aristocratic atmosphere in **The Churchill Bar & Cigar Divan** *(30 Portman Square)*, which has an extensive selection of cigars and single malts. The stylish **Steam** *(1 Eastbourne Terrace)*, technically within Paddington Station, offers fabulous cocktails, unusual beers and a simple English bar menu. **Match** *(37–38 Margaret St)* fills up with an urban chic crowd for classic cocktails. Winelovers enjoy the old-world **Dock Blida** *(50–54 Blandford St)*, where rare vintages can be ordered with 24-hours' notice. A popular gastropub is **The Street** *(58 Crawford St)*, which serves great risottos, beer-battered cod and chips in a Moroccan-souk interior. One of the oldest and best pubs in the area is the **Barley Mow** *(8 Dorset St)*, with two quirky former pawnbroking booths for private drinking. Monarchists (and lovers of regal kitsch) can admire the memorabilia at **Windsor Castle** *(29 Crawford Place)*. In an exclusive mews **Dover Castle** *(43 Weymouth Mews)* offers reasonably priced beers and plenty of old-fashioned leather sofa seating. For a Scottish experience try a Nessie's monster sandwich and a choice single malt at the **William Wallace** *(33 Aybrook St)*. For a daytime treat tuck into a luscious gateau at **Patisserie Valerie at Sagne** *(105 Marylebone High St)*, where the outdoor tables are good for people-watching.

Fish and Chips

*When the fish is fresh, the batter crisp and the chips nice and chunky,
this no-nonsense classic British dish is supremely satisfying*

Fish and chips is one of Britain's few great and original contributions to the world's repertoire of classic dishes. Though a cabinet minister recently claimed that chicken tikka masala should now be regarded as Britain's premier national dish, fish and chips has outlived boiled beef and carrots and still rivals roast beef and Yorkshire pudding or steak and kidney pudding as an all-time national favourite.

Extraordinary, then, to find that in London at least, and often throughout the UK, it is seldom Britons who prepare and sell the dish. There are only 8,600 fish and chip shops left in Britain today (in the 1930s there were more than 30,000) and the future of those that remain is threatened by dwindling fish stocks and ever-increasing competition from more new-fangled fast-food alternatives. Surprisingly, no-one has yet succeeded in fashioning a popular restaurant chain founded on fish and chips. The nearest approach is Harry Ramsden's (established in 1928 in Leeds and now owned by a catering conglomerate), which has just launched a fresh assault on city centres and the takeaway trade, so it may yet happen.

Fish and chips originated as long ago as the 1850s. Before that, some street vendors sold hot potatoes, others fried fish. When the two were offered together, their popularity as a cheap staple was quickly assured. Historians argue that fish and chips played a vital role in the First World War, saving Britain from military defeat, socialist revolution and famine. *The Frier*, a trade magazine, claimed at the time that fish and chips 'had stood more than any other trade in the country, between the very poorest of our population and famine and revolt'.

Mushy peas, a traditional accompaniment to fish and chips

Traditionally, cod is the fish of choice in London and the south, while haddock is preferred in the north, but many fryers offer other varieties such as rock, plaice, skate, halibut, swordfish, scampi, trout, lemon or Dover sole, sea bass or even grilled salmon, conger eel or sardines. More still have diversified into chicken portions, battered sausages, reheated pies and pasties, Chinese spring rolls, kebabs and even the ubiquitous burger, archrival to the traditional dish.

Golden rules

As a general rule you will get much better value for money at a real fish and chip restaurant (attached to a shop offering takeaway service) than at pubs or restaurants that offer fish and chips alongside their meat menus. Beware the smell of stale oil (a sure warning sign of a dire chippy), and uniform triangular – or rhomboidal – shaped pieces of fish that are evenly battered. The latter are reconstituted fish steaks, processed and long frozen, and devoid of flavour. Beware also even-cut or long, thin and pallid chips (either frozen, or fashioned by extrusion of mashed or reconstituted potato).

Choose a chippy that offers the widest possible selection of fish and fewer meat alternatives. The posher fish and chip restaurants should also offer suitably fish-based starters, fresh salads, decent desserts, and a range of side orders such as pickled gherkins, onions or eggs, and mushy peas or baked beans.

The top test, apart from truly fresh fish and crisp batter, is that you should be given fresh lemon instead of, or at least as an alternative to, the coarse-flavoured malt vinegar or (worse) the dreadful non-brewed condiment (a euphemism for chemically created acetic acid) still found all too often marring the taste and freshness of otherwise perfectly good fish and chips.

Top-ranking chippies

For whatever reason, many of the best fish and chip shops and their associated restaurants remain under immigrant management to this day. Among the best are **Rock & Sole Plaice** in Covent Garden *(47 Endell St, WC2; daily noon–10pm)*, the **Golden Hind** in Marylebone *(73 Marylebone Lane, W1; L and D Mon–Fri, D only Sat)*, **Costa's** in Notting Hill *(18 Hillgate St, W8; L and D Tues–Sat)* and the **Fryer's Delight** in Holborn *(19 Theobald's Rd, WC1; Mon–Sat noon–10pm)*; they are all owned and staffed by Italians. **Nautilus** in West Hampstead *(27–29 Fortune Green Rd, NW6; L and D Mon–Sat)* is so Jewish that its fish are coated in matzo flour, and throughout London and the rest of Britain you will easily find well-run fish and chip shops and restaurants in the charge of Chinese, Cypriots (Greek or Turkish) or Central Europeans.

Among other top-rank addresses worth mentioning are the long-standing fashionable favourites **Sea Shell** in Marylebone *(49–51 Lisson Grove, NW1; L and D Mon–Fri, noon–10.30pm Sat)* and **Geales** in Notting Hill *(2 Farmer St, W8; L and D Mon–Sat, D only Sun)*. **Fish Central** near the Barbican Centre *(149–151 Central St, EC1; L and D Mon–Sat)* is a blessing to concert- and theatre-goers. **Seafresh** *(80–81 Wilton Rd, SW1; noon–10.30pm Mon–Sat)* is handy for Victoria Station, and **Masters Superfish** *(191 Waterloo Rd, SE1; L and D Tues–Sat, D only Mon)* for Waterloo. The **North Sea Fish Restaurant** in Bloomsbury *(7–8 Leigh St, WC1; L and D Mon–Sat)* is pleasantly old-fashioned. More far flung are **Two Brothers Fish** in Finchley *(297 Regent's Park Rd, N3; L and D Tues–Sat)* and **Toff's** in Muswell Hill *(38 Muswell Hill Broadway, N10; 11.30am–10pm Mon–Sat)*, while **Brady's** in Wandsworth *(513 Old York Rd, SW18; D only Mon–Sat)*, **Olley's** in Herne Hill *(67 Norwood Rd, SE24; L and D Tues–Sat, D only Sun, Mon)* and the **Sea Cow** *(37 Lordship Lane, SE22; L and D Tues–Sat)* in East Dulwich fly the flag in south London.

All the above-mentioned restaurants offer a takeaway service. Prices for a basic plate of fish and chips start at around £5. Most lunch sittings run from between 11am or noon to around 2.30pm. Dinner is served from around 5pm or 6pm until 10pm to 11pm.

Vintage fryer at the Golden Hind, one of London's oldest and best chippies

KENSINGTON AND CHELSEA

Though well endowed with top-end restaurants, this well-heeled borough has a surprising number of good, reasonably priced eateries

Most visitors to London will, at some point or another, be drawn to Kensington and Chelsea, whether it's to discover the museums, walk in Kensington Gardens, shop on the King's Road or simply experience the thriving restaurant scene. Here you'll find London's only three-starred Michelin restaurant, the eponymous Gordon Ramsay run by the super-chef, as well as renowned and feted eateries such as Bibendum, Zaika, English Garden and Tom Aikens. It also has an abundance of good neighbourhood restaurants and gastropubs, along with cafés, bars, delicatessens and food shops aplenty.

South Kensington

The Royal Borough of Kensington and Chelsea is one of the most fashionable and well-to-do districts of London. At its epicentre is Brompton Cross, the point at which Brompton Road, Fulham Road, Sloane Avenue and Walton Street meet. Scattered among the stylish designer boutiques are culinary hotspots Daphne's, The Collection and Bibendum. The area typically attracts young, well-heeled professionals and showbusiness types that come here to shop as much as they do to eat out. If you are feeling indulgent, the Bibendum Oyster Bar situated in the beautiful Art Deco Michelin building is the perfect place to go for a glass of champagne and some seafood.

Opposite: Bibendum, Michelin House Below: a sunny Zaika cocktail

To the north lies South Kensington. Its main street, Old Brompton Road, is unprepossessing, and the area, which is home to the French Institute and the Lycée Français Charles de Gaulle, has more of a Gallic influence, with patisseries selling exquisite gateaux and pastries, a charcuterie and a delightful French bistro, La Bouchée. South Kensington is also home to three of London's most popular (and free) museums: the Natural History Museum, the Science Museum, and the Victoria and Albert. They were the brainchild of Prince Albert, following the success of his Great Exhibition in 1851. His aim was to create a permanent showcase for the arts and sciences. He didn't live to see his dream come to fruition, but the museums today attract several million visitors a year.

King's Road

While Brompton Cross is the place where beautiful people go to be seen, King's Road is more low-key. Created by Charles II (1660–85) as the private royal route to link St James's Palace to his rural retreat Hampton Court, King's Road rose to its pinnacle of fame in the Swinging Sixties. Ground-breaking designers such as Mary Quant and Ossie Clarke had their boutiques on King's Road and it became the hip place to hang out. The restaurant scene was then limited to a few small bistros such as Thierrys at No. 342 (still running today), Malita's, then frequented by Christine Keeler and Mandy Rice Davies – the prostitutes at the centre of the 1963 Profumo sex scandal that rocked the establishment – and No. 235, popular with actors working at the Royal Court Theatre on Sloane

Square. In the 1970s the outlandish designers Vivienne Westwood and Malcolm McLaren opened their designer shop, Sex, at No. 430, after which it became the mecca for punk rockers.

Gradually, the independent fashion-leading boutiques have been replaced by high-street chains such as Monsoon, Jigsaw and Marks & Spencer. King's Road now follows rather than sets the trends. Sadly, this in part is reflected in its restaurant scene. Chains such as Spiga, Ed's Easy Diner, Stockpot, New Cultural Revolution and Benihana jostle for attention among the many coffee shops owned by Starbucks, Coffee Republic, Caffè Nero and the like. Even Bluebird's oversized, upmarket food hall has recently been taken over by supermarket chain Sainsbury's. A couple of gems still remain – most notably the Bluebird restaurant, The Big Easy and Italian restaurants Pucci Pizza and Bacio.

However, from a shopper's perspective King's Road excels. It has a thriving café scene, and large stores such as Peter Jones, Designer's Guild and Habitat all have good in-store cafés or restaurants. Oriel's on Sloane Square, Patisserie Valerie on Duke of York Square and the Bluebird Café are good meeting places, whether for tea and cake or a long lunch. Chocolate lovers should make a beeline for Rococo at 321 King's Road or L'Artisan at 89 Lower Sloane Street; both sell mouthwatering creations.

Kensington High Street

Kensington High Street is another major shopping area, a mixture of the trendy and the traditional, bounded at its western end by Kensington Gardens, once the private garden of Kensington Palace, now a sedate place where uniformed nannies push the babies of rich parents around in the latest-model prams. The Orangery in the grounds of Kensington Palace, which was built for Queen Anne as a summer dining room, has been described as the best place to experience a proper English tea *(see page 127)*.

Restaurants of note include the Michelin-starred Zaika, serving superb Indian cuisine, and Babylon, which overlooks Europe's largest roof garden, both of which are on Kensington High Street, and Clarke's Kensington Place on Kensington Church Street.

Kensington Church Street, which leads up to Notting Hill, is renowned for its antique shops – it has over 80 dealers selling pieces from the Tang Dynasty to the Victorian era – as well as many good specialist food shops including The Fish Shop at Kensington Place at No. 199a, Mrs Keefe's Sausage Shop at No. 27, and Clarke's café and shop at No. 122, which sells more than 25 different varieties of freshly baked breads. Kensington Church Street is also the venue of the Kensington Farmer's Market, held in the car park behind Kensington Place every weekend. Here you can buy fresh bread, organic meat, regional cheeses, fruit and vegetables and talk to the farmer to find out how the food was produced.

Celebrity Chefs

Britain's top chefs have joined the ranks of film stars, footballers and pop idols to become household names and hot paparazzi property

In these celebrity-obsessed times, Britain's appetite for celebrity chefs is unstoppable. Ten years ago such a phenomenon was unthinkable – chefs kept firmly behind their stoves and it was the restaurants that grabbed the headlines. Today Gordon (Ramsay), Marco (Pierre White), Jamie (Oliver), Antony (Worrall Thompson), Brian (Turner) and Giorgio (Locatelli) are household names.

Multimillionaire entrepreneur **Marco Pierre White** was the first of the new-wave super-chefs, with an uncompromising devotion to success. From child poacher, when he claims his love of food began, he became a kitchen porter in Harrogate, persuaded the Roux brothers and Raymond Blanc to employ him, and opened his first restaurant Harvey's in the 1980s. Controversially, after winning three Michelin stars at the Oak Room, Piccadilly, he hung up his chef's whites. MPW, as he calls himself, is now a restaurateur running an astonishing number of top establishments.

The notoriously outspoken **Gordon Ramsay**, current darling of the culinary world, set out to become a football star before injury forced him to turn his hand to cooking. His name is now synonymous with fine dining. Ramsay has opened restaurants in London's landmark hotels including Claridge's and provided the backing for his protégés Marcus Wareing at the Savoy Grill *(see page 38)* and Angela Hartnett at the Connaught *(see page 68)*. For a fascinating insight into cooking at this level, book the chef's table in the kitchen of Claridge's *(see page 71)*.

Jamie Oliver was spotted during a TV series about the River Café *(see page 164)* and shot to fame on our screens as the Naked Chef, a cheeky chappie on a serious mission to get us cooking and eating well, which appealed far beyond the usual market for cookery programmes. Jamie Oliver now has his own restaurant, Fifteen *(see page 137)*, where he trains groups of disadvantaged young adults to work in the kitchen and launch their own culinary careers.

Giorgio Locatelli's soulful good looks only reinforce his brilliance in the kitchen of his restaurant Locanda Locatelli *(see page 80)*, an instant hit with diners and critics alike as well as with celebrities, from Madonna to Tony Blair. His deceptively simple yet beautifully balanced home-made pasta, gnocchi and tiramisu are incomparable.

Gordon Ramsay at Claridge's, one of the many restaurants in his culinary empire

As well as a huge TV personality, **Antony Worrall Thompson** is a genius of reinvention to suit the prevailing foodie trends, from running a novel restaurant, Ménage à Trois, in the 1980s which served only starters and desserts, to his present Notting Grill *(see page 120)* specialising in rare-breed steaks.

Brian Turner rose to fame on TV's 'Ready Steady Cook'. His devotion to the cause of reviving British culinary traditions is reflected in the menu of his flagship Brian Turner Mayfair at the Millennium Hotel *(see page 64)*, which includes classics such as steak and oyster pie, and trifle.

A

Kensington Pl.
Kensington Place
Clarke's
Peel Street
Campden St.
Bedford Gdns.
Sheffield Ter.
Hornton
Holland Street
Ffiona's
Maggie Jones's
Kensington Church Street
Palace Gardens
Brunswick Gdns.
Kensington Gate

B

Kensington Palace
Kensington Palace Gardens
The Broad Walk
The Dial Walk
KENSINGTON
Round Pond
Bandstand
GARDENS
The Flower Walk
Albert Memorial

C

Peter Pan Statue
Physical Energy
Temple Lodge
Serpentine Bridge
Serpentine Gallery
Alexandra Gate

Holland Street
Argyll Road
Phillimore
Kensington High Street
Babylon
HIGH STREET KENSINGTON
Kensington Sq.
Walk
Verna Gdns.
Abingdon Villas
Allen
Earls
Court
Scarsdale Villas
Stratford Place
Lexham
Pembroke Rd
Gardens

Zaika
Kensington Road
Palace Gate
Queen's Gate
Kensington Gore
Royal Albert Hall
St. Alban's Gro.
Wódka
Pasha
Kensington Gate
Queen's Gate Ter.
Petersham Pl.
Elvaston Pl.
Petersham M.
Queen's Ga.
Lay Mews
Kensington Gore
Prince Consort Rd
Imperial College of Science, Technology & Medicine
Imperial College Road
Science Museum
Geological Museum
Natural History Museum

Kynance Mews
Cornwall Gdns.
Cornwall Gdns.
McLeod's M.
Grenville Pl.
Queen's Ga.
Queen's Ga. Gdns.
Road
Cromwell
GLOUCESTER ROAD
Gloucester Road
Stanhope Gdns.
Daquise
SOUTH KENSINGTON
W. Cromwell Rd
Redfield Lane
Kenway Road
Howarth Road
Collingham Rd.
Courtfield Road
Bombay Brasserie
Harrington Gdns.
Wetherby Pl.
Hereford
Rosary Gdns.
Clareville St.
Harrington Rd
La Bouchée

4
EARL'S COURT
Longridge Road
Nevern Pl.
Templeton Pl.
Nevern Sq.
Warwick
Trebovir Road
EARL'S COURT
Penywern Road
Barkston Gdns.
Hesper Mews
Bramham Gdns.
Earl's Ct. Sq.
Earl's Ct. Rd.
Bolton Gdns.
Mr Wing
Old Brompton Road
SOUTH KENSINGTON
Cambio de Tercio
Nam Long
Creswell Place
Drayton Gardens
Roland Wy.
Cranley Mews
Thistle Grove
Roland Gdns.
Old Brompton Road
Onslow Gdns.
Evelyn Gdns.
Neville St.
Onslow
Le Colombie

Earl's Court Exhibition Building
Eardley Cres.
Kempsford Gdns.
Earl's Ct. Rd.
The Little Boltons
The Boltons
The Boltons
Gilston Road
Cranley Gdns.
Grove
Old Church Street
Elm Park Road

5
Lillie Road
WEST BROMPTON
BROMPTON
WEST BROMPTON CEMETERY
Seagrave Rd
Tamworth Farm La.
Finborough Road
Redcliffe Gardens
Redcliffe Sq.
Harcourt Ter.
Hollywood Road
Cathcart
Ifield Road
Fawcett
Netherton Gro.
Brinkley's Wine Gallery
Fulham Road
Limerston St.
Park Wk.
Sophie's Steakhouse
Aubergine
Bluebird
Eight Over Eight
Chelsea Bun
Ed's Diner
Vama
Chutney Mary
The Big Easy
Thierry's

A   **B**   **C**

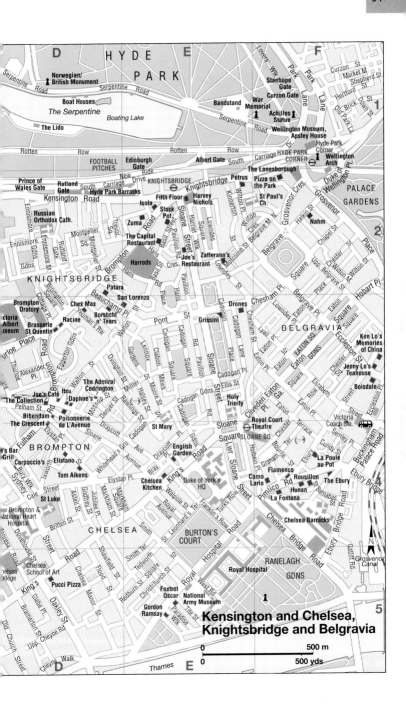

Listings

Brinkley's back garden

American

The Big Easy

332–334 King's Rd, SW3 [C5]. Tel: 7352 4071. Open: noon–11.30pm Mon–Thur, until 12.30am Fri–Sat, until 10.30pm Sun. £££ www.bigeasy.uk.com

Taken in the right spirit, it's hard to fault this boisterous American restaurant, which dishes out enormous portions of the usual American fare: groaning platters piled with prawns, chicken wings, ribeye steaks and giant burgers that are nearly impossible to finish. Those with bigger appetites should enter the ongoing spare-rib contest. There's live music in the basement every night, but if you want a quieter meal eat upstairs.

Ed's Diner

362 King's Rd, SW3 [C5]. Tel: 7352 1956. Open: daily until 11pm. £

One of a small but successful chain of mock-1950s American diners, serving juicy burgers, wonderfully thick milkshakes and delicious cheese-covered chips. You can watch your burger sizzling away and pick out a classic tune from the jukebox on your table while you wait.

PJ's Bar and Grill

52 Fulham Rd, SW3 [D4]. Tel: 7581 0025. Open: daily until midnight, Br Sat–Sun. ££

This loud and lively bar/restaurant is always heaving with locals who come here to drink after work or have dinner with friends. The food is good and well executed but there are few surprises – grilled tuna steak, salads and burgers are among the choices.

British

Brinkley's Wine Gallery

47 Hollywood Rd, SW10 [B5]. Tel: 7351 1683. Open: L and D daily. ££ www.brinkleys.com

This popular, lively restaurant serves appetising modern British food in smart, stylish surroundings. In summer, tables spill out onto the pavement and into the delightful garden at the back. Its real selling point, though, is the incredibly low mark-up on its excellent wines.

Chelsea Bun

9a Lamont Rd, SW10 [C5]. Tel: 7352 3635. Open: Mon–Sat 7am–midnight, Sun 9am–7pm. £

Small but perfectly formed, this café just off the King's Rd serves one of the best breakfasts in London. Whether it's waffles and maple syrup, a full English or simply marmite on toast that takes your fancy, they'll do it. At night it dims its lights, puts candles on the tables and takes on a bistro feel. BYOB; corkage charge.

Chelsea Kitchen

98 King's Rd, SW3 [E4]. Tel: 7589 1330. Open: daily until 11.45pm. £

This no-frills restaurant has changed little since it opened in the 1960s and is still going strong. Most enduringly popular among the basic, unrefined but filling dishes is the good old spaghetti bolognaise and escalopes. The menu may not be remarkable but the prices certainly are.

Ffiona's

51 Kensington Church St, W8 [A1]. Tel: 7937 4152. Open: D only Tues–Sat, L and D Sun. ££
Walking into this homely candle-lit bistro is a little like going to a dinner party. The friendly proprietor, Ffiona, always greets you warmly and makes you feel like an honoured guest. The food may not be refined, but dishes such as pork and herb sausages, and saddle of lamb are hearty, appetising and extremely good value.

Foxtrot Oscar

79 Royal Hospital Rd, SW3 [E5]. Tel: 7352 7179. Open: L and D Mon–Sat, L only Sun. ££
This cosy restaurant is a favourite among well-heeled locals who come for reassuring comfort food rather than a culinary experience. Bangers and mash, burgers and chips, fishcakes and club sand-wiches all feature, and its wine list is good and inexpensive. Kick off with a Bloody Mary, which are excellent here.

Maggie Jones's

6 Old Court Place, Kensington Church St, W8 [A2]. Tel: 7937 6462. Open: L and D daily. £££
Once a favourite of the late Princess Margaret, this quirky but cosy restaurant, with its paraphernalia-filled nooks and crannies, is a wonderful place to eat with friends. Traditional British dishes, such as guinea fowl in red wine sauce and baked mackerel with gooseberries, are always beautiful-ly cooked and there's no skimping on the portions. Wine is served in huge carafes and you pay for what you drink.

Sophie's Steakhouse 🍴

311–313 Fulham Rd, SW10 [C5]. Tel: 7352 0088. Open: Mon–Sat until 11.45pm, Sun until 11pm. ££ www.sophiessteakhouse.com
A relative newcomer to the so-called 'Fulham Beach' scene, this large restaurant prides itself on sourcing only meat of the highest quality. It's not just for carnivores though and offers an excellent choice of fish dishes, including fresh Cornish crab salad and swordfish steak. The wine list is interesting, and while it doesn't take bookings, the wait at the bar with one of its generously sized cocktails is never long.

Slap-up breakfast at the Chelsea Bun

Listings

TIP

Chef Andrew Turner has moved from 1837 at Brown's to **1880 at The Bentley** (27–33 *Harrington Gardens, SW7; tel: 7244 5555; D only Mon–Sat; ££££) and taken his famous grazing menus with him. A fabulously decadent experience, as you get to try everything. Needless to say, such indulgence comes at a price.*

Chinese

Mr Wing
242–244 Old Brompton Rd, SW5 [B4]. Tel: 7370 4450. Open: daily 12.30pm–midnight. £££ www.mrwing.com
This eccentric Chinese restaurant, with its huge aquarium, cascading waterfall and jungle foliage, makes most other eateries look quite dull. The food is tasty, but it takes very few dishes to make your bill shoot up. Service is good, the waiters charming and on Friday and Saturday you can listen to jazz while you eat.

Fish

Poisonnerie de L'Avenue
82 Sloane Ave, SW3 [D3]. Tel: 7589 2457. Open: L and D Mon–Sat. ££ (set menu), £££
Run by the same family for over 20 years, this smart but stuffy restaurant continues to serve an excellent choice of fish dishes, with over 20 different main courses to choose from. The meat dishes are limited to a choice of three.

French

Aubergine
11 Park Walk, SW10 [C5]. Tel: 7352 3449. Open: L and D Mon–Sat. £££ (set lunch), ££££
Gordon Ramsay is a hard act to follow, but chef William Drabble makes a noble attempt. His New French cooking, which includes dishes such as pigeon boudin, and sea bass on Mediterranean roasted artichokes, is well executed and beautifully presented. The service is faultless, though the atmosphere is a little austere. Booking is essential, and £50 is deducted from your credit card if you don't show.

La Bouchée
56 Old Brompton Rd, SW7 [C4]. Tel: 7589 1929. Open: L and D daily. ££ (set lunch), £££
Across the threshold of this bistro lies a corner of France. The candlelit, dark wooden interior has a romantic feel, and the menu offers a great choice of traditional dishes such as coq au vin, and snails in garlic butter, plus there's a treat in store for chocolate mousse aficionados. It also has a specials

Maggie Jones's for traditional British comfort food

This cosy French bistro may be one of the old names on the block but it is still good for celebrity-spotting – Eric Clapton lives round the corner and is a regular, and Bill Wyman has also been spotted here. The food is good, especially its coq au vin, and the ambience lends itself to a romantic meal. The best seats for people-watching are in the arched windows that frame the doors.

Tom Aikens 🍴
43 Elystan St, SW3 [D4]. Tel: 7584 2003. Open: L and D Mon–Fri. ££ (set lunch), ££££ www.tomaikens.co.uk
This modern French restaurant, opened by precocious chef Tom Aikens, and recently awarded its first Michelin star, is for the more adventurous diner. Intensely flavoured dishes such as frogs' legs with poached lettuce, rabbit confit with carrot and Sauternes jelly, and pig's head braised with spices and ginger demonstrate Aikens' culinary craftsmanship and flair for unusual, some say exciting, cuisine.

Indian

Bombay Brasserie
Courtfield Rd, SW7 [B3]. Tel: 7370 4040. Open: L and D daily, last orders midnight. ££ (set lunch), £££ www.bombay brasserielondon.com
Legend has it that Tom Cruise ordered a takeaway curry to be flown to his film set in Italy from here. While some complain that the food is dated compared to restaurants such as Zaika *(see over)*, this classy restaurant still deserves its reputation for good, if expensive, food. When booking, try and get a table in the huge, airy conservatory.

board that changes daily. If there are any complaints it is the over-enthusiastic waiters.

Le Colombier
145 Dovehouse St, SW3 [C4]. Tel: 7351 1155. Open: L and D daily. £££
The Chelsea set adore this 'bourgeois' restaurant, with its starched white linen and French-speaking waiters. The menu of rich Gallic fare is accompanied by a good, predominantly French wine list with some interesting half bottles. Booking is essential if you want the guarantee of a seat on the delightful terrace.

Thierry's
342 King's Rd, SW3 [C5]. Tel: 7352 3365. Open: L and D Tues–Sat, L only Sun. £££ www.trpplc.com

Did you know?
South Kensington has its own French community. At its hub is the French Institute *(17 Queensbury Place)*, which has a regular programme of films, plays and cultural events. In the neighbourhood there's a French lycée, a French bookshop and a cluster of patisseries and brasseries.

Listings

TIP

If you're out and about and feeling hungry at a time when all other kitchens are closed then head for the stylish 24-hour diner **Vingt-Quatre** (352 Fulham Rd, SW10; ££). Its menu is simple and appealing, with dishes like eggs benedict, freshly made soup, burgers and omelettes, for which people are prepared to queue outside, even in the early hours. No bookings.

Chutney Mary

535 King's Rd, SW10 [C5]. Tel: 7351 3113. Open: D only Mon–Fri, Br and D Sat–Sun. ££ www.realindianfood.com

This smart Indian restaurant is in a league of its own. Recently refurbished, the decor is stylish and smart, the service impeccable and the cuisine exceptional. The chefs come from across the subcontinent, so you can take your pick of regional dishes from Goa to Delhi and Kerala to Bombay. The Sunday jazz brunch is popular as ever.

Vama

438 King's Rd, SW10 [C5]. Tel: 7351 4118. Open: L and D daily. £££ www.vama.co.uk

Refined and elegant, this Indian restaurant is noted for its distinctive and flavoursome North Indian/Punjabi cuisine, with dishes such as adaraki gosht (cubes of baby lamb marinated in ginger and coriander) and saag paneer (spinach and cheese flavoured with nutmeg and ginger). The atmosphere is relaxed but the service can be unpredictable.

Zaika

1 Kensingston High St, W8 [B2]. Tel: 7795 6533. Open: L and D Sun–Fri, D only Sat. £££ (set menu), ££££ www.cuisine-collection.co.uk

Situated in a converted high-street bank, this Indian restaurant has a stylish and luxurious feel, with high ceilings and beautiful furnishings. Ground-breaking chef Vineet Bhatia turns out imaginative dishes that are both fragrant and subtle. The coconut soup and grilled lobster tail with spiced lobster jus is a taste sensation. Take advantage of the good-value set lunch menu or head to **Zaika Bazaar** *(Pond Place)*, an offshoot of the restaurant where you can shop and eat simultaneously.

Italian

Carpaccio's

4 Sydney St, SW3 [D4]. Tel: 7352 3433. Open: L and D Mon–Sat. ££ (set lunch), £££

This relaxed Italian joint has a versatile menu, which allows you to have starters as main courses and vice versa. And as the name suggests, it offers a good choice of carpaccio, including tuna and sea bass and classic beef. The service is attentive and the atmosphere bustling.

Daphne's

112 Draycott Ave, SW3 [D3]. Tel: 7589 4257. Open: L and D daily. ££££ www.daphnes-restaurant.co.uk

This charming Italian restaurant is low-key, but the food is exquisite and authentic. In summer the best place to dine is in the conservatory, which has a retractable roof, but people-watching from the front is just as appealing. The atmosphere is easy-going, and you will feel comfortable whether you dress up or come in jeans.

Elistano

25–27 Elystan St, SW3 [D4]. Tel: 7584 5248. Open: L and D daily. £££

The food here is unfussy but good – the regular Italian clientele is a

Japanese fast-food chain, Itsu

Left and below: Zaika

testament to its authentic menu – and the atmosphere is loud and lively. Portions are generous and prices reasonable. There are pavement tables for alfresco dining. Not the place for a quiet tête-à-tête.

Pucci Pizza

205 King's Rd, SW3 [D5]. Tel: 7352 2134. Open: L and D Mon–Sat, until 12.30am, D only Sun, closed Aug. ££

The warm and friendly staff apart, the appeal of this Italian restaurant is debatable – its pizzas are nothing special, and the noise levels are often so high that it's difficult to hear yourself talk – yet it is always buzzing with groups of beautiful young things, and Ferraris and Porsches are regularly parked outside.

Japanese

Itsu

118 Draycott Ave, SW3 [D3]. Tel: 7584 5522. Open: until 11pm Sun–Thur, until midnight Fri–Sat £ www.itsu.co.uk

Itsu introduced the Chelsea set to the delights of conveyor-belt eating. However, if the offerings on the colour-coded plates don't appeal then you can try a dish from the hot grill, such as chicken teriyaki or hot eel sushi. The popu-

lar upstairs bar doubles up as the waiting area. Outside is a refrigerated cabinet where you can buy sushi to take away.

Modern European

The Admiral Codrington

17 Mossop St, SW3 [D3]. Tel: 7581 0005. Open: daily until 11pm. £££

A popular pub in the 1960s, the Admiral Codrington continues to be a favourite meeting place and restaurant – so much so that you need to book even on a Monday night. Its large extension seats about 60 and, if you want an intimate meal, ask for a booth. The modern European dishes are generally good and it always has appealing specials. Bar snacks include home-made soup, fish and chips, and chicken Caesar salad.

Babylon

The Roof Gardens, Seventh Floor, Kensington High St, W8 [A2]. Tel: 7368 3993. Open: L and D Sun–Fri, D only Sat. ££££ www.roofgardens.com

You can't help but be impressed by the surroundings of this lofty restaurant, owned by Richard Branson. Situated on the seventh floor, it overlooks one and a half acres of mature gardens, with a

pond that is home to pink flamingos. However, its offerings, such as tagine of red mullet with couscous or chorizo sausage and caramelised celeriac and spring vegetables, look impressive on the menu but don't always live up to expectations, and the staff are either overattentive or ignore you.

Bibendum ⑪

Michelin House, 81 Fulham Rd, SW3 [D3]. Tel: 7581 5817. Open: L and D daily. £££ (lunch menu), ££££ www.bibendum.co.uk

The best time to visit is on a sunny day when the light streams through the glorious stained-glass windows of this landmark restaurant. Chef Matthew Harris maintains high standards. Dishes such as grilled oysters with curried sauce and courgette linguine were faultless, the wine list impressive and the service excellent. Take advantage of the popular and extremely reasonable lunchtime prix fixe menus, but make sure you book at least a week in advance.

Bibendum Oyster Bar

Michelin House, 81 Fulham Rd, SW3 [D3]. Tel: 7581 5817. Open: L and D daily, bar meals served from noon all day. £££ www.bibendum.co.uk

On the ground floor, below Bibendum, this beautiful tiled oyster bar often has a queue of people waiting patiently for a table. Once you have one, the service is thankfully very quick. Rock oysters, prawns and dressed crab are best washed down with a chilled glass of wine or bubbly. At the entrance you can buy fresh crustaceans to take away.

Bluebird

350 King's Rd, SW3 [C5]. Tel: 7559 1000. Open: L and D daily, Br Sat–Sun. ££ (set menu), ££££ www.conran.com

Owned by Sir Terence Conran, this huge restaurant, housed in what was once Europe's largest motor garage, can seat up to 230 diners at any one sitting. However, unless it's busy, the restaurant can lack atmosphere. The food varies from being wonderfully delicious to disappointing, and the service is equally unpredictable. The best tables are next to windows overlooking King's Road.

Clarke's

124 Kensington Church St, W8 [A1]. Tel: 7221 9225. Open: D only Mon, L and D Tues–Sat, Br Sat. ££££ www.sallyclarke.com

Owned by Sally Clarke, this delightful restaurant differs from

From left to right: Bluebird, Babylon, Bibendum and Bibendum Oyster Bar

most in that it only offers a set menu in the evenings, which changes daily. The cuisine is Mediterranean-influenced, and only fresh, seasonal ingredients are used. The week's menus are posted in the restaurant window or on the website. Next door is a small shop and café, which sells fresh bread baked in the restaurant kitchens, quiches, cheeses and wines.

The Collection
264 Brompton Rd, SW3 [D3]. Tel: 7225 1212. Open: D only Mon–Fri, L and D Sat–Sun. ££££ www.the-collection.co.uk
A vibrant restaurant and bar which is a magnet to a hip, young designer-clad crowd. Diners have the choice of eating light meals in the high booths by the bar or a three-course meal on the mezzanine above. The food is a hit-and-miss combination of European and Asian influences, but a lively ambience is guaranteed. More suited to groups than for a romantic meal à deux. Booking is advisable.

The Crescent
99 Fulham Rd, SW3 [D4]. Tel: 7225 2244. Open: L and D Mon–Sat. ££
This tiny restaurant, which prides itself on its extensive and impressive wine list, is a good place to

go if you are meeting a friend and just want a quick bite to eat with a glass of choice wine. Spread over two floors, it has a specials board, which changes daily, and another one with wine recommendations. Dishes vary from smoked salmon and scrambled eggs to Provençal chicken and delicious stir-fry vegetables. No bookings. Open for coffee and bar snacks all day.

English Garden
10 Lincoln St, SW3 [E4]. Tel: 7584 7272. Open: L and D Tues–Sun, D only Mon. £££ (set menu), ££££ www.lindsayhouse.co.uk
There's not much that's typically English on the menu, and there's no garden to speak of, but Richard Corrigan's cosy restaurant in a Georgian townhouse is a great place to go if you want appetising modern European food in beautiful surroundings. The service is impeccable, and the irregular rooms – many of them private dining rooms – add to the charm. There's a small terrace for outside dining.

Gordon Ramsay
68–69 Royal Hospital Rd, SW3 [E5]. Tel: 7352 4441/3334. Open: L and D Mon–Fri. £££ (lunch menu), ££££ www.gordonramsay.com

TIP
If you are visiting the Royal Court Theatre on Sloane Square, you can pre-order your meal in its commendable basement restaurant before the play starts. *(L and D Mon–Sat; tel: 7565 5061; ££).*

Gordon Ramsay's reputation as London's top chef shows no signs of slipping. This is *the* place to dine. The front is unobtrusive, and the decor minimalist, but the gastronomic experience is exquisite. The food can only be described as perfect – with such inventive delights as lobster tortellini, carpaccio of Bresse pigeon or roast tranche of foie gras – and the service by maître d' Jean-Claude Breton, is charming and attentive. If the price is too much to swallow then take advantage of the excellent lunchtime set menu (£35 for three courses, without wine).

Joe's Café

126 Draycott Ave, SW3 [D3]. Tel: 7225 2217. Open: B and L daily. £££

Well-groomed lunching ladies form the core clientele of this offshoot of the chic fashion label Joseph. The menu is surprisingly unexciting, but reassuring all the same. Typical dishes include tuna niçoise, Joe's burger, and scrambled eggs and smoked salmon. No bookings at the weekend.

Kensington Place

201–209 Kensington Church St, W8 [A1]. Tel: 7727 3184. Open: L and D daily. £££
www.kensingtonplace.co.uk

Above: Cambio de Tercio
Right: Wódka

A trailblazer of the modern European scene, Kensington Place is still going strong. The high noise levels and the goldfish-bowl effect of floor-to-ceiling windows may not be to everyone's taste, but the food, under chef Rowley Leigh, is simple yet inventive and consistently good.

Moroccan

Pasha

1 Gloucester Rd, SW7 [B2]. Tel: 7589 7969. Open: L and D Mon–Sat, D only Sun. £££
www.pasha-restaurant.co.uk

Cushion-stacked alcoves and low lighting make this sumptuous Moroccan restaurant a joy to dine in. The atmosphere is wonderfully relaxed and romantic. Opt for the mezze starter, a great way of experiencing some of the different Moroccan flavours, and its generous tagine dish as a main.

Pan-Asian

Eight Over Eight

392 King's Rd, SW3 [C5]. Tel: 7349 9934. Open: L and D daily. ££££
www.eightovereight.nu

Although locals were sad to see the demise of the Man in the Moon pub, which had occupied this King's Road corner for decades, the stylish Chinese restaurant that has taken its place is attracting a following of its own. It offers Asian dishes with a modern twist. Open crab won tons in green pasta, foie gras and shiitake dumplings, and banana and sesame ice cream are just some of the dishes on the menu. Everything is beautifully presented, from the food to the decor. Booking essential Thursday to Saturday.

Polish

Daquise

20 Thurloe St, SW7 [C3]. Tel: 7589 6117. Open: daily until 11pm. ££

Dating from the late 1940s, this charming Polish restaurant has a loyal following among locals who come for its good home cooking, laid-back, unpretentious atmosphere and make an exception for its worn and faded decor. Typical dishes include pork knuckle and stuffed cabbage, and the house speciality is its tasty potato pancakes.

Wódka

12 St Alban's Grove, W8 [B2]. Tel: 7937 6513. Open: L and D Mon–Fri, L only Sat–Sun. £ *(lunch menu),* £££ *www.wodka.co.uk*

In what was once the dairy to Kensington Palace, this sophisticated but fun Polish restaurant offers delicious food and an amazing range of vodkas – over 30 different kinds – which come served in frozen glasses. Inevitably, as the vodka in the bottles diminishes so the noise volume increases.

Spanish

Cambio de Tercio

163 Old Brompton Rd, SW5 [B4]. Tel: 7244 8970. Open: L and D daily. ££££

This small restaurant has won many accolades for its exciting food and consistently high standards. It sources ingredients of the highest quality and its chefs are not afraid to experiment – duck liver mousse with Coca Cola sauce being one of the dishes on the menu when we visited. The atmosphere is bright and cheery, and service impeccable.

Vietnamese

Nam Long

159 Old Brompton Rd, SW5 [B4]. Tel: 7373 1926. Open: daily, D only. £££

London's first Vietnamese restaurant is today best known for its bar and infamous 'Flaming Ferrari' cocktail. The food may be adequate and the restaurant on the cramped side of cosy, but it still has its fans, Kylie Minogue and Hugh Grant among them.

PUBS, BARS AND CAFÉS

Most of the best pubs in Kensington and Chelsea are tucked away down the borough's smart residential streets. The following are great for sampling English ales and mixing with locals: the **Anglesea Arms** *(15 Selwood Terrace)*, the **Cross Keys** *(1 Lawrence St)*, the **Front Page** *(35 Old Church St)*, **The Sporting Page** *(6 Camera Place)*, **The Duke of Clarence** *(148 Old Brompton Rd)*, **The Abingdon** *(54 Abingdon Rd)*, the **Lots Road Dining Rooms** *(114 Lots Rd)* and the **Admiral Codrington** *(17 Mossop St)*. In summer, **Henry J Beans** *(195 King's Rd)*, a cross between a bar and a pub, has the advantage of a huge garden, with heat lamps to keep you warm on cool nights.

If it's a cocktail or a glass of champagne that you're after, the best places to go are the **190 Bar** *(190 Queensgate)*, the upstairs bar of **Itsu** *(118 Draycott Ave)*, **Nam-Long Le Shaker** *(159 Brompton Rd)*, the bar of **Sophie's Steakhouse** *(311 Fulham Rd)*, **The Collection** *(264 Brompton Rd)* and **Apartment 195**, which has more of a members' club feel than buzzy Henry J Beans below. **Oriel's** on Sloane Square, **PJ's** *(52 Fulham Rd)* and **The Crescent** *(99 Fulham Rd)* are also good places for a cool glass of wine after work, while **Bar Cuba** *(11–13 Kensington High St)* and **Lomo** *(222 Fulham Rd)* both hold a late-night licence.

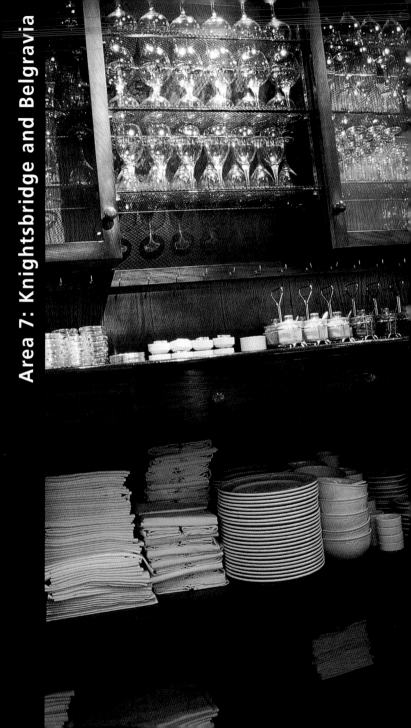

KNIGHTSBRIDGE AND BELGRAVIA

Here, in the Queen's back yard, purveyors of fine food and elite chefs maintain high standards for a demanding and moneyed clientele

Back in the 18th century, Belgravia was the haunt of highwaymen and the site of many duels. It was later described by prime minister Benjamin Disraeli as being 'so contrived as to be at the same time insipid and tawdry'. How times have changed. With its huge Regency houses, Belgravia is now one of London's most exclusive and expensive residential areas. It is better known by visitors for its foreign embassies, of which there are more than 25, but the flourishing food shops and top-class restaurants also make it a place for foodies to step out in the evening. Stately Belgravia and its less strait-laced sister Knightsbridge are *the* places in London to dress up rather than down for. Don't expect the hip and happening scenes of Notting Hill or Clerkenwell. This area has a quiet aura of wealth and privilege, where young moneyed Europeans take their place alongside the British Establishment, with plenty of elbow room between them. Nobody runs or jostles in Belgravia, people conduct themselves discreetly and at a dignified pace. It is British manners at their best. Just don't forget your credit cards.

Elizabeth Street to Ebury Street

Despite its proximity to Victoria Station, Belgravia retains a distinct air of refinement. The side streets are lined with pristine Edwardian and Georgian townhouses trimmed with smart window boxes, and there is surprisingly little traffic. Elizabeth Street, an unassuming road behind Sloane Square that begins in smart Eaton Square, is a row of one-off boutiques and upmarket food shops. Aficionados of Parisian baker Poilane's distinctive bread will travel the length of the city for a big round loaf of *pain poilâne* and a fresh batch of melt-in-the-mouth croissants from the boulangerie at No. 46. A few doors down, the Chocolate Society (No. 36) stocks the finest of all things chocolate, and the wine merchant Jeroboams (No. 51) has some classic vintages in its stores.

Opposite: Knightsbridge brasserie, Racine

Below: a fragrant welcome at the Cinnamon Club

About half way down, Elizabeth Street crosses Ebury Street, Belgravia's main road for restaurants, which sweeps from Pimlico Road, near Sloane Square to the garden walls of Buckingham Palace. It is dotted with genteel old-world restaurants, such as La Poule au Pot *(see page 108)* and Ken Lo's Memories of China *(see page 107).*

Westminster and Pimlico

To the south and southeast of Belgravia, between Victoria Station and the river, lie the relatively quiet backwaters of Pimlico and Westminster. While not bursting with shops and restaurants, they are pleasant places to walk around and ideal for visitors who wish to see a bit of characteristic London on foot.

Pimlico was built on reclaimed marshland and has many grand stuccoed houses, originally built for the Duke of Westminster. The area has a neighbourhood feel, with squares, small shops and pleasant walks down to the river. Pimlico Gardens, between Vauxhall Bridge and Chelsea Bridge, is a romantic place to view river traffic on a lazy day. Opposite Pimilico Gardens is Dolphin Square, where many a politico and diplomat keeps an apartment. If you're feeling flush, Dolphin Square Hotel has a smart new restaurant, Allium *(tel: 7798 6767)*, run by ex-Savoy chef Anton Edelmann, where you can round off your walk.

Westminster has an altogether different atmosphere. Despite the fact that some of London's top sights are here – Big Ben, the Houses of Parliament, Westminster Abbey, Tate Britain – it is not blessed with many eateries. Rather than get caught up in the busy melee of Parliament Square, canny visitors can take a detour to Great Smith Street next to Westminster Abbey and find some superb food in the beautifully designed Cinnamon Club *(see page 109)* or the more down-to-earth Paviour's Arms pub on Page Street. A little further up Marsham Street, in Marsham Court, is Shepherd's, the lunchtime haunt of parliamentarians who wolf down simple British dishes between sessions. The concert halls of nearby St John's Smith Square, housed in a former 18th-century church, have fine acoustics and a reputation for classical music, not to mention a good wine bar-cum-restaurant in the crypt.

A 15-minute walk further down Millbank, beyond Lambeth Bridge, is Tate Britain, the storehouse for a vast collection of British art from 1500 to the present day, including the paintings bequeathed to the nation by prolific seascape and landscape artist JMW Turner. It has an excellent restaurant by gallery standards *(see page 106)* and is decorated with a specially commissioned mural by Rex Whistler with the intriguing title, *The Expedition in Pursuit of Rare Meats* (1927).

> Map of Knightsbridge and Belgravia on page 90–91

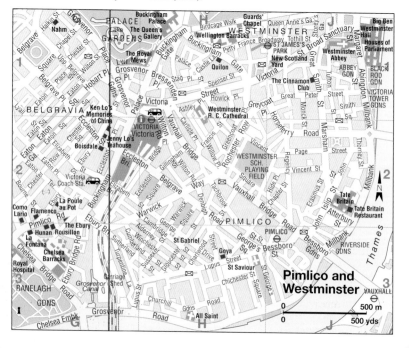

Pimlico and Westminster

| 0 | 500 m |
| 0 | 500 yds |

Harrods Food Hall

Knightsbridge

In Knightsbridge, things are livelier. Big department stores populate the busy streets, and the roar of traffic heading for every London driver's hell – Hyde Park Corner – forces you to pay attention at pedestrian crossings. Food-lovers are rewarded with two of the best food halls in two of the most famous department stores in the world – Harrods and its more sleekly designed neighbour Harvey Nichols *(see page 114)*. Harrods Food Hall boasts that it can source any food in the world. Its different galleries for meat, fish, dairy and wine give the impression that you are browsing at an indoor market designed for royalty. The tiled walls, elaborate murals, lighting and, of course, the trademark green bags, turn even the smallest purchase into an event. Harrods also has seven restaurants, one on every floor (except the fifth), all of which have a reputation to uphold.

Harvey Nichols concentrates all its food efforts on to the fifth floor where its restaurant is a birthday treat to spoil a friend, while fans of the television comedy show *Absolutely Fabulous* will recognise the round bar, propped up in many a scene by Patsy and Edina (played by Joanna Lumley and Jennifer Saunders). Less formal is the brasserie next to the food hall, where Harvey Nichols' own brand of coffee, nuts, chocolates and pasta are bought by the design-fixated for their sleek silver packaging.

Knightsbridge is where moneyed shoppers head for. Gucci, Browns, Valentino, Louis Vuitton, Salvatore Ferragamo *et al* are all lined up along the top end of Sloane Street, and the restaurants in the vicinity reflect the taste and style of the lunching ladies they cater to. Beauchamp Place and Brompton Road are the two main areas for eating out. Restaurants around here rarely disappoint. You will always be treated with the utmost courtesy, assumed to have a large bank account whatever your current credit rating and fed with food from modern Europeans who know how to live and eat well.

It's not all swanky restaurants, though. Knightsbridge and Belgravia have an extraordinary number of good, unpretentious pubs, such as the Grenadier in Old Barrack Yard off Wilton Row. Even the much-feted gastropubs, such as the Swag and Tails in Fairholt Street, serve good food for around £12 per main course. As the owner Anne Marie Boomer-Davies says, 'The Swag and Tails is what Americans think all British pubs should be like, but aren't'. When talking about London as a whole, the same could be said for Knightsbridge and Belgravia.

British

Boisdale

15 Eccleston St, SW1 [F3]. Tel: 7730 6922. Open: L and D Mon–Fri, D only Sat. £££ www.boisdale.co.uk

Boisdale would call itself Scottish, not British, and all the fresh produce and menu items, not to mention the decorative tartan touches, reflect this pride in its heritage. Feast on Hebridean lobster bisque, Macsween haggis and Aberdeen Angus steaks. There is always a fresh fish and game of the day and a full malt whisky line-up. The next-door Macdonald Bar features jazz every evening except Sunday and offers a mind-numbing choice of cocktails and malt whiskies.

Tate Britain Restaurant

Millbank, SW1 [J2, page 104]. Tel: 7887 8825. Open: L only daily. £ (set menu), ££ www.tate.org.uk

Perfect for combining with a morning or afternoon gallery viewing, the Tate Britain Restaurant has a reputation for wine as well as food. Seasonal dishes, such as sauté of wild mushrooms or roast cod fillet with herb crust, are offered on a set menu (£16.75 for two courses and £19.50 for three) with a wine list the size of a telephone directory. The Whistler mural is the icing on the cake.

Did you know?
The Zander Bar *(Buckingham Gate)*, where shaken and stirred Martinis are a speciality, has the longest bar in Europe.

Boisdale, for Scottish specialities

Chinese

Hunan

51 Pimlico Rd, SW1 [F4]. Tel: 7730 5712. Open: L and D Mon–Sat. £££

Few places are dominated by the personality of the proprietor to the extent that Hunan is. Mr Peng won't hesitate to tell you where you are going wrong with your ordering and brings dishes that you didn't order as well as those you did, but those who know what's good for them don't object and just submit to the feast. Menus for a minimum of two people start at £30 per head. A1 food and amusing service.

Jenny Lo's Teahouse

14 Eccleston St, SW1 [F3]. Tel: 7259 0399. Open: L and D Mon–Sat. £

For a cheap, healthy and filling meal, this modern, bright and minimalist cafeteria-style restaurant is hard to beat. The menu is subdivided into soup noodles, wok noodles, and rice dishes. Everyone is polite, the food is fresh and delicious, and cleansing teas are suggested for afters.

Ken Lo's Memories of China

67–69 Ebury St, SW1 [F3]. Tel: 7730 7734. Open: L and D Mon–Sat, D only Sun. ££ (set lunch), ££££

After 20 years, Ken Lo's menus, skewed towards Western tastes, have lost none of their popular appeal, despite the fact that the final bill invariably comes as a costly surprise. The newly refurbished interior is elegant, the service good, the ambience always

Ken Lo's
Memories
of China

lively, and deep-fried fresh prawns and crispy duck with home-made pancakes always on order.

French

The Capital Restaurant ⑪
Capital Hotel, 22–24 Basil St, SW3 [E2]. Tel: 7589 5171. Open: L and D Mon–Sat, D only Sun. £££ (lunch menu), ££££ www.capitalhotel.co.uk
In January 2001, Michelin awarded The Capital two stars, turning the French chef Eric Chavot into something of a celebrity. The hotel itself won Small Hotel of the Year in August 2003, so guests need not stray far from their beds to sample fine food. This is traditional dining at its very best. Dishes such as truffle and pecorino risotto, Dover sole, veal, and sculpted puddings all ooze exquisite flavour. The set lunch menu is excellent value for such a prestigious establishment.

Chez Max
3 Yeoman's Row, SW3 [D3]. Tel: 7590 9999. Open: L and D daily. £££ www.whitestarline.org.uk
Another feather in Marco Pierre White's cap, this classy Knightsbridge restaurant, formerly the Parisienne Chophouse, has at the helm Max Renzland, who runs a tight but very hospitable ship. The Gallic bistro food is authentic and served in refreshingly large portions. From the black and white tiled floor and Parisian posters to the *assiette de charcuterie*, asparagus with hollandaise sauce to the *confit de canard*, delectable cheeses, and superlative wine list, it's all *très français*.

Drones
1 Pont St, SW1 [E3]. Tel: 7235 9555. Open: L and D Mon–Fri, D only Sat, L only Sun. £££ www.whitestarline.org.uk
Any restaurant owned by Marco Pierre White has a reputation to uphold, and Drones – a Belgravia institution – does the Michelin-starred chef proud. The dining room is atmospherically lit, and the black and white photos of stars of the silver screen add a touch of glamour. The unfussy food is

The Cinnamon Club, set in a refurbished Victorian library

TIP

For a more affordable taste of Gordon Ramsay's cooking, try the stylish but informal **Boxwood Café** at the Berkeley Hotel *(Wilton Place, SW1; tel: 7235 1010; L and D daily; £££).*

expertly prepared; smoked haddock colcannon is the chef's signature dish. Set lunch menus, the Sunday lunch in particular, are popular, so book ahead.

Pétrus
The Berkeley, Wilton Place, SW1 [E2]. Tel: 7235 1200. Open: L and D Mon–Fri, D only Sat. ££££ www.petrus-restaurant.com
The transfer of Marcus Wareing's flagship restaurant from St James's Street to The Berkeley was well publicised, but critics have been mixed. Some maintain that Britain's brightest young chef star (Gordon Ramsay's protégé) is trying too hard for his second Michelin star. The menu reads like poetry, but such inventiveness comes at a price. As you would expect from a restaurant named after one of the world's most famous wines, the wine list is inspirational.

La Poule au Pot
231 Ebury St, SW1 [F4]. Tel: 7730 7763. Open: L and D daily. ££ (set lunch), £££
A far cry from the haute cuisine refinement of The Capital *(see page 107)*, those in search of a more down-to-earth yet authentically French experience can't go wrong with La Poule au Pot. This charming and romantic corner of France has occupied its Pimlico address for 30 years. Daily specials are decided as deliveries are made, and those opting for the £16 fixed-price lunch menu could be biting into *escargots* or *soupe de poisson*, with a perfect plate of *bifteck et frites* to follow. A good place to exercise your rusty French.

Racine 🍴
239 Brompton Rd, SW3 [D3]. Tel: 7584 4477. Open: L and D daily. ££ (set menu), £££
One of the most welcome additions to London's restaurant scene. The beautiful glass exterior to Racine promises a classy meal, though the understated brown interior gives no indication of the delights to come. Chef Henry Harris rarely misses a beat with his menu, which is innovative yet firmly rooted in the French tradition. The chilled cucumber and mint soup, warm garlic and saffron mousse with mussels and grilled rabbit were all perfectly executed. Take advantage of the three-course set menu that operates before 7.30pm. Great value for this part of town.

Rousillon
16 St Barnabas St, SW1 [F4]. Tel: 7730 5550. Open: L and D Wed–Fri, D only Sat–Mon. ££ (set menu), ££££ www.rousillon.co.uk
Dedicated to seasonal dishes and with an array of set menus promising food for foodies, Rousillon deserves all the awards it has won over the past couple of years. The watchword is seasonal. In autumn, for example, fruit and vegetables are cooked together in a pot with

aged balsamic. Fish such as monkfish or John Dory cooked in delicious rich sauces are a reliable choice. There is a separate chocolate pudding list for chocoholics.

Indian

The Cinnamon Club 🍴
Old Westminster Library, 30 Great Smith St, SW1 [J1, page 104]. Tel: 7222 2555. Open: L and D Mon–Fri, D only Sat. ££ *(set lunch),* ££££
www.cinnamonclub.com
The large bowl of rose petals by the door marks the entrance to a rarefied world. The Cinnamon Club is set in a beautifully refurbished Victorian library full of light and space. The shelf-lined galleries and antechambers, where you can sip aperitifs, give it a distinctly clubby feel. The menu offers a fine selection of sub-continental specialities, from Nile perch to Keralan curry, and East-meets-West dishes, such as spiced banana tarte tatin, with good vegetarian options. First class.

Quilon
41 Buckingham Gate, SW1 [H1, page 104]. Tel: 7821 1899. Open: L and D Mon–Fri, D only Sat. ££ *(set lunch),* £££
www.thequilonrestaurant.com
Quilon is the smartest of smart Indian restaurants. The service is attentive but respectful, with plenty of staff running around in the middle of the dining area, and one chef who cooks nothing but delicious rice pancakes. The lunch menu is very good value at £15.95 for three courses, though an evening meal of Coorg chicken, pepper shrimps or Cananra lamb curry will set you back around £40 a head.

Italian

Como Lario
22 Holbein Place, SW1 [F4]. Tel: 7730 2594. Open: L and D Mon–Sat. £££
Booking is advisable in this traditional Italian trattoria, which attracts so many regulars, largely for its daily specials. Side dishes of salads and spinach are best

Classy Knightsbridge brasserie, Racine

Suave and sophisticated Zafferano's

ordered liberally from the many waiters present, and expect 'ladies' to be treated as such in this old-fashioned spot.

La Fontana

101 Pimlico Rd, SW1 [F4]. Tel: 7730 6630. Open: L and D daily. £££
La Fontana never changes. The decor may be dated to say the least, but the ever-attentive waiters and old-fashioned staples like zabaglione will hopefully remain as good and comforting as they have since the '60s. The fish is particularly good, while the steaks are favoured by Establishment regulars. A warm, comfortable atmosphere.

Grissini

Carlton Tower Hotel, Cadogan Place, SW1 [E3]. Tel: 7858 7171. Open: L and D Mon–Fri, D only Sat. £££ www.carltontower.com
So often hotel restaurants above ground level lack atmosphere, but Grissini is an exception. The pasta is particularly good – the tagliolini with prosecco and lobster sauce is delicious, and sauces use well-matched ingredients. Meat and fish dishes abound, and there are pretty views over the square. Slow paced and pleasant.

Isola

145 Knightsbridge, SW1 [E2]. Tel: 7838 1055. Open: L and D Mon–Sat. £££
The combination of stunning interiors and good, if heavy, Italian food makes Oliver Peyton's Isola a

popular primetime venue. The red and white bar upstairs serves good cocktails, and the chic restaurant downstairs has an Italian wine list unparalleled in London.

Pizza on the Park

11 Knightsbridge, SW1 [F2]. Tel: 7236 6853. Open: L and D daily, until midnight Mon–Sat. ££
If you need somewhere to go with the family, then Pizza on the Park, the flagship restaurant of the Pizza Express chain, offers live jazz music in the evenings and plenty of space and freshly made pizzas tossed on the spot for an extremely reasonable lunch or dinner. Opposite Hyde Park, it's perfect for children in the daytime.

San Lorenzo

22 Beauchamp Place, SW3 [E3]. Tel: 7584 1074. Open: L and D Mon–Sat. ££££
The swanky Knightsbridge office cafeteria for fashion, music and media moguls, with beautiful waif-like waiting staff to match. The food pioneered the popularity of 'eating Italian' in this country. These days, it may not be as adventurous as some of its followers, but quality is maintained with wholegrain risottos, freshly made pastas and creamy home-made yoghurts and ice creams. Always an occasion, but one you pay for.

Zafferano's

15 Lowndes St, SW1 [E2]. Tel: 7235 5800. Open: L and D daily. ££ (set lunch), ££££

TIP

The Grenadier pub in Old Barrack Yard was once frequented by the Duke of Wellington and is said to mix the best Bloody Mary (vodka and tomato juice) in the area.

This is Italian food at its most sophisticated, with every attention to detail taken care of at a price that will make you remember the meal for ever. Set lunch is good value at £28.50. The set dinners come at a heftier price, but you will be rewarded with exquisite black truffle salads, risottos, fresh pasta dishes, sirloin steaks, and faultless tarts and home-made ice cream, topped with impeccable service.

Japanese

Zuma 🍽

5 Raphael St, SW7 [E2]. Tel: 7584 1010. Open: L and D daily. ££££ www.zumarestaurant.com
Designed by Tokyo's ultra-hip Super Potato company, Zuma is one of London's hottest restaurants and has become a serious rival to Nobu, the lofty Mayfair restaurant that put Japanese cooking firmly on the map. Zuma's extensive menu offers excellent sushi and sashimi, delicious skewers from the robata grill, along with more complex, flavour-packed dishes, not to mention 22 varieties of sake. For the virtuous, there's an enticing list of non-alcoholic 'cleansing' cocktails. This is A-list territory and reservations need to be made well in advance, or you could try your luck getting a seat at the bar, which doesn't take reservations.

Middle Eastern

Joe's Restaurant

16 Sloane St, SW1 [E2]. Tel: 7235 9869. Open: L only Mon–Sat, open until 6pm. ££
The variety of Mediterranean dishes, Arabic specialities and salads makes this a popular little boutique diner for a mid-shop spot of lunch. Main courses are reasonable and, although there is no set menu, favourites such as chicken chermoula with couscous are always sought after. Alternatively, pop in for afternoon tea and a slice of sticky date pudding.

Modern European

Brasserie St Quentin

243 Brompton Rd, SW3 [D3]. Tel: 7589 8005. Open: L and D daily. ££ (set lunch), £££ www.brasseriestquentin.co.uk

Did you know?
Harrods, London's best-known department store, was started by the tea merchant Henry Charles Harrod in 1849 and boasts that it can source and send any item to anywhere in the world. The food hall is open Monday to Saturday until 7pm. The Harrods Sushi Bar (pictured left) is one of 25 in-store eateries.

Nahm at Halkin Hotel

In its 1980s heyday, this was *the* place to be seen. It has changed hands several times since, but the brasserie still excites newcomers. The latest owners have injected a freshness into the decor and brought the menu closer to home. Dishes like smoked Irish eel, Dorset crab, and bangers, mash and English asparagus sit comfort-ably alongside oysters, *soupe de poisson* and seared foie gras.

The Ebury

11 Pimlico Rd, SW1 [F4]. Tel: 7739 6784. Open: L and D daily. £££ www.theebury.co.uk
The latest in Tom Etridge's success-ful line of gastropubs. The ground floor has a brasserie and seafood bar where you can have a simple salad, down a dozen British or Breton oysters or tuck into a ribeye steak and chips. The upstairs dining room offers a more sophisticated set menu. Good value all round.

Fifth Floor, Harvey Nichols

109–125 Knightsbridge, SW1 [E2]. Tel: 7235 1839. Open: L and D Mon–Sat, L only Sun. ££ (set menu), ££££ www.harveynichols.com

Despite the departure of celebrated chef Henry Harris who, after many years of innovative cooking, went to Racine *(see page 108)*, this ele-gant restaurant atop London's most fashionable department store retains its reputation. The decor is chic, the lighting system state of the art, and the food always dec-orative but decidedly average. The best thing on the menu is the patis-serie and puddings made by the dedicated pastry chef. The bill is the hardest part to swallow.

Russian

Borshtch 'n' Tears

45–46 Beauchamp Place, SW3 [D3]. Tel: 7589 5003. Open: D only daily. ££
With its vast range of vodkas this raucous restaurant is more a des-tination for party animals than gourmets. The food is run-of-the-mill Russian fare, with the usual diet of blinis, cod's roe, borshtch, and beef stroganoff, but if you're in the mood, the cosy velvet and red interior and cheerful young crowds make for an enjoyable night out.

nation of draft beer and cheery bow-tied waiters keeps regulars coming back.

Thai

Nahm

Halkin Hotel, Halkin St, SW1 [F2]. Tel: 7333 1234. Open: L and D Mon–Fri, D only Sat–Sun. ££££ www.halkin.co.uk
First-rate Thai-fusion cuisine by Australian chef David Thompson, who led the restaurant to receive the first-ever Michelin star awarded to a Thai place. Expect such delicacies as minced prawns with chicken served on tiny slices of pineapple and mandarin, and a green curry of guinea fowl. The one complaint regularly levelled at the restaurant is its lack of atmosphere.

Patara

9 Beauchamp Place, SW3 [D2]. Tel: 7581 8820. Open: L and D daily. ££ www.patara.co.uk
Classic Knightsbridge dining for remarkably un-Knightsbridge prices. Recommended are the raw tuna in lemongrass for starters, duck breast for main, sorbet for dessert and tea to finish.

Spanish

Goya

34 Lupus St, SW1 [H3, page 104]. Tel: 7976 5309. Open: L and D daily. ££ www.goyarestaurants.co.uk
If you need a quick bite that won't break the bank, you could do worse than this keenly priced restaurant. The oily patatas bravas and Galician-style octopus are not to everyone's taste, but the combi-

PUBS, BARS AND CAFÉS

The best bars are found in the area's many grand hotels, where extravagant cocktails are mixed in the elegant and refined spaces of sumptuous upper-class living. Places like the **Polo Lounge**, one of Madonna's favourite London haunts, in the Lanesborough Hotel on Hyde Park Corner, the **Blue Bar** in the Berkeley Hotel in Wilton Place and the **Mandarin Bar** in the Mandarin Oriental in Hyde Park will all thoroughly spoil visitors with long drinks lists and unlimited nibbles.

For those who want something a little less refined and a little more funky, the **Isola Bar** (145 Knightsbridge), the **Townhouse** (Beauchamp Place) and the **Zander Bar** (45 Buckingham Gate) promise a little more buzz.

Good cafés are hard to come by in this area, which is dominated by chains like Starbucks, Aroma and Costa Coffee, particularly around tourist traps such as Parliament Square. Opt instead for afternoon tea at any of the high-class hotels. It will be a truly English affair, with cucumber sandwiches on silver stands, scones and porcelain tea services, even tea dances in some (see page 126 for suggested venues). For those with a caffeine aversion, **The Chocolate Society** shop on Elizabeth Street serves the best hot chocolate in the capital.

London's Best Food Shops

*From Fortnum & Mason, the royal grocer, to busy Borough Market,
London's food stores are a feast for all the senses*

Britain is gaining a reputation for good food in its own right, and London
has an unparalleled variety and concentration of cosmopolitan food
shops specialising in the best of British and world cuisine ingredients.
Discerning foodie visitors can shop for specialist items, from artisan cheeses
to exceptional chocolates, kosher biscuits to single-estate leaf tea, and talk to
knowledgeable retailers passionate about their ingredients.

First stop has to be the food halls of the major stores. **Harrods** *(Brompton
Road, SW1)* originated as a grocer, and food remains a major player in the
success of the mammoth Knightsbridge store. The magnificent food hall,
nearly 24,000 sq ft (2,200 sq metres) and clad in Doulton tiles, has spectacular displays of food (the wet fish display incorporates a new design each day).
Highlights include more than 150 types of bread, a wonderful chocolate
room, a definitive wine and spirit department – including many own labels –
and beautifully packaged teas, biscuits and other gifts.

Nearby, under the ducted ceiling of the food hall in **Harvey Nichols**
(Knightsbridge, SW1), you can shop for esoteric sauces and relishes, pastas
and noodles, including Harvey Nichols' own-label products, and stop for
kaitean sushi.

At **Fortnum & Mason** *(181 Piccadilly, W1)*, established as a grocer in
1707, male shop assistants wear full morning dress. Everything is highly
desirable, from a choice of over 120 decorative tins of tea to a vast range of
regional British foods and many chocolatiers whose wares are exclusive to
the store. Hugely fashionable **Selfridge's** *(400 Oxford St, W1)* attracts a large
number of celebrity customers. Highlights include the astonishing array of
smoked fish, Middle Eastern pastries and excellent traiteur for picnics. If all
the food shopping makes you hungry, numerous dining possibilities, from
oyster bar to salt-beef bar, provide tempting refreshments.

*Harrods'
spectacular
Food Hall*

Specialist shops

The Seven Dials area in Covent Garden is home to **Neal's Yard Dairy** *(17 Short's Gardens, WC2)*, with its wonderful variety of artisan cheeses. Buy a truckle of English Colston Bassett Stilton or Montgomery Cheddar or an unpasteurised cheese bought directly from tiny farms and matured and ripened in the dairy's own cellars. Tasting is encouraged. Other excellent cheese stores are **Paxton & Whitfield** *(93 Jermyn St, SW1)*, established over 200 years ago, **Rippon Cheese Stores** *(26 Upper Tachbrook St, SW1)* near Victoria, stocking over 500 cheeses, and **La Fromagerie** *(4 Moxon St, W1)* in Marylebone.

Carluccio's *(28a Neal St, WC2)*, owned by the well-known wild mushroom enthusiast Antonio Carluccio, has a carefully selected and exquisitely packaged range of top Italian foods. From the traiteur, try risotto balls, delicious mushroom tarts, and Piedmontese sweetmeats. Within Soho are two much loved old-fashioned Italian delis where salami and panettone (Italian Christmas and Easter cake) hang from the ceiling: **Lina Stores** *(18 Brewer St, W1)* and **I. Camisa** *(61 Old Compton St, W1)*. The hub of shopping activity in nearby Chinatown is Gerrard Place. Besides the grocers, check out the Chinese cake and pastry shops such as **Far East** *(13 Gerrard St, W1)*, the place to try a mooncake – a sweet bun made from lotus seed and red bean with a salted duck egg inside.

London has some particularly fine chocolate shops. The capital's oldest (established in 1902) is **Prestat** *(14 Princes Arcade, Piccadilly, SW1)*, purveyor of chocolates to Her Majesty the Queen. The **Chocolate Society** *(36 Elizabeth St, SW1)* in Knightsbridge also operates as a café (try the divine hot chocolate) and stocks the entire range of Valrhona as well as their definitive handmade truffles. The prettiest chocolatier is **Rococo** *(321 Kings Rd, SW3)*, which has an original Victorian frontage; not to be missed are its chocolate bars flavoured with organic essential oils, such as orange and geranium. The chocolate cognoscenti head for **L'Artisan du Chocolat** *(89 Lower Sloane St, SW1)* in Chelsea where exquisite handmade chocolates with unusual flavours such as aromatic Sechuan pepper and Earl Grey tea are displayed like jewels in a smart boutique and wonderfully witty chocolate sculptures mark the seasons. Gordon Ramsay uses its chocolates in his restaurants.

Borough Market (by London Bridge) on Fridays and Saturdays is highly recommended for London's resident foodies. You'll find everything from fabulous bread to obscure Arab condiments, Sardinian cheeses and myriad olives. For lunch on the hoof queue up for a bap filled with char-grilled chorizo and rocket from Spanish specialists **Brindisa**. There are several good foodie shops on the market's perimeter, including a second Neal's Yard Dairy *(6 Park St, SE1)* and stylish baker **Konditor & Cook** *(10 Stoney St, SE1)*, which has branches in Waterloo and Holborn.

More off the beaten track is **The Hive Honey Shop** *(93 Northcote Rd, SW11)* with the largest selection of honeys and honey products in London. The main attraction is owner James Hamill's honeys flavoured with ginger, cognac and rum and raisin. In the middle of the shop is a startling glass-fronted working hive of 2,000 bees.

Brick Lane Beigel Bakery *(159 Brick Lane, E1)*, open 24 hours at weekends, is great for snacks in the early hours or when you are shopping in Brick Lane Market on Sunday morning.

Finally, **Books for Cooks** *(4 Blenheim Crescent, W11)* is the place to go to be inspired by cookery books covering every conceivable area of the globe.

Top: sweet treats from Rococo Above: Prestat supplies chocolates to the Queen

NOTTING HILL AND BAYSWATER

This area is a melting pot of all classes and races, its cultural mix reflected in a mind-expanding range of exotic food on offer

Between them, Notting Hill and Bayswater can satisfy most food cravings. The range of exotic cuisines on offer goes beyond the Indian, Chinese and Thai norm. If you ever had the desire to sample authentic southern-fried crab cakes, Tirolean fondue, Polish pork and dumplings, a Brazilian barbecue, Armenian black bread or Jamaican jerk chicken, this is the place to come. Most of the restaurants recommended are concentrated in three different areas. The finer restaurants associated with the area sit between the grand houses on Kensington Park Road. Westbourne Grove and Portobello Road offer an eclectic mix of trendy bars and cheaper eateries, while some of the best ethnic food can be found around Queensway in Bayswater.

Notting Hill Gate (the road) extends into Holland Park Avenue at its western end, and Bayswater to the east. These stretches of wide road form the southern boundary of our restaurant area.

Notting Hill Gate to Portobello Road

The scene that unfolds as you emerge from Notting Hill tube station is not a promising one. Notting Hill Gate, the main four-lane thoroughfare, is flanked with scruffy newsagents, supermarkets, banks and building societies. But appearances are deceptive. Beyond the din of traffic lie warrens of quiet, residential streets and leafy crescents, lined with Georgian townhouses and intermittent clusters of ultra-hip galleries and bars, as well as grungy shops and cafés.

The main north-south artery, Ladbroke Grove, is the parade route for the Notting Hill Carnival, a massive three-day Caribbean festival which takes over the area in the last weekend of August. The first carnival, a small affair, was held in St Pancras Town Hall in 1959 in an attempt to unite the local communities after appalling race riots. The annual party moved to Notting Hill in 1964, and over the decades has grown into one of Europe's largest street parties – a rowdy and colourful weekend of music, costume parades, dancing, and, of course, eating and drinking.

Opposite: Ashbells, for gourmet soul food

Below: daily specials at the Cow Dining Room

The rest of the year, Notting Hill is relatively quiet, though the weekend markets pull in the crowds. The Farmer's market (behind Waterstone's bookshop on Notting Hill Gate), was one of the first to open in the capital. Everything on sale here is grown or produced by the seller. Anyone looking for variety in British food would do well to taste one of 122 different varieties of English apples or a slice of any number of British cheeses. Most stalls have samples to try before you buy.

Portobello Market on Portobello Road attracts a steady stream of tourists in search of elusive bargains. It is more famous for its bric-a-brac and antiques than food, but the middle section, on a level with the old Electric Cinema, has many stallholders selling fruit and vegetables.

Eating in London

Heading up through Notting Hill towards the Westway, an elevated highway that marks the northern boundary, you enter a grittier landscape, reminiscent of a more run-down bohemian Notting Hill before its reincarnation into one of London's most desirable districts. Northeast of the flyover, Golborne Road, with a conglomeration of stalls, exotic cafés and shops, has an atmosphere all of its own and is a good place to stop for refreshment after trawling the market.

Bayswater

Westbourne Grove runs east of Portobello Road to intersect with Queensway, Bayswater's main drag. Both have a Continental flavour, with immigrants from Germany, Italy, Greece and the Middle East, and are packed with eating places – especially Chinese (the largest concentration outside Soho's Chinatown) and Indian – buzzy cafés and patisseries. Shops are open late, and evening strollers encompass an amazing range of nationalities. Where Bayswater looks over the park, three international hotels make useful pit-stops for afternoon tea or morning coffee while planning your day.

This is a particularly child-friendly area. The wide pavements and the proximity of Kensington Gardens, with its green expanses and the huge adventure play area in the Princess Diana Memorial Garden on Bayswater, make it a reliable destination for those burnt out by the intense urban experience of the West End.

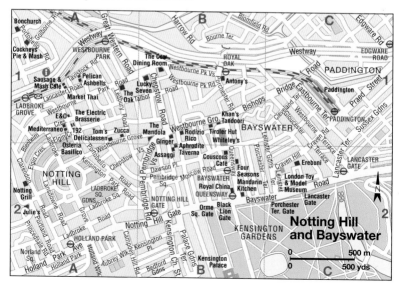

Soul food champion, Ashbell McElveen

and spicy seafood gumbo, served up with creamy grits and collard greens, are all made with the freshest ingredients according to traditional recipes and without the least hint of pretension. Save room for a portion of Sharon's pound cake. For £12.50, the 'Josephine Baker' or 'Paul Robeson' brunch are good value. Reservations necessary.

African

The Mandola
139–141 Westbourne Grove, W11 [B1]. Tel: 7229 4734. Open: Tues–Sun, D only Mon. £ www.mandolacafe.com
This relaxed restaurant serves authentically spicy Sudanese food, a blend of Middle Eastern and African influences, with a choice of tasty salads (there's an option to sample them all in a mezze-type spread), spicy lamb and chicken dishes, and a good few vegetarian options. People travel from all over town for the Sudanese spiced coffee, but bring your own champagne or wine as the place is unlicensed.

American

Ashbells 🍴
29 All Saints Rd, W11 [A1]. Tel: 7221 8585. Open: D only Mon–Sat, Br Sat–Sun. ££ (brunch menu), £££ www.ashbells.co.uk
For a real taste of black southern home cooking, South Carolina chef Ashbell's heart-warming menu is the very definition of soul food. His Maryland crab cakes, pulled pork

Lucky Seven
127 Westbourne Park Rd, W2 [B1]. Tel: 7727 6771. Open: B, L and D daily. £
With its gleaming stainless-steel kitchen running along the back of the room and cosy dining booths, Tom Conran's New York-style diner is a hit with the Notting Hillbillies. The menu is simple, its classic burgers, salads and daily specials reasonably priced. Back by popular request are their 'fat' fries, a delicious alternative to their French cousins. Also open for American breakfast. Great pancakes.

Austrian

Tiroler Hut
27 Westbourne Grove, W2 [B1]. Tel: 7727 3981. Open: D only Tues–Sun. £££ www.tirolerhut.co.uk
For a full-on Austrian experience, complete with lederhosen, alpine

TIP

Fill up on authentic Jamaican patties and jerk chicken from the popular Caribbean takeaway **Yum Yum's** *(312 Ladbroke Grove; tel: 8968 1477).*

The Tiroler Hut

scenes, accordion players, and fräuleins serving foaming beer, the Tiroler Hut is one of a kind. Most people go for the fondues, and the cheese and chocolate are firm favourites – just don't yodel for the waiter.

Brazilian

Rodizio Rico

111 Westbourne Grove, W2 [B1]. Tel: 7792 4035. Open: D only Mon–Fri, L and D Sat–Sun. £
Waiters circle the room with huge skewers of meat ('Rodizio' means 'rotating') from which they lop off chunks of lamb, ham, pork, chicken, beef – rump and fillet – while you help yourself to vegetables and other side dishes from the buffet – all for £18 a head. Popular, despite the slack service.

British

Cockney's Pie and Mash

314 Portobello Rd, W10 [A1]. Tel: 8960 9409. Open: 11.30am–5.30pm Tues–Sat. £
One of the few Victorian pie and mash shops that's not yet fallen victim to London's gentrification epidemic. For less than a fiver, you can tuck into a meat pie, mashed potatoes and green liquor (a fluorescent green parsley sauce), while those with a more iron constitution can opt for stewed or jellied eels, all washed down with a mug of strong tea. Sample this slice of working-class life while you still can.

Notting Grill

123a Clarendon Rd, W11 [A2]. Tel: 7229 1500. Open: D only Mon–Fri. L and D Sat–Sun. £££
www.nottinggrill.com
Antony Worrall Thompson has taken up residence in this new fashionable steakhouse where

every kind of rare breed and organic beast is on offer grilled, skewered, roasted or stewed. Its motto 'well bred, well fed, well hung' is born out by the sheer variety of red meat on the menu, with a few salads and fish dishes to keep dieting co-diners happy. Vegetarians should steer clear.

Pelican

45 All Saints Rd, W11 [A1]. Tel: 7792 3073. Open: L and D Tues–Sun, D only Mon. ££
www.thepelicanpublichouse.co.uk
This gastropub is the place to head for generous, wholesome meals. The unpretentiousness of stripped wood and wooden bench surroundings matches the menu, which offers hearty soups, baked potatoes and free-range ham, fish pies, and asparagus with broad bean salads. Worth the walk if you find yourself on the wilder side of the Hill.

Sausage and Mash Café

268 Portobello Rd, W10 [A1]. Tel: 8968 8898. Open: daily, 11am–10.30pm. £
Elevating sausage and mash into an art form (wait until you see how your meal is served), this

Sausage and Mash Café

and steamed bass are among the favourites at this cheap, friendly and ever-popular venue.

Royal China
13 Queensway, W2 [B2].Tel: 7221 2535. Open: L and D daily. ££
The ambience is nothing special, but Royal China's menu is first rate, offering superb dim sum, delicious lobster with noodles, and delicate crispy spring rolls. The queues of Chinese who flock here every weekend from all over town are all the recommendation you need.

imaginative little restaurant puts lots of thought into its variety of gravy, mash and sausages from all over the world. And all for around £6 a main – unbeatable.

Chinese

Four Seasons
84 Queensway, W2 [B2]. Tel: 7229 4320. Open: daily noon–11pm. £
The roast duck cooking in the window is the most enduringly popular dish at this busy restaurant, where queues form every day of the week. As much effort goes into presentation as taste, making this a memorable meal all round. Try the chef's recommendations to vary your order.

Mandarin Kitchen
14–16 Queensway, W2 [B2].Tel: 7727 9012. Open: L and D daily. ££
Those too tired to queue at the next door Royal China can pop in here for some of the most delicious seafood served in a time-honoured Chinese fashion. Lobster, steamed scallops and razor clams, deep-fried baby squid,

French

Bonchurch Brasserie
349 Portobello Rd, W10 [A1]. Tel: 8968 5828. Open: L and D Tues–Sat, L only Sun. ££
This is a wonderful place to wind up for lunch or weekend brunch after a trawl down the Portobello Road. Choose from a host of wholesome starters, followed by seared venison carpaccio, crab-meat and spaghetti, grilled sword-fish, a fillet steak or a juicy burger and chips. Highchairs available for tired tots.

The Electric Brasserie
191 Portobello Rd, W11 [A1]. Tel: 7908 9696. Open: B, Br, L and D daily. ££ (lunch menu), £££ www.electricbrasserie.com
This former cinema has been restored as a members' club, with a very decent bar and brasserie open to the public. The steak sandwich served with a cone of chips on a chopping board is tender and tasty, and the set lunch menus very reasonable. If you can't find a seat inside, the outdoor tables command perfect pavement viewing of fashionable Portobello Market-goers.

Portobello Road

Electric Brasserie in a converted cinema

TIP

West of Notting Hill, the streets around Holland Park, with their expensive stuccoed houses shaded by plane trees, make for a pleasant strolling ground. Holland Park itself has some wide open spaces and a cosy café.

Greek

Aphrodite Taverna

15 Hereford Rd, W2 [B2]. Tel: 7229 2206. Open: L and D Mon–Sat. ££

One look at the tired decor might tempt you to dismiss this old-fashioned Greek taverna, but once inside the warmest welcome in London awaits you. Greek hospitality overflows with the retsina, and mezes of aubergine, tsatsiki and grilled calamari are rustled up in the kitchen quickly. Excellent falafels, sweet sticky puddings, and generous portions of everything. Not surprising then that it's often crowded with loyal regulars.

Indian

Ginger

115 Westbourne Grove, W2 [B1]. Tel: 7908 1990. Open: L and D daily. £££

www.gingerrestaurant.co.uk

For a reasonable price, diners are treated to immaculately presented genuine Bangladeshi dishes, not sweetened and soured for British palates. Fish is a speciality, with chunks of imported freshwater fish served in delicious broths. -

Old-fashioned service and considered wine list.

Khan's Tandoori

13–15 Westbourne Grove, W2 [B1]. Tel: 7727 5420. Open: L and D daily. £

www.khansrestaurant.com

Something about the huge high ceilings painted sky blue, and the polite waiters in traditional dress makes you love the chaos and noise of Khan's. The Indian fare is more fast-food than refined, but it's always served with style. If you find it impossible to choose from the extensive menu, don't hesitate to ask the waiter for recommendations. No alcohol is served here, but there's a huge range of fresh halal drinks.

Italian

Assaggi

39 Chepstow Place, W2 [B2]. Tel: 7792 5501. Open: L and D Mon–Sat. ££££

Its unexceptional position above The Chepstow pub belies the exceptional Italian food served within. The menu is simple and rustic, but ingredients such as scallops, veal chops and buffalo mozzarella are all painstakingly selected for freshness and quality. Delight in the authentic flavours and bask in the attentiveness of the waiters. Book up to four weeks ahead for dinner, and a few days ahead for lunch.

Mediterraneo
37 Kensington Park Rd, W11 [A1]. Tel: 7792 3131. Open: L and D daily. £££

The atmosphere is usually cheerful in this modern rustic trattoria, though it can get cramped at peak times. Daily specials of seared tuna, langoustine, sea bass, prawns and squid come in generous portions. Only the biggest appetites find room for the rich puddings in this busy local haunt.

Osteria Basilico 🍴
29 Kensington Park Rd, W11 [A1]. Tel: 7727 9372. Open: L and D daily. £££

Superb pizzas and the mixed antipasto buffet (for £6 you help yourself to an array of traditional titbits laid out on a counter) make this one of the most popular venues on this busy street. Everything is generously served, specials change daily, and you get the impression that the cheery waiters all live here. Celebrity spot from the window tables.

Zucca
188 Westbourne Grove, W11 [A1]. Tel: 7727 0060. Open: L and D Mon–Fri, D only Sat. ££ (set menu), £££

Zucca is that rare Italian place, stylish without being pretentious, quiet without being empty, friendly without being over the top, and with all the best attributes of eating Italian – simple ingredients and unfussy menus that include a few fresh pasta, pizza, meat and fish dishes. Some good, reasonably priced wines on the list. Booking is essential for dinner, especially if you want a table outside.

Modern European

192 🍴
192 Kensington Park Rd, W11 [A1]. Tel: 7229 0482. Open: L and D daily. ££ (set lunch), £££

Although 192 saw its heyday in the 1990s, it has consistently produced excellent dishes from fresh ingredients for a discerning crowd that still cram into its upstairs room every evening. The windows are thrown open on warm summer evenings giving the place a grand and decadent feel, and the perfectly cooked lamb and fish dishes rarely disappoint.

The Cow Dining Room 🍴
89 Westbourne Park Rd, W2 [B1]. Tel: 7221 5400. Open: L and D daily. £££

For discerning Guinness drinkers Tom Conran's busy downstairs boozer pours the perfect pint, the obligatory accompaniment to the fresh oysters and shrimps served at the bar. The upstairs dining room is a much quieter affair, with an informal atmosphere where the smarter residents like to gather. The daily changing menu has an English bias

Modern Italian trattoria, Mediterraneo

with a euro twist, and the food is simple but expertly prepared. Booking essential for the restaurant but no bar reservations.

Julie's

135–137 Portland Rd, W11 [A2]. Tel: 7229 8331. Open: L, T and D Sun–Fri, D only Sat. ££ (bar and lunch menus), £££ www.juliesrestaurant.com

This romantic haunt, full of cosy nooks and crannies and mellow jazz sounds, is a long-standing Notting Hill fixture. The food on the health-conscious menu is 90 percent organic, and the meat from free-range, British-reared stock. The children's Sunday lunch menu and crèche is a godsend for well-heeled Holland Park mums on the nanny's day off. The elegant wine bar offers a number of choices by the glass.

The Oak

137 Westbourne Park Rd, W2 [A1]. Tel: 7221 3355. L and D daily. £££

While the downstairs Italian gastropub continues to turn out wood-fired pizzas and pasta dishes, the classy new upstairs restaurant has made an auspicious start with chef Mark Broadbent at the helm

Cow Dining Room

impressing Notting Hill's discerning diners with his inventive and seasonal menu.

Moroccan

Couscous Café

7 Porchester Gardens, W2 [B2]. Tel: 7727 6597. Open: L and D daily, until midnight Fri–Sat. £

Once you have filled your boots with tagines and couscous, you may wonder why you don't eat Moroccan more often. The effusive service, pretty pottery, complimentary pastries and mint tea offered between courses, and palatable Morrocan wines puts you in the mood for soft sofas. Very moreish.

Pan-Asian

E&O

14 Blenheim Crescent, W11 [A1]. Tel: 7229 5454. Open: L and D daily. £££ www.eando.nu

The acclaimed 'Eastern and Oriental' has applied the same winning formula to its cuisine as in its equally successful sister restaurants (Great Eastern, Cicada and Eight over Eight), fusing standard oriental

ingredients with Pacific Rim flavours. The decor is minimalist, all dark wood and clean lines, and the staff glide between tables effortlessly taking and bringing orders. Portions are not huge, but they don't need to be. Everything from the prawn sesame rolls to the curries and desserts is beautifully presented and full of fresh taste-bud tingling flavours. Book ahead.

Polish

Antony's
54 Porchester Rd, W2 [B1]. Tel: 7243 8743. Open: D only Mon–Sat. **££**
Polish fare is not often found in these parts, but Antony's *pirogi* (savoury turnovers) and pork dishes are definitely worth a trek. The restaurant may be stuck in a 1970s time warp, with its candlelit tables and terracotta walls, but for many that's half the appeal. Live music in the bar at weekends. Vodka and Polish brandy flows.

Russian

Erebuni
London Guards Hotel, 36–37 Lancaster Gate, W2 [C2]. Tel: 7402 6067. Open: D only Mon–Sat. **££** *(set menu),* **£££** *www.erebuni.ltd.uk*
Tucked away in the basement of a hotel and crammed with Russians and Armenians, this cheerful back-street venue is a real find. The menu is full of Russian and Central European dishes, even if the decor is a little too authentically Soviet, with beetroot, gherkin and excellent *pelmeni* (Russian dumplings). Black bread, Baltika beer and complimentary vodka helps wash down the soups.

Thai

Market Thai
First Floor, The Market Bar, 240 Portobello Rd, W.11 [A1]. Tel: 7460 8320. Open: L and D daily. **£**
It's not often that a Thai restaurant offers a reasonable set menu, but at £13.95 per person the Market Thai special is unbeatable. Standard Thai dishes such as satay and spring rolls for starters, with tasty tom yam soups, pad thai noodles, sweet and sour pork, and green and red curries to follow. A relaxed, authentic atmosphere. Takeaways also available.

PUBS, BARS AND CAFÉS

Notting Hill, rather than Bayswater, is the place to enjoy a little café society. To mix with serious foodies, head for **Books for Cooks** *(4 Blenheim Crescent; 10am–6pm Tues–Sat)*, the largest supplier of cookbooks in London, and hope that one of the six tables are free. The choice of food is limited to only one starter, main and cakes baked in the tiny test kitchen that day, but it's guaranteed to be delicious. **Tom's Delicatessen** *(227 Westbourne Grove; 8am–8pm Mon–Sat, 10am–4.30pm Sun)* is where the beautiful people hang out. It's a fine deli, and the café serves decent snacks, best eaten in the back garden on sunny summer days. Otherwise, there are plenty of posey pubs to see and be seen in: **Westbourne** *(101 Westbourne Park Villas)*, **The Oak** *(137 Westbourne Park Rd)* and **The Cow** *(89 Westbourne Park Rd)* are all within staggering distance of each other and packed with chattering wannabes. Those who like playing pool and swigging beer from a bottle should head for **The Elbow Room** *(103 Westbourne Grove)*.

Afternoon Tea

*This is a luxurious and quintessentially English tradition,
but, like many traditions, it doesn't come cheap*

Afternoon tea was at once synonymous with gentility and decadence. In the Roaring Twenties bandleader Victor Sylvester used to play for the Savoy's demure *thés dansants*, while in the 1930s the audacious dancing at the hotel's infamous 'Tango Teas' created a scandal. Tearooms may hark back to a world gone by, yet afternoon tea is the closest most of us come to enjoying the trappings of luxury in an old-world setting. As the ditty goes: *"I'm feeling sublime for I've passed back in time, surrounded by glamour and glitz. As I sip my Earl Grey, all life's cares pass away. For I'm having tea at the Ritz".*

Hotel teas

Afternoon tea in a top London hotel is an experience that everyone should have at least once. In the case of the top hotels, be prepared to dress smartly, including a jacket and tie for men. The strict dress code is justified by the tone set by the Spode china and Victorian silver salvers: who would wish to be outshone by a piece of chinaware? Reservations are essential for all up-market high teas, in particular the Ritz, Brown's and Claridge's.

Claridge's *(55 Brook St, W1; tel: 7629 8860; ££)* is a bastion of the Establishment, which combines Classical grandeur and Art Deco styling. High tea (later than afternoon tea) is an elegantly presented ritual served with urbane charm by liveried footmen. The backdrop is the Foyer and the Reading Room, where the proceedings unfold to the sound of a string quartet. **Fortnum & Mason** *(Picccadilly, W1; tel: 7734 8040; ££)*, a grand gastronomic emporium dating back to 1707, is steeped in tea-drinking tradition. A sumptuous tea can be sampled below paintings of colonial tea-planters.

Le Meridien Waldorf *(Aldwych, WC2; tel: 0870 400 8484; ££)*, currently being revamped, is in a state of flux, part Edwardian splendour, part fussy fashion victim. Traditionalists will spurn the modern lobby in favour of the studied elegance of the Edwardian Palm Court, designed by the architect of the *Titanic*.

A cosy setting at Raffles Brown's

Raffles Brown's Hotel *(Albermarle St, W1; tel: 7493 6020; ££)* is one of London's most traditional hotels, graced with wood-panelling, antiques and log fires. Its famed afternoon tea has been staged in the Drawing Room for over 160 years. Tea includes cucumber sandwiches, scones with clotted cream, and dainty pastries served on Victorian silver cake stands.

The Ritz *(150 Piccadilly, W1; tel: 7493 8181; ££)*. Afternoon tea at the Ritz has an undeniable cachet. The lavish but unintimidating setting of the Palm Court could be the backdrop for a Noel Coward play.

The Savoy *(The Strand, WC2; tel: 7836 4343; ££)*. The Savoy's Thames foyer is a reliable choice. Egg and cress sandwiches, French pastries, tea cakes and scones served with clotted cream are served to the accompaniment of clinking spoons and tinkling Chopin. As soothing as it sounds.

Museums, galleries and churches

London's best museums, galleries and churches represent some of the loveliest yet quirkiest places for tea. Value for money is an additional draw.

The Bramah Tea and Coffee Museum *(40 Southwark St, SE1; tel: 7403 5650; £)* covers the history of tea and coffee from 1600 to 1950. Its café (free admission) serves cakes and pastries, as well as the finest coffees and teas.

Café Bagatelle, The Wallace Collection *(Hertford House, Manchester Square, W1; tel: 7563 9505; £–££)* provides the perfect excuse to explore a mansion showcasing art by Canaletto and Gainsborough. A sunny courtyard overlooks palms and an ornamental pool, protected by a glass roof. The tasty tea includes finger sandwiches, scones and home-made cakes.

The Orangery at Kensington Palace

Café in the Crypt *(St Martins-in-the-Fields, Trafalgar Square, W1; tel: 7839 4342; £)*. Tourists and locals alike enjoy the café's quirky character while tucking into a set tea of chocolate fudge cake, scones and cream.

The Court Restaurant, The British Museum *(Great Russell St, WC1; tel: 7323 8990; £)*. The restaurant, set below Norman Foster's stunning glass dome, offers a moody, modern setting for tea. Alongside the normal fare, a champagne tea includes salmon sandwiches, scones and brownies.

Somerset House *(The Strand, WC2; tel: 7845 4670/4646; £)*. The 18th-century buildings of the former tax office have been transformed into a glorious art gallery and performance space. Sip tea overlooking the Thames or the main courtyard, which doubles as a water garden.

The cream of Kensington

Whether it's the royal cachet or the profusion of 'ladies who lunch', Kensington is awash with delightful venues. Here are a few:

Kandy Tea *(4 Holland St, W8; tel: 7937 3001; £)* offers an intimate William Morris sitting room, with silver strainers and tiered cake stands. Fruit tarts and chocolate cake are available in addition to set teas.

The Orangery at Kensington Palace *(Kensington Gardens, W8; tel: 7376 0239; £–££)* provides a pastoral backdrop for various themed teas. The grandest combines a glass of kir royale with smoked salmon sandwiches, Belgian chocolate cake, and scones spliced with fresh strawberries and cream.

Patisserie Valerie *(27 Kensington Church St, W8; tel: 7937 9574; £)*. The belle epoque-style patisserie champions classic French pastries, from éclairs to millefeuilles, macaroons, fruit tarts and chocolate gateaux.

Costs per person: £ under £12; ££ £12–30 (more for champagne teas).

AT THE BAR
CAULIFLOWER SOUP
RABBIT OFFAL & LENTILS
QUAIL & AIOLI - 6:00
BRILL BREAD & GREEN SAUCE
GREEN BEANS & SHALLOTS
CHEESE & CHUTNEY SANDWICH
WELSH RAREBIT
ANCHOVY TOAST - 4:50
CHEESE & BISCUITS
SWEETCORN
6X

CITY AND CLERKENWELL

City slickers, urban hipsters and East Enders are well served by a host of up-market restaurants, upbeat diners and working-class canteens

Incredible though it may seem, people have lived in the area now called the City for 15,000 years. From their original settlements on Ludgate Hill and Cornhill, separated by the now hidden Walbrook stream, Londoners have been trading in earnest since Roman times. Now a shifting population of City workers, tourists, meat tradesmen and clubbers works and plays within the confines of the 'Square Mile' and beyond its ancient borders to Clerkenwell in the north and Spitalfields in the northeast.

The City

The City's past isn't readily accessible through its buildings. It has been devastated twice: once by the Great Fire of 1666 and again during the Blitz in the winter of 1940–41, which left one third smoking in ruins. Its ancient history is visible in the scattered remnants of its ancient walls and echoes in the street names – Aldersgate, Fleet Street, Cheapside, London Wall. Historical monuments cast heavy shadows among the glass and steel banks and trading centres. The top three attractions here are William the Conqueror's Tower of London, built with white brick from Normandy, Sir Christopher Wren's St Paul's Cathedral, which miraculously escaped devastation in the Blitz, and Monument, a glorious obelisk raised to commemorate those who died in the Great Fire. The latest addition to the cityscape is the Swiss Re building, Norman Foster's glass 'gherkin', a soaring capitalist temple that dominates the skyline.

Opposite: Clerkenwell's St John
Below: Bangla Beer, Brick Lane's top brew

Around these monolithic structures works a powerful and energising force for change; for things to be better, bigger, bolder. Cranes are as much a part of the skyline as ancient monuments. Here work is like oxygen, and everyday needs such as eating are more a necessity than a leisure activity. Lunch hour is a luxury. The City has a high concentration of sandwich bars to feed the swarms of suited stockbrokers and dealers who spill out of their offices for a quick bite on the hoof. Entertaining clients is a different matter. There are plenty of top-class expense-account restaurants and wine bars in which to ply them with good food and wine and clinch that deal over a long and well-lubricated meal.

Clerkenwell

A small hop beyond the old city gates are the newly desirable environs of old Smithfield Market. Here you can find New York City-style loft living, mega club Fabric, and out along St John Street, the address of many a good restaurant, the young movers and shakers of diligently cool advertising agencies such as Mother. The market itself, where meat is still sold, Clerkenwell Green and the environs of St Barts hospital define an area historically associated with food, frivolity and crime. It has long been a haunt for night revellers who rub shoulders in the pubs and cafés with market workers while pursuing the high-cholesterol breakfasts that are the market porters' dinners – the meat-market day ends as most people's begins. Clerkenwell also has a reputation as a refuge for outsiders and free thinkers. On the green, Papists were hung, drawn and quartered. And in offices just off the green, Lenin edited a paper during the early 19th century called *Spark*. The daily *Morning Star* once peddled communist-friendly journalism from its offices in Farringdon Road. Now, in a neat sign of the times, *The Guardian* – the left's most popular daily – is sited on the same road. Nearby, hungry hacks are fed at the pioneering gastropub, The Eagle *(see page 137)*.

Spitalfields and Brick Lane

To the east of Bishopsgate, one of the oldest thoroughfares out of the City of London, lies Spitalfields. Once the site of a medieval hospital, St Mary of Spital, and another famous market-place still trading to this day, Spitalfields is increasingly under siege by the development of new office buildings. However, the grand 18th-century Huguenot houses can still be found in and around the roads off Brick Lane. Their original inhabitants settled here and in Soho after

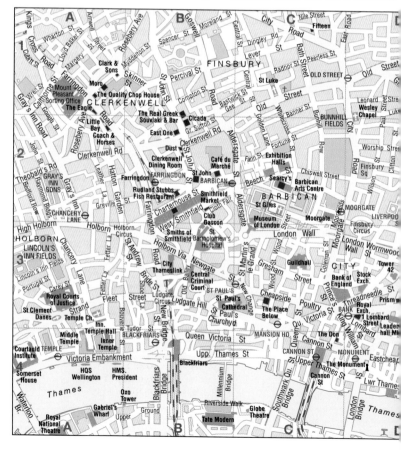

escaping persecution in their homelands, bringing their silk-weaving skills with them. Their arrival signalled the onset of waves of migrants both from abroad and within the country, including European Jews, Bangladeshis, and latterly

Above:
Brick Lane

artists, all of whom have left their mark in the silk-trading outlets, bagel shops, curry houses, art galleries and trendy bars. Keep your eyes peeled and you might spot the eccentric gait of artists Gilbert and George walking along Brick Lane to their house in Fournier Street, or Tracey Emin drinking a pint, or Turner Prize winner Wolfgang Tillmans snapping a picture in one of the local clubs. On a Sunday, with its markets, cafés and fascinating characters, Brick Lane is a great place to hang out. It has been called the New Camden, has had a novel named after it, and is one of the most interesting and vibrant areas in London.

FIVE OF THE BEST 🍽

Moro: Moorish food, a wood-fired oven and excellent Spanish wines and sherries

Cicada: predominantly Thai, with Chinese and Japanese thrown into the mix

St John: Fergus Henderson continues to perform his magic, transforming offal and odd cuts into eminently edible dishes

Club Gascon: fine modern French cuisine served tapas style

Coach & Horses: homely, friendly, with an inventive but unpretentious menu – one of the best gastropubs in town

*Clerkenwell
Dining
Room*

British

Clark & Sons
*46 Exmouth Market, EC1 [A1].
Tel: 7837 1974. Open: Mon–Sat,
all day. £*
One of the few remaining pie and mash shops standing its ground among the global fast-food chains that dominate London's high streets. The worn wooden pews, tiled floors, gut-busting food, low prices and no-nonsense service keep the working-class tradition alive. Cash only.

Clerkenwell Dining Room
*69–73 St John St, EC1 [B2]. Tel:
7253 9000. Open: L and D
Mon–Fri, D only Sat, L only
Sun. ££ (set lunch), £££
www.theclerkenwell.com*
An inviting smell of wine welcomes you into this small but well-presented restaurant. Predictable modern British mains like corn-fed chicken and ribeye of beef are on offer alongside more adventurous combinations, such as saddle of rabbit with black pudding and parsnip purée. The service is efficient, but the atmosphere rather staid. The upstairs dining room with its own bar is popular for private parties, offering reasonable set menus for groups of 20 or more.

Dust
*27 Clerkenwell Rd, EC1 [B2].
Tel: 7490 5120. Open: L and D
Mon–Fri, D only Sat, bar open
until 2am, food served until
10pm. £££ www.dustbar.co.uk*
For a fun evening of cocktails, food and music, this trendy lounge bar in a converted sewing factory is a good choice. The downstairs bar, which has regular weekend DJs, is partnered by a small dining room upstairs serving modern British dishes such as wild boar sausages and mash, and salmon fillets in a lime crust.

The Quality Chop House
*94 Farringdon Rd, EC1 [A1].
Tel: 7837 5093. Open: L and D
Sun–Fri, D only Sat. £££*
Take an old Victorian café, buff up its original features, charge £9 for a plate of traditionally cheap corned beef hash and hey presto, you have a successful restaurant with working class chic. Over-pricing apart, the food is undeniably good and wholesome, particularly the fish and seafood dishes, and the atmosphere warmly nostalgic.

St John 🍴
*26 St John St, EC1 [B2]. Tel:
7251 0848. Open: L and D
Mon–Fri, D only Sat. ££££
www.stjohnrestaurant.com*

A stone's throw from Smithfield meat market, this little restaurant in an old smokehouse is a Clerkenwell favourite. The white brick interior with its lofty skylights is stark but elegant. On entering, a bar and bakery serve up fresh bread, wine and snacks along the lines of Welsh rarebit, beef ribs and oysters. In the main dining room, the meat and offal-heavy menu changes with the season offering simple but unusual pairings such as Middlewhite belly and dandelion, rabbit and lentils, goose and watercress. Chef Fergus Henderson's signature roast bone marrow and parsley salad is always on the menu. Some fish dishes, but not for vegetarians.

St John Bread and Wine

94–96 Commercial St, E1 [E2].
Tel: 7247 8724. Open: B, L and
D daily. £££
www.stjohnbreadandwine.com
It seems that St John's quirky offal and odd-cuts formula has taken off here in its smaller sibling opposite Spitalfields market where the smell of freshly cooked bread wafts onto the pavement of drab and dingy Commercial Street. Food is served all day, but the best time to come is in the morning for their delicious bacon sandwiches. The dinner menu is best sampled in the less cramped St John's original *(see above).*

Smiths of Smithfield

66–67 Charterhouse St, EC1 [B2].
Tel: 7251 7950. Open B, L and D
daily. ££ (brunch menu), £££
www.smithsofsmithfield.co.uk
Brunch on a Saturday or Sunday is great fun in this lively and buzzy post-industrial complex. Those not monitoring their cholesterol intake can tuck into a cooked breakfast, grilled minute steak, or corned beef hash. Lighter options and fresh fruit juices and smoothies are on

offer for the health conscious. The more refined (and more expensive) upstairs restaurant offers a range of solid well-sourced meat and fish dishes complemented by views over Smithfield Market. Very popular with Clerkenwell and city folk both day and night.

Fish

Aquarium

Ivory House, St Katherine's
Dock, E1 [E4]. Tel: 7480 6116.
Open: L and D Mon–Sat.
££ (set lunch menu), £££.
www.theaquarium.co.uk
Smart St Katherine's Dock eatery with outside tables overlooking the little port. All the fish is well sourced and guaranteed fresh. Waiters are charming and very attentive. Upstairs at the Bang Bar young city types bray loudly about profit-related bonuses.

St John,
Clerkenwell

Fishmarket

Great Eastern Hotel, Bishopsgate, EC2 [D3]. Tel: 7618 7200. Open: L and D Mon–Fri. ££££
www.conran-restaurants.co.uk
Fishmarket is a small but perfectly formed space within the ground-floor confines of Terence Conran's Great Eastern Hotel. Its centrepiece is a chrome swish of a circular bar around which patrons quaff champagne and pick at the variety of fishy fodder, from roast halibut and potted shrimps to oysters and Canadian lobster. However, the restaurant feels a bit too like a hotel bar to make it an interesting evening venue.

Rudland Stubbs Fish Restaurant

35–37 Greenhill Rents, Cowcross St, EC1 [B2]. Tel: 7253 0148. Open: L and D Mon–Fri. £££
In the winding streets off Smithfield's northern flank, this cute fish restaurant in a converted sausage factory does a busy lunchtime trade. Rudland Stubbs prides itself on the freshness of its fish served in unfussy dishes like tuna niçoise, crab Caesar salad, and of course fish and chips.The cool lemon-and-lime tiled interior and ceiling fans create a relaxed environment.

Café du Marché

French

1 Lombard Street

1 Lombard St, EC3 [D3]. Tel: 7929 6611. Open: L and D Mon–Fri. ££££
www.1lombardstreet.com
Close to the Bank of England, this grand, cathedral-like banking hall-turned-restaurant, crowned with its own glass dome, is a hive of serious city dealing by day and boisterous entertaining by night. The menu ranges across a fine fish selection to well-executed brasserie-type meat dishes such as steak and liver, with enough caviar and champagne to impress the most successful trader.

Café du Marché

22 Charterhouse Square, Charterhouse Mews, EC1 [B2]. Tel: 7608 1609. Open: L and D Mon–Fri, D only Sat. £££
The delightful entrance to this restaurant leads into a countrified courtyard complete with hanging flower baskets. Inside, the rustic theme continues, in both decor and in the traditional French menu. The food is a little on the rich side but enjoyable nonetheless and a pleasant surprise in such an urban area. Ideal for a romantic meal or lunchtime treat.

Club Gascon 🍴

57 West Smithfield, EC1 [B2]. Tel: 7796 0600. Open: L and D Mon–Sat. £££
Though tradition is not totally dispensed with, there's more to this Michelin-starred Gascon restaurant than the requisite foie gras, cassoulet and magret de canard standards. Dishes and ingredients of southwestern France are lovingly prepared with an inventive modern touch and served tapas style, with a fine selection of regional wines to match. Booking essential.

Greek

The Real Greek Souvlaki & Bar

140 St John St, EC1 [B1]. Tel: 7253 7234. Open: L and D daily.
££ *www.therealgreek.co.uk*
More compact than its bigger Shoreditch brother *(see page 160)* and stuck on the grim edge of St John Street, this is not a recommendation based on appearances. Nevertheless, the intense tastes that Theodore Kyriakou has originated deserve as much experimentation here as they do in the roomier, more established branch. This is the place to discover what real taramasalata tastes like. Better for lunch than dinner.

Bollywood comes to Bangla Town at Café Naz

Indian

Café Naz

46–48 Brick Lane, E1 [E2]. Tel: 7247 0234. Open: daily, all day.
£ *(set lunch),* **££**
A big and brash antidote to the unanimity of curry houses on Brick Lane, Café Naz is an attempt to bring some modern design into the area. Stainless steel, big windows and a predominance of black are a far cry from the standard flock wallpaper and garish lighting. A busy and lively venue frequented by a stylish, young Asian crowd, serving modern takes on traditional Bangladeshi cuisine.

Café Shan

26 Hanbury St, E1 [E2]. Tel: 7247 4102. Open: daily, all day. **£**
This contemporary restaurant specialises in Bangladeshi cuisine. Kormas are delicately flavoured, meat dishes freshly cooked, and the service is impeccable. Shan has the added advantage of being neither as beer-swilling or noisy as its more run-of-the-mill neighbours.

Nazrul

130 Brick Lane, E1 [E2]. Tel: 7247 2505. Open: daily, all day. **£**
Comfortingly predictable, despite the frequent changes in banquette coverings. Groups of friends with a craving for an early-evening or late-night biriyani will find much to please here, but you'll need to bring your own beer, which the friendly staff will open for you. A recently installed cash machine beckons, just in case your eyes get bigger than your belly.

International

Café Mediterraneo

14 Horner Square, Old Spitalfields Market, E1 [E2]. Tel: 7377 8552. Open: L daily. **£**
Under the cover of Spitalfields Market you'll find an enviable variety of food outlets from Italian and Chinese to Moroccan. This is one of the more interesting lunchtime cafés, with a range of hearty dishes from lasagne and mousaka to couscous layered with

TIP

In the wee small hours early risers and party animals who have worked up an appetite on the dance floor, make a beeline for the long-established **Brick Lane Beigel Bake** at no 159, open 24/7.

Caravaggio, a serious City lunch venue

with aubergine and gorgonzola is exquisite, if rich. Very good and very expensive.

Sweet Basil

Brushfield St, E1 [D/E2]. Tel: 7375 3484. Open: L and D Mon–Fri, L only Sun. ***£££***
Recently relocated to the 'saved' part of Spitalfields Market, Sweet Basil has undergone something of a white-linen makeover. Tried and tested favourites, such as fettucine al salmone and veal escalopes, are impeccably presented in a bright and airy interior catering for a City lunch crowd. The service is attentive, and the food top-notch if not ground-breaking. The downstairs pizzeria is more imaginative with its toppings.

Modern European

Coach & Horses 🍴

26–28 Ray St, EC1 [A2]. Tel: 7657 8088. Open: L and D Mon–Fri, D only Sat, L only Sun ***££***
Of the many gastropubs trying to make their mark across the city, this Clerkenwell newcomer really gets it right. The scrubbed wood decor is simple, but homely, the food (masterminded by ex-Alastair Little chef, Paul Adams) inventive, but unpretentious, the wines excellent value and the service extremely good-natured. All in all, this gastropub is one of the best of its kind – let's hope it stays that way.

The Don

20 St Swithin's Lane, EC4 [C4]. Tel: 7626 2606. Open: L and D Mon–Fri. ***£££***
Hidden in a courtyard off St Swithin's Lane, The Don is a cosy and welcoming brick-walled bistro, formerly a madeira cellar (it gets its name from the trademark figure of Sandeman port). The food is a flavour-packed melange

your choice of meat or vegetables. Perfect if you've a yen for a cheap filling meal.

Italian

Caravaggio

107 Leadenhall St, EC3 [D3]. Tel: 7626 6206. Open: L and D Mon–Fri. ***£££*** *(set menu),* ***££££***
www.etruscagroup.co.uk
This grand and rather showy Italian restaurant in a converted bank, with mezzanine, is a busy business dining zone and the kind of place only dedicated gastronomes cross town for. Head chef Jonathan Lees brings new life to classic Italian dishes, with the emphasis on freshness and authenticity, and there is plenty of variety on the menu. Fish is always a good option, and the fillet steak

of influences, with a strong French bias, and the wine list laudable. The wooden-floored upstairs restaurant offers finer fare: Scottish salmon, venison, foie gras, and rich puddings. Popular at lunchtime so book ahead.

The Eagle
159 Farringdon Rd, EC1 [A1].
Tel: 7837 1353. Open: L and D
Mon–Sat, L only Sun. ££
It has all the outward signs of being a perfectly ordinary pub: noise, bar queues, smoke, scruffy seats and a well-worn bar. But the Eagle is more than your average boozer. This was the pub that launched a thousand gastropubs with its pioneering menu of the type of inventive but satisfying dishes you now see chalked up on trendy gastropub boards across London. The food, which has a Mediterranean bias, is complemented by an extensive range of European beers. However, it is tiny, and invariably crowded, so get there early. No bookings.

Fifteen
15 Westland Place, N1 [C1]. Tel:
7251 1515. Open: L and D
Mon–Sat. ££££
www.fifteenrestaurant.com
Visited by the great and good, including Tony Blair and his wife, Fifteen is certainly living up to its hype. Food is carefully prepared by Jamie Oliver's now famous trainees, who you can gawp at through an open kitchen in the basement (if you're lucky enough you might catch a glimpse of the man himself). The sourcing is imaginative (the lamb is Hardwick, a rare breed) and the desserts accomplished, though the mains can be disappointing. The bar upstairs, with its retro chandelier, is lovely. Book well in advance.

Little Bay
171 Farringdon Rd, EC1 [A2].
Tel: 7278 1234. Open: daily, all
day. £
For honest food honestly priced, this bizarre little bistro, lit by hand-crafted copper sculptures encrusted with droplets of coloured glass, is hard to beat. The dishes are surprisingly sophisticated, with starters such as smoked gammon and foie gras terrine, and mains like Barbary duck breast, red cabbage, honey and ginger. All are carefully cooked and nicely presented by sweet staff. A great budget address to have up your sleeve.

Prism
147 Leadenhall St, EC3 [D3].
Tel: 7256 3888. Open: L and D
Mon–Fri. ££££
www.harveynichols.com
A rich dining experience in both senses of the word. The sea bass and roast salmon are very good, indeed the fish menu as a whole is great. But the main attraction here is the grand 1920s architecture – it was once the Bank of New York – refitted with a contemporary minimalist interior for Harvey Nichols, who own it. There is a very stylish bar in the basement.

Pioneering gastropub, The Eagle

Listings

Cicada

Searcy's
Level 2, Barbican, Silk St, EC2 [C2]. Tel: 7588 3008. Open: L and D Mon–Fri, D only Sat. £££ (set menu), ££££
www.searcys.co.uk

Searcy's occupies one of the best spots in the Barbican, overlooking the soothing stretch of water at the heart of the complex. It's a classy restaurant that serves up surprisingly well-executed dishes for an arts centre restaurant. The sea trout with fennel, and duck with prunes and asparagus sampled for this review were fresh and flavoursome. A relaxed and indulgent experience.

Terminus Bar & Grill
40 Liverpool St, EC2 [D3]. Tel: 7618 7400. Open: B, L and D daily. ££££
www.terminus-restaurant.co.uk

Yet another restaurant that calls the Great Eastern Hotel its home, Terminus is a bustling, noisy venue. On one side a long, busy bar dominates, and an open kitchen fills the bottom end. Between them sits a business crowd served an interesting-sounding but often bland (and expensive) range of fish and meat dishes.

Pan-Asian

Cicada
132–136 St John St, EC1 [B2]. Tel: 7608 1550. Open: L and D Mon–Fri, D only Sat. £££
www.cicada.nu

This side of St John Street can feel desolate, but Cicada is a little oasis of trendy eating in what remains an entertainment desert. Split into two areas, the bar and restaurant follow Clerkenwell's battered (and over-used) school table and dark leather aesthetic, brightened by large, round 1970s light shades. The menu offers a range of well executed pan-Asian dishes like chilli-crusted tofu, and roast teriyaki cod, with sumptuous sorbets for dessert. Kick off with an enticing cocktail mixed at the bar.

East One
175–179 St John St, EC1 [B2]. Tel: 7566 0088. Open: daily, all day. £££ www.eastone.co.uk

In an unprepossessing post-war building, East One packs a young party crowd into its bright, easy and clean interior. It follows the do-it-yourself formula – you pick the ingredients and sauces, and the wok-wielding chef will stir-fry them up for you in a matter of minutes. This is a noisy, busy venue that may lack intimacy, but good fun can be had with friends.

consistently surprise: lamb is charcoal grilled, tuna is wind dried, monkfish wood roasted, manzanilla sherry used to partner prawns and garlic. Dining is unhurried.

Spanish

Moro

34–36 Exmouth Market, EC1 [A1]. Tel: 7833 8336. Open: L and D Mon–Fri, D only Sat. £££ www.moro.co.uk

Those who haven't discovered this fashionable, laid-back restaurant have a treat in store. On the part shabby, part quirky Exmouth Market, Moro has quickly gained a reputation for excellent food and friendly service. The food on the lively Spanish–North African menu really is as exciting as all the critics claim (owners Sam and Sam Clark have a cracking cookbook), with an intensity of tastes and textures that

Vegetarian

The Place Below

St Mary-le-Bow, Cheapside, EC2 [C3]. Tel: 7329 0789. Open: B and L Mon–Fri. ££ www.theplacebelow.co.uk

A godsend for hungry vegetarians is this uplifting café in the cool crypt of St Mary-le-Bow church, with seats in the churchyard in summer. Dishes are of the simple quiche and salad variety, and there is always a hot dish of the day. With pastries from posh deli Comptoir Gascon, breakfast is an inviting suggestion too. Popular at lunchtimes so best to visit before or after the peak midday–1.30pm slot.

PUBS, BARS AND CAFÉS

Given that some of London's oldest streets as well as its newest buildings are here, the mix of watering holes is accordingly diverse, ranging from achingly hip bars and contemporary cafés to quaint pubs full of character and history. Some cater for a 9–5 city slicker crowd, others for late-night clubbers. Fewer and farther between are the no-nonsense Victorian pubs, but with a bit of effort traditionalists or anyone craving a quiet pint and a packet of peanuts can root them out. On a foggy winter's night, nip into the cosy **Pride of Spitalfields** (3 Heneage St), a tiny old-style pub just off Brick Lane with an interesting mix of East End locals and Brick Lane trendies. A short walk away, opposite Spitalfields Market, is **The Golden Heart** (110 Commercial St), whose landlady, Sandra, is an influential figure in today's art scene, as she plays host (and lends an ear) to many of Hoxton's bright young artistic things. If you're in the area on a Sunday, take a trip up

Brick Lane and visit **Café @** (154 Brick Lane) and exchange some bad jokes with Adrian, the characterful and proud owner of this successful indie challenge to the invasion of the big bland coffee-shop chains.

Over in Clerkenwell, **Smiths of Smithfield** (67–77 Charterhouse St) is a cavernous and oh-so-trendy lounge venue, which changes mood throughout the day. For a more low-key atmosphere **Match** (45–47 Clerkenwell Rd) is a dimly lit original '90s bar with great cocktails. Refreshingly unhip and oozing with history, the **Jerusalem Tavern** (55 Britton St; weekdays only) is an intimate little pub dating from 1720, with cubicles, Georgian-style furniture and a good selection of real ales and fruit beers. **Ye Olde Mitre** (1 Ely Court, Ely Place) is a quaint pub full of character and history, with a warren of small, dark-panelled rooms. The original 1547 inn was built to service the needs of the nearby palace belonging to the Bishops of Ely.

Riverside Pubs

London's best riverside pubs provide good food, real ales, great views and fascinating insights into the city's history

One of the most enjoyable ways of passing time in London is to have lunch or supper in one of the Thames-side pubs. Although some are off the usual tourist trail, nearly all of them have an interesting history.

The oldest and most photogenic pub on the river is the **Prospect of Whitby** *(57 Wapping Wall, E1)*. Built in 1520, it was once a popular haunt for river thieves and smugglers. Samuel Pepys and Charles Dickens were regulars, and the artist JMW Turner came to paint its view of the Thames. In the 1950s the pub opened a fine new restaurant and began to attract an up-market crowd, including the late Princess Margaret and the actor Kirk Douglas.

Nearby is the **Town of Ramsgate** *(62 Wapping High St, E1)*, named after the fishermen from Ramsgate who used to unload their catch on the steps beside

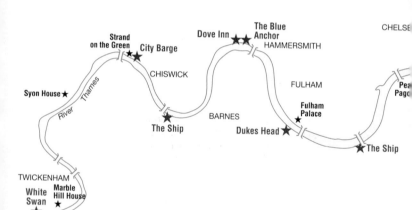

the pub. It stands next to the so-called execution dock, where reprobates were once hanged and then chained to allow the tide to wash over them three times. Later, more fortunate offenders were kept in holding cells in the pub's basement, to be shipped to Australia and America. Today, this long, narrow pub, with its waterside terrace, is mostly frequented by office workers and journalists working on the national newspapers produced close by.

Further east, **The Grapes** *(76 Narrow St, E14)* has a good seafood restaurant and serves fish and chips and sandwiches at the bar. Some say The Grapes was Dickens's inspiration for his pub Six Jolly Fellowship Porters in *Our Mutual Friend*; certainly another pub mentioned in the same novel is the picturesque **Trafalgar Tavern** *(Park Row, Greenwich, SE10)*. Close to the *Cutty Sark* and the National Maritime Museum, it offers a good choice of real ales, great food and has live jazz in the evenings at weekends.

Also on the south bank is **The Mayflower** *(Rotherhithe St, SE16)*. Parts of the pub date back to 1560, but it wasn't renamed The Mayflower until 1957 to mark the departure of *The Mayflower* from here in 1620. Its tiny rooms with low, black-beamed ceilings and narrow settles are fascinating. It serves real ales and dishes such as salmon supreme, and T-bone steak.

Close by, overlooking Tower Bridge, **The Angel** *(101 Bermondsey Wall East, SE16)* prides itself on being one of London's first riverside pubs, as it lies on the site of a small inn built by the monks of Bermondsey Abbey in the 15th century. Further west, close to Tate Modern and The Globe, **The Anchor** *(34 Bankside, SE1)* is a labyrinth of rooms, with five bars, a dining room and accommodation. Samuel Pepys took refuge here during the Great Fire of London of 1666, noting in his diary: "All over the Thames,

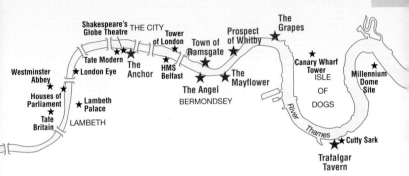

ATTERSEA

with one's face in the wind, you were almost burned with a shower of fire drops… When we could endure no more upon the water, we moved to a little ale-house on the Bankside".

In Wandsworth, further west, **The Ship** *(41 Jews Row, SW18)* has a huge verandah where barbecues are often held at weekends. It also has two bars: according to an unstated rule, locals are welcome in the front bar and visitors in the lively back room. Its popular restaurant serves good food and wine.

Downriver at Hammersmith is **The Blue Anchor** *(13 Lower Mall, W6)*, first licensed in 1722 during the reign of King George I. It was here that Gustav Holst wrote his *Hammersmith Suite*. Today, under the upturned rowing boats that hang from the ceiling, you can choose from a menu ranging from simple jacket potatoes or a ploughman's to lamb rogan josh.

A stone's throw away is the tiny **Dove Inn** *(19 Upper Mall, W6)*, noted in the *Guinness Book of Records* as having the world's smallest snug bar. It is associated with several famous people: James Thomson, who wrote *Rule Britannia*, lived in a room above the bar; William Morris lived a couple of doors away; and Ernest Hemingway and Graham Greene would often pop in for a drink. Its vine-covered terrace is a delightful place to watch passing boats and sample the appetising food.

Upstream, other pubs worth visiting are **The Ship** at Mortlake *(10 Thames Bank, SW14)*, a good spot to watch the finish of the annual Oxford/Cambridge boat race in April, The **City Barge** *(27 Strand-on-the-Green, W4)* in Chiswick, and **The White Swan** *(The Riverside)* in Twickenham.

SOUTH BANK AND BOROUGH

Work up an appetite sniffing out the area's best eateries scattered along the riverfront and hidden down Dickensian lanes and alleys

Anyone enjoying the restaurants in this chapter has a crack at the ultimate foodie fantasy – eating superbly *and* burning off the calories, for this sprawling, chaotic area covers nearly two pages in the London A–Z. Walking at a brisk clip from the western border in Kennington, SE11, to its eastern edge in Bermondsey, SE1, would easily burn enough carbs for a scoop of cherry-vodka ice cream in the stylish eatery Baltic, about half-way in between.

Within these ragged borders you can dine elegantly, with crisp linen tablecloths and a river view of St Paul's Cathedral, or plentifully, sharing fish and chips with a drove of cabbies and cadging a lift home afterwards. There are restaurants in the precincts of one London's oldest gothic churches, Southwark Cathedral, and in one of its newest institutions, Tate Modern.

Fine wines figure highly here, too. Vinopolis, City of Wine, covers nearly 3 acres of old warehouses in Borough and is Britain's only museum where you can educate yourself with four hours of recorded commentary and get merry along the way. Tastings are included in the tour, and Vinopolis also has a restaurant and wine bar, where you can quaff by the glass from 100 different varieties.

On the riverfront

The district is anchored at the northern end by the River Thames. In 1176 work began on a stone London Bridge linking it to the City of London on the other side. From the 15th century the south was a notorious den of vice and bear-baiting, and theatrical entrepreneurs built some of the first playhouses here, considered too disreputable for the precincts of the City. Dining in the attractive restaurant of the reconstructed Globe Theatre is now a civilised experience, but in the backstreet pubs of this twilight area, a hint of impropriety still glows.

The South Bank runs from Westminster Bridge to Blackfriars Bridge, flanked at each end by imposing buildings from the 1920s: County Hall and the Oxo Tower. In between is London's cultural playground, including the South Bank concert halls, the National Theatre and the Hayward Gallery. London's educated elite had few dining possibilities until the People's Palace in the Royal Festival Hall was relaunched to make the best of its stunning river views. The style brigade followed close behind, posh Knightsbridge store Harvey Nichols leading the pack by managing the Oxo Tower Restaurant.

For years Waterloo was little more than a battle, a railway station and a sunset. As recently as a decade ago, the only food worth ordering near The Cut was from Konditor & Cook's takeaway on Cornwell Road. The locale and the locals were so starved that each new restaurant was pounced upon instantly: one resident ate both lunch and dinner in the Fire Station on the day it opened and then did the

Opposite: fish! restaurant for upmarket fish and chips

same at the original Livebait. Now a stroll down The Cut is an exercise in international gastronomy, with Chinese, Spanish, Turkish and Polish cuisine among the choices.

Around Borough Market

Borough Market, across Cathedral Street from Southwark Cathedral, has nearly 1,000 years of history. The market – known as 'London's Larder' – was sited on London Bridge (for centuries the only bridge spanning the Thames) until 18th-century traffic jams forced a move to its current premises. It is primarily a wholesale fruit and veg market supplying the hotel and restaurant trade, and a couple of local pubs still open from 6am to 8.30am for thirsty marketeers to grab a pint. A few years ago, independent food traders set up stalls during the slack daytime hours, selling quality produce to city traders and the media minions who inhabit the newly resurgent area.

Now, on Fridays from noon until 6pm and on Saturdays from 9am until 4pm, you can find everything from wild boar sausages to Isle of Wight smoked tomatoes, from GM-free fish to tangy Spanish olives, with snacks as you go along. Catching the attention of *The New Yorker* magazine, the market has seeded a bloom of food shops (open Mondays to Saturdays) in the neighbouring streets. There are creamy British cheeses from Neal's Yard Dairy, great bread from the 'artisan bakers' De Gustibus, fresh fish from Applebee's and free-range chicken from the Wyndham House Poultry Company, either French-style (small, with no meat on the legs) or English (plump and succulent).

To picnic in the grounds of Southwark Cathedral is one of the area's pleasures, and local merchants are eager to cater. A trio of first-rate takeaways line Stoney Street, offering sushi, Asian fusion, and mouthwatering cakes. Further up the street, true carnivores can pick up a spit-roast hog sandwich to eat on the hoof. True Brits head for Hobbs in nearby Bedale Street, a pie and mash stall that featured in the film *Bridget Jones's Diary*.

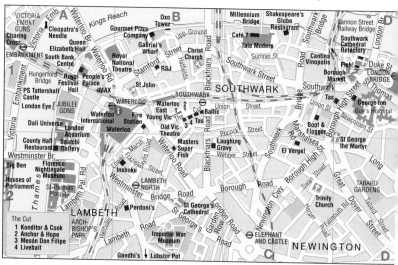

Bermondsey

The transformation of Borough from seedy suburb to trendy enclave encouraged the growth of next-door Bermondsey – designers at one end, desolate alleyways at the other. Dress designer Zandra Rhodes's pink-and-orange fronted Fashion and Textile Museum on Bermondsey Street paved the way, and now cutting-edge arrivistes tip-toe through litter-blown streets from gallery to restaurant. Or, at the trendy watering hole Delfina, to a gallery *in* a restaurant. With

---

FIVE OF THE BEST

Anchor and Hope: fresh produce and value-for-money menu make this gastropub a welcome addition to The Cut
Blue Print Café: views of Tower Bridge enhance the always excellent food
Champor-Champor: exotic Malaysian food with an eccentric decor to match
Baltic: the sleek interior, tasty Polish food and vast range of vodkas attract lounge lizards and media types
Tentazioni: tucked-away Italian with authenticity built into every bite

---

new places opening all the time, Bermondsey is definitely an area to watch.

It was another design guru, Terence Conran, who took charge of run-down Butlers Wharf. Conran, who appropriately cut his style teeth on the South Bank, took one look at the location – in the shadow of Tower Bridge – and promptly created the Design Museum. To capitalise on the excellent view from the top of the building, he opened the Blue Print Café *(see page 150)*, followed shortly by Le Pont de la Tour *(see page 151)*, the high-end eatery where Tony and Cherie Blair entertained Bill and Hillary Clinton, and the mayor of London dined with the mayor of New York. Le Pont de la Tour's food shop is a place to find epicurean eccentricities and tangy olive oil.

Soon, Conran and others had turned the entire Butlers Wharf waterfront into a long alfresco dining room, where promenading South Bankers can sashay between pizzeria, wine bar, down-home or up-market restaurants. A peek at the menus, though, shows that the only people likely to burn calories off here are the waiters.

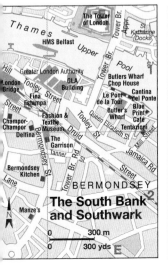

Culture vultures need never go hungry on the South Bank, which has restaurants, bars and cafés in all its theatres and concert halls

British

Boot and Flogger

10–20 Redcross Way, SE1 [C1]. Tel: 7407 1116. Open: L and D (until 8pm) Mon–Fri. ££

This tucked-away wine bar, named after a simple corking device, recalls a bygone era with its leather chairs, wine barrels and whiff of cigar smoke. The traditional food is adequate rather than memorable (think roast beef or cod) but the only-in-Britain atmosphere is matchless, and the selection of ports, sherries and wines excellent. A gentleman's club where women are welcome.

Butlers Wharf Chop House

Butlers Wharf Building, 36e Shad Thames, SE1 [E1]. Tel: 7403 3403. Open: L and D Mon–Sat, D only Sun (restaurant). ££ (set menu), ££££ www.conran.com

The Chop House flies the flag for classic English food. Service is generous, with constant replenishments of four kinds of bread. Carnivores should head straight for the roast suckling pig with tangy apple sauce and lots of crackling.

TIP

The charming **Bramah Tea and Coffee Museum** *(40 Southwark St)* tells the story of the world's two favourite hot beverages, and its adjoining café *(pictured below)* serves the finest cup of tea. If you come in the afternoon between 3pm and 6pm, the full works are laid on, with fine China tea and towering platters of cakes.

Bramah Tea and Coffee Museum café.

For vegetarians there's a fish dish. For afters, the bread and butter pudding comes smothered in custard. With luck, if the weather's fine, you might get a terrace table (bookings aren't taken for riverside seating). The set-price bar lunch is great value and has the same stunning river view.

Manze's

87 Tower Bridge Rd, SE1 [D2]. Tel: 7407 2985. Open: L only Mon–Sat. £

Michele Manze opened this Bermondsey pie and mash shop in 1902. Now his three grandsons keep this endangered cuisine alive, dispensing stewed and jellied eels, mash and home-made beef pies laden with liquor (electric-green, parsley-based gravy). Visit this delightfully old-fashioned place, with tiled walls and marble-top tables, while you still can.

Chilean

El Vergel

8 Lant St, SE1 [C2]. Tel: 7357 0057. Open: B and L Mon–Fri. £ www.elvergel.co.uk

Crispy tostadas and perfect tortillas are served up by cheerful staff in this pleasant café. Mainstays include churrasco palta (steak, avocado and tomatoes in Chilean bread) and empanadas (vegetable or meat turnovers). Crowded at lunchtime, so you might want to try the Latin breakfast instead. No credit cards. No smoking.

Fish

fish!

Cathedral St, SE1 [D1]. Tel: 7407 3803. Open: L and D daily. £££ www.fishdiner.co.uk

With its expansion plans floundering like a fish out of water, this

fish!

flagship eatery has dropped the attitude and now concentrates on what it does best – dispensing tasty GM-free fish swiftly, if a little offhandedly. The seats at the counter are too noisy for conversation, so sit outside or away from the kitchen to admire the views of Southwark Cathedral.

Livebait

43 The Cut, SE1 [B1]. Tel: 7928 7211. Open: L and D Mon–Sat. ***£££*** *www.santeonline.co.uk*

Actors from the Old and Young Vic theatres cram into the cool, tiled rooms of this, the original Livebait. Although the service and standards can vary, Livebait still offers killer cocktails and a calm oasis to lovers of good fish, prepared in creative ways. Monday special: a free lobster upgrade with every classic seafood platter. Booking advised.

Lobster Pot

3 Kennington Lane, SE11 [B2]. Tel: 7582 5556. Open: L and D Tues–Sat. ***££*** *(set menu),* ***£££*** *www.lobsterpotrestaurant.co.uk*

Service is hit and miss at this quirky place, but the food rarely fails to impress. Heavily French influenced and established long

before upscale fish restaurants had franchise opportunities, the Lobster Pot's eccentric decor and authenticity have netted devoted fans over the years. Booking advised.

Masters Superfish

191 Waterloo Road, SE1 [B2]. Tel: 7928 6924. Open: L and D Tues–Sat, D only Mon. ***£***

Need a taxi? You'll find cabbies galore in Masters, tucking into huge portions of freshly prepared fish and chips in this old-fashioned eatery. With a canny nod to the modern, though, it's also licensed, has air conditioning and accepts credit cards.

French

RSJ

13a Coin St, SE1 [B1]. Tel: 7928 4554. Open: L and D Mon–Fri, D only Sat. ***££–£££***

This pretty two-storied restaurant offers smooth service, paintings on the walls and pleasant dishes like Gressingham duck with golden beetroot salad, but the real attraction is the wine. The owner lectures on wines and vineyards of the Loire Valley, and the extensive list reflects his passion.

Did you know?

The Anchor pub *(34, Park St)* has stood on the same Bankside site for 800 years and was a haunt of diarist Samuel Pepys and Dr Samuel Johnson. The riverside terrace has great views of St Paul's cathedral.

The Laughing Gravy

TIP

Butlers Wharf's Conran restaurants operate a "first-come" policy for riverside seating. Increase your chances by booking a late lunch or dinner, when there are also fewer tourists walking past.

Indian

Gandhi's

347a Kennington Rd, SE11 [B2]. Tel: 7735 9015. Open: L and D daily. ££

The decor is unremarkable, but the food is above average, and there's the added attraction of the locals who dine here. Many a politician has been known to dash straight from Parliament to debate issues and careers over a Gandhi's prawn *jalfrizi*. Tables are small and within close eavesdropping distance.

International

County Hall Restaurant

County Hall, SE1 [A2]. Tel: 7902 8000. Open: B, L and D daily. ££££

Located in a grand riverside building, with views of Westminster, County Hall should be a class act. Unfortunately, sharing premises with the Marriott Hotel, it's fallen victim to 'hotel-itis'; the menu is a confusing mish-mash, as if the chef were in a conference call. Go instead for a leisurely weekend breakfast, or for a stylish afternoon tea in the Library Lounge.

Delfina

50 Bermondsey St, SE1 [D1]. Tel: 7357 0244. Open: L Mon–Fri, coffee until 5pm. ££–£££ www.delfina.org.uk

Lunchtime trendies and foodies flock to be wooed and soothed by head chef Maria Elia's honeydew melon soup, followed by an Australian fish of the day. The cool, sophisticated interior has art on the walls, and tables so far apart you could rollerblade.

The Laughing Gravy

154 Blackfriars Rd, SE1 [B2]. Tel: 7721 7055. Open: L and D Mon–Fri, D only Sat. £££

The decor is 1950s Paris, the menu 1980s California, the clientele a friendly mix of southeast Londoners and arrivistes from the trendy workshops and galleries nearby. Food is imaginative (try the warm duck salad with stem ginger and orange oil dressing) but pricey; inexpensive house wine keeps the bill down, or eat at the bar.

Italian

Cantina del Ponte

Butlers Wharf Building, 36c Shad Thames, SE1 [E1]. Tel: 7403 5403. Open: L and D daily. £££ www.conran.com

A young crowd animates the least expensive of Conran's river-front restaurants, enjoying pizzas, risotti and dishes like roast rabbit leg with prosciutto, or grilled squid with chillies. Keeping with the Italian theme, there's a huge, bright mural inside to admire while tasting freshly-made ciabatta or the help-yourself antipasti table.

Gourmet Pizza Company

Gabriel's Wharf, 56 Upper Ground, SE1 [B1]. Tel: 7928 3188. Open: L and D daily. ££
www.gourmetpizzacompany.co.uk
Although service can be indifferent, and wilder ingredients have been tamed (only the Chinese duck and buffalo mozzarella California pizzas remain from the original menu), the Thames flowing in the front and cute Gabriel's Wharf shops in the back have made this pizzeria a popular stop since 1989. Large salads provide a fresh alternative.

Perdoni's

18–20 Kennington Rd, SE1 [B2]. Tel: 7928 6846. Open: 7am–6.30pm Mon–Fri, until 2.30pm Sat. £
This Italian eatery has everything a 'caff' should have: leatherette banquettes, huge portions, fast and friendly service. Spezzatino di manzo (beef stew with rice) is a house special. No credit cards.

Tentazioni Ⓨ

2 Mill St, SE1 [E2]. Tel: 7237 1100. Open: L and D Tues–Fri, D only Mon and Sat. ££££
www.tentazioni.co.uk
'Temptations' is the perfect name for this hidden Italian gem. Greetings and service come with smiles and consideration. Dishes, like carpaccio with truffled cheese, are something to savour. The menu *degustazione* offers five courses chosen by the chef – pricey but divine – and a three-course menu highlights an Italian regional cuisine, changing monthly.

Malaysian

Champor-Champor Ⓨ

62 Weston St, SE1 [D1]. Tel: 7403 4600. Open: D only Mon–Sat. £££
www.champor-champor.com
A tiny spicebox of a place, Champor-Champor is a Malay expression loosely translated as 'mix and match'. Chef Adu Amran Hassan combines flavours as creatively as an artist mixing colours. Asian cuisines are grafted onto Malay village roots, then cooked European style to produce fragrant and innovative dishes that linger on the palate. Imagine king prawns with miso, curry leaf and mango.

Middle Eastern

Tas

33 The Cut, SE1 [B1]. Tel: 7928 2111. Open: L and D daily. ££
www.tasrestaurant.com
Tas is a local favourite. Service is

Tas, by the Globe Theatre

quick but friendly, and the menu is long enough to cater to most tastes – even vegetarian dishes are given a Turkish twist. It's easy to go overboard on the mezzes, all of which come with home-made bread, but save room for the Tas special (lamb with potatoes). The Tas at 72 Borough High St *(tel: 7403 7200)* also has a next-door café for lunch snacks to eat in or take away. Tas Pide by the Globe Theatre *(tel: 7928 3300)*, arguably the nicest, has a slightly different menu (*pide* is a pizza-like dish).

Modern European

The Anchor and Hope ⑪
36 The Cut, SE1 [B1]. Tel: 7928 9898. Open: L and D daily. ££
Chefs formerly of St John in Clerkenwell and The Eagle in Farringdon have banded together

Above: the Fire Station
Right: Cantina Vinopolis

to open this gastropub. All produce is British, and the meat – featured strongly on the menu – is butchered on the premises. Foie gras with grapes melted on the tongue, while ratatouille made a fine accompaniment to perfectly cooked roast neck of lamb. With keen prices, hefty portions and friendly staff, the Anchor is a definite winner (though perhaps not for vegetarians). Even the bar snacks are inventive.

Bermondsey Kitchen
194 Bermondsey St, SE1 [D2]. Tel: 7407 5719. Open: L and D Mon–Sat, Br Sun. ££
www.bermondseykitchen.co.uk
The emphasis here is on excellent vegetables. Leek and ricotta tart was the hit of the starters, red onion platter came dressed with moutabal and feta, to please the vegetarian. Heavenly desserts include poached peach with apricot cream, and hot chocolate pudding. A stylish, satisfying eatery.

Blue Print Café ⑪
28 Shad Thames, SE1 [E1]. Tel: 7378 7031. Open: L and D Mon–Sat, D only Sun. ££££
www.conran.com
First and the prettiest of the Butlers Wharf Conran restaurants, chef Jeremy Lee's menu changes daily. Grilled, marinated pigeon comes perfectly cooked; warm clam salad had a hint of samphire. River activity is on view for the stylish clientele, who often arrive from the Design Museum below, using the cute binoculars provided at table. Booking advised.

Cantina Vinopolis
1 Bank End, SE1 [C1]. Tel: 7940 8333. Open: L and D Mon–Sat, D only Sun. £££
www.vinopolis.co.uk
Full marks to the wine, with over 150 choices at this Italianate

Blue Print Café, for fantastic river views

restaurant in London's only wine museum. Then comes the decor – soaring cathedral-style arches of polished, palest brick. The food is fine, and the wait-staff are unfailingly patient, offering expert sommelier advice to the uninitiated.

Fire Station

150 Waterloo Rd, SE1 [B1]. Tel: 7620 2226. Open: L and D daily. ££

Energetic cooking, huge portions and a changing menu of pleasant pub grub are the attractions of this restaurant in a converted fire station. Dishes are chalked up on a huge board and prepared in view in the large kitchen. The acoustics are terrible, though, so choose a quiet spell or visit on Sunday night. Avoid Friday night, when it's mobbed by office workers.

The Garrison

99–101 Bermondsey St, SE1 [D/E2]. Tel: 7089 9355. Open: L and D daily, Br Sat–Sun. ££

Snacks like corn on the cob and chipolatas are augmented on the short menu by more ambitious dishes including cullen skink (Scottish fish soup) and roast guinea fowl. However, the decidedly pub atmosphere and uncomfortable chairs make this best for a quick stop rather than luxurious lingering.

Oxo Tower Restaurant

Oxo Tower Wharf, Barge House St, SE1 [B1]. Tel: 7803 3888. Open: L and D daily. ££££ www.harveynichols.com

Overpriced
e**X**ceptional views
Ok food

still attracts the suits and wannabes long after this was *the* place to be. Service ranges from attentive to snobbish. Dishes like poached Scottish wild salmon are pleasant enough. However, the view of the Thames through the huge windows is magnificent. For a similar, less expensive experience, eat at the brasserie next door. Booking advised.

The People's Palace

Level 3, Royal Festival Hall, Belvedere Rd, SE1 [A1]. Tel: 7928 9999. Open: L and D daily. £££ www.peoplespalace.co.uk

One of the first upscale restaurants to capitalise on its river setting, the Palace's decor now looks positively retro next to its chrome-and-steel culinary neighbours. The clientele is cultured, the waiters wear proper attire, tables are far apart and the food is well-prepared. A tendency towards old-fashioned dishes is vigorously

TIP

A public viewing platform on the eighth floor of the Oxo Tower has lovely river views, but it's in the middle of the haughty Oxo Tower Restaurant. Exercise your right to use it.

fought: think escargots, but jazzed up with cumin and fennel. Booking advised.

Le Pont de la Tour
Butlers Wharf Building, 36d Shad Thames, SE1 [E1]. Tel: 7403 8403. Open: L and D daily. ££££ www.conran.com
Prime ministers and presidents vie with lovers and movie stars for the romantic view of Tower Bridge. Service is impeccable, the crystal gleams, and the wine list is comprehensive. Chef Tim Powell presents a polished blend of styles, like braised pig's trotter garnished with pomme purée and truffles. A pianist plays in the terraced bar and grill next door, where the emphasis is on seafood. Booking advised.

Shakespeare's Globe Restaurant
New Globe Walk, SE1 [C1]. Tel: 7928 9444. Open: D only Mon, L and D Tues–Sat, L only Sun in winter. ££ (set menu), £££ www.shakespearesglobe.org
The Globe's restaurant is a pretty room with mullioned windows that open to views of St Paul's Cathedral. 'Elizabethan dishes' have been thankfully dropped for a hearty selection of modern European fare. The set menu is lighter on the palate and, for the location, good value.

Tate Modern, Café 7
Bankside, SE1 [C1]. Tel: 7401 5020. Open: L daily, D Fri–Sat (last order 9.30pm). £££ www.tate.org.uk
The modern European food, the views and an arty, good-looking crowd make dining in London's trendiest national institution fun. During the day, expect queues. On weekend evenings the food and the clientele are more sophisticated, and if you are one of the last to leave, you get to walk unescorted through the echoing, dimly lit gallery. Spooky. Café 2 is another cool spot for lunch, though it doesn't have the views.

Pan-Asian

Inshoku
2304 Lower Marsh, SE1 [B2]. Tel: 7928 2311. Open: L and D Mon–Fri, D only Sat. ££
A large room with spartan decor, this excellent-value restaurant in Waterloo's Lower Marsh Market is rarely full. The cooking is thoughtful – a combination of traditional sushi or sashimi, with more exotic dishes like beef Yakiniku (sizzling Korean barbecue), and Japanese-style curry. Bring a crowd to liven things up.

Peruvian

Fina Estampa

*150 Tooley St, SE1 [D1]. Tel:
7403 1342. Open: L and D
Mon–Fri, D only Sat. £££*
For over a decade, the Jones have
been serving first-rate Peruvian
food in an unassuming venue near
Tower Bridge. Bianca is from
Lima and cooks; Richard is British
and maintains front of house. The
famous Peruvian *cuy* (guinea pig)
isn't on the menu, but don't miss
the *arroz de mariscos*, sky-high
with shellfish. Sweet potatoes
embellish almost everything.

Polish

Baltic ⓦ

*74 Blackfriars Rd, SE1 [B1]. Tel:
7928 1111. Open: L and D daily.
£££ www.balticrestaurant.co.uk*
A cool grey bar filled with lounge
lizards from LWT-TV and other
media types leads to the skylit dining room of this award-winning
restaurant. The menu changes
regularly, featuring hearty golonka
(roast pork shank) and kololik
(spiced lamb and beef meatballs).
For those who like to pose or pick
at food prettily, there are 32 kinds
of vodka, plus blinis, at the bar.
Booking advised.

Spanish

Mesón Don Felipe

*53 The Cut, SE1 [B1]. Tel: 7928
3237. Open: L and D Mon–Sat,
D only Sun. ££*
Stage hands from the nearby theatres, office workers and locals
flock to this long-established eatery
for its feel-good atmosphere and
tasty tapas. Tables near the door get
bumped by the flow of traffic, so sit
at the counter or in the back for
comfort. The drinks list is an edu-
cation in Spanish wines.

PUBS, BARS AND CAFÉS

In Chaucer's *Canterbury Tales*, the Miller apolo-
gises in advance: 'And if the words get mud-
dled in my tale, just put it down to too much
Southwark ale.' Sobriety has never been a
characteristic of this area, which still has an
extraordinary number of pubs. The historic
George Inn *(77 Borough High St)*, rebuilt in
1676, is London's only galleried coaching inn.
The Market Porter *(9 Stoney St)* is famous for
opening its doors from 6am to 8.30am for the
Borough Market workers. The nearby
Wheatsheaf *(6 Stoney St)* is a local cockney
boozer with two bars, and a lunchtime menu
which offers above-average pub grub.

Among the more contemporary bars are
The Old Vic theatre's **Pit Bar** *(The Cut, closed
Sun)* which has a pianist. The **Cubana bar** in
the Cubana restaurant *(48 Lower Marsh)*
attracts a young crowd lured by salsa sounds
and margaritas. The **Wine Wharf** *(Stoney St,*
closed Sun), part of the Vinopolis Museum of
Wine, offers a choice of more than 150 wines,
plus tapas.

Of the area's many quirky and original
cafés, these are worth seeking out: **The
Bermondsey** *(63 Bermondsey St)* – any caff
that serves bacon, eggs and Veuve Clicquot is
OK by us; **House of Crepes** *(56 Upper Ground)*
for sweet or savoury pancakes under outdoor
umbrellas in cutesy Gabriel's Wharf; **Marie's**
(90 Lower Marsh) serves fry-ups in the daytime and tasty Thai food from 6pm to
10.30pm; the uniquely located **Southwark
Cathedral Refectory** *(Montague Close)* feeds
clergy, tourists and local office workers in its
airy cafeteria and courtyard; **Konditor & Cook**
(The Young Vic, 66 The Cut) prepares delicious
savoury snacks, but it's the organic cakes they
are known for *(takeaway available at 22
Cornwall Rd and 10 Stoney St).*

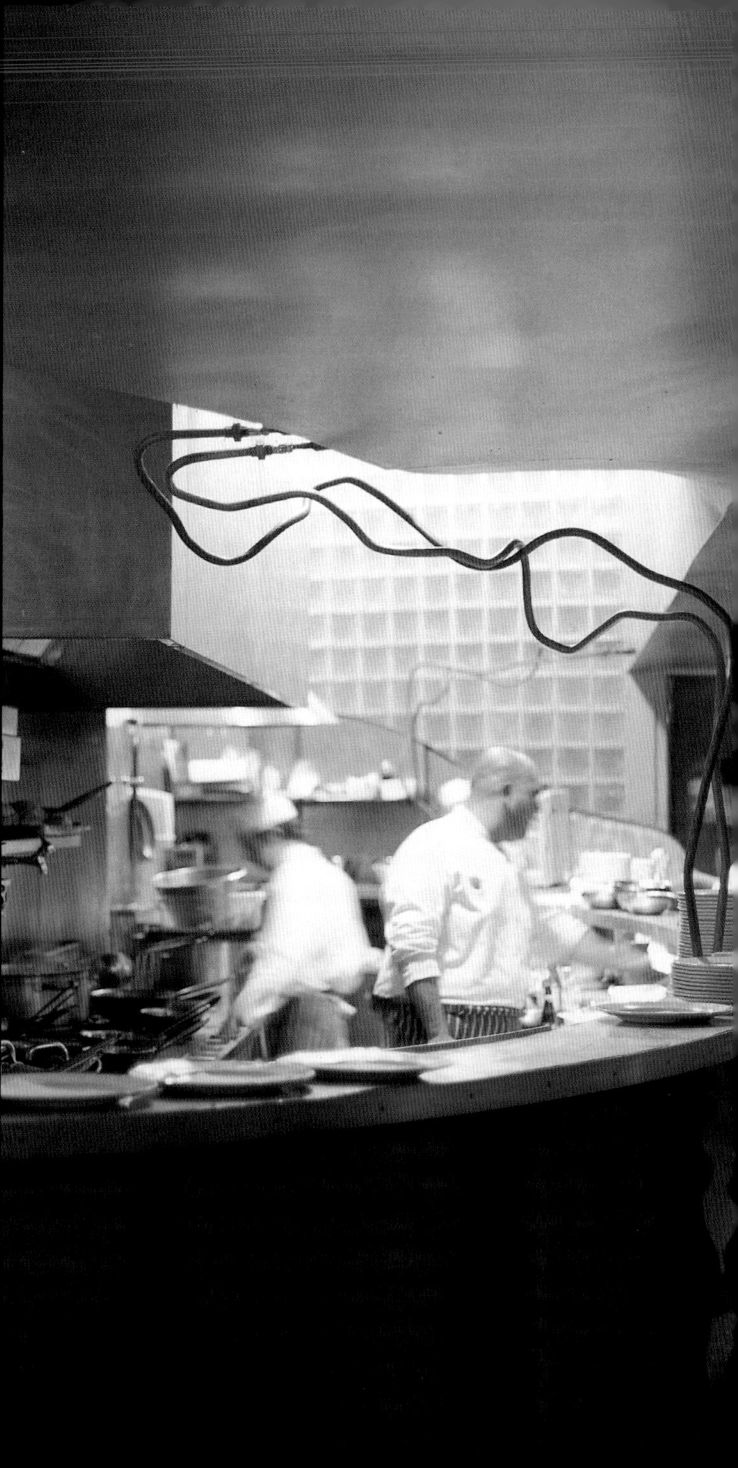

CAMDEN TOWN TO HAMPSTEAD

Camden Town is a curious mixture of the smart and the seedy, best known for the vast market that draws young bohemians, fashion victims and tourists in their droves. Camden offers a wide range of lively restaurants, bars and cafés, which do a brisk weekend trade. Neighbouring Primrose Hill, with its pretty tree-lined streets, is smarter and more sedate. Chichi cafés are interspersed with one-off shops, and the park has great views over London. Further north, perched on a hill, lies exclusive Hampstead. It is a popular destination both for its fashionable shops and the sprawling heath. Bars, cafés and pubs are plentiful, but of the many chain restaurants that dominate the area, only a couple are of note.

Belgo Noord
72 Chalk Farm Rd, NW1. Tel: 7267 0718. Open: L and D daily. ££ www.belgo-restaurants.com
One of the two survivors of the quirky Belgian-themed restaurant, where waiters in monk-like aprons serve up mountains of moules. Despite some inventive variations on the mussels and chips theme, such as mussels in Thai red curry sauce, the food tends to be mediocre, but the range of Belgian beers on offer is a big plus point.

Camden Brasserie
9 Jamestown Rd, NW1. Tel: 7482 2114. Open: L and D daily £££
Celebrating 20 years in Camden, though with a recent change of venue, this local restaurant delivers accomplished brasserie fare. The space is elegantly decorated, and dishes, particularly the grills, are satisfyingly tasty.

Crown and Goose
100 Arlington Rd NW1. Tel: 7485 2342. Open: L and D daily. ££
A popular gastropub serving familiar dishes with a flourish. The dining area to one side of the main bar is cosy, and the candlelit wooden tables lend an intimate feel to this busy local watering hole.

The Engineer
65 Gloucester Ave, NW1. Tel: 7722 0950. Open: B, L and D daily. £££ www.the-engineer.com

This stylish gastropub serves a sophisticated menu, with such offerings as char-grilled squid with green papaya, cucumber and mint salad with lime, peanut and palm sugar dressing. A walled garden and lively bar offer more relaxed settings for eating and drinking. It's a short and scenic walk along the canal from Camden Market.

Galangal
25–31 Parkway, NW1. Tel: 7485 9933 Open: L and D daily. £
This modern Thai canteen, serving flavoursome, keenly priced food, is a good option for a quick meal before heading to the cinema opposite. Refreshing juices such as lime, mint and ginger are a welcome accompaniment to the spicy curry and noodle dishes.

Lemonia
89 Regents Park Rd, NW1. Tel: 7586 7454. Open: L and D Mon–Fri, D only Sat, L only Sun. ££
A Camden institution that's always packed at weekends with locals as well as visitors sharing tasty mezze and typical Greek char grills. A bona fide family restaurant that works for parties or intimate dinners. Set menus are available for group bookings.

Little Basil
82 Hampstead High St, NW3. Tel: 7794 6238. Open: L and D daily. ££

TIP

Camden has a wide range of pubs, from gastro to grunge. Almost every street corner has a pub for a drink or quick bite. Inverness Street, terminating in the legendary **Good Mixer** pub (No.30) where Brit poppers hung out in the 1990s, has a string of trendy bars, most of which serve food. **Bar Gansa** (No. 2) serves great tapas and **Bar Vinyl** (No. 6) is the place for serious drinking with the in-crowd.

Opposite: Belgo Noord

Camden Lock

This Thai restaurant has large communal tables at the front and smaller, more intimate ones in the atmospheric dark wood interior. An extensive menu offers standard Thai dishes and more, all freshly prepared in the open kitchen. A good option on a Sunday when a buffet spread allows you to try all those things you couldn't decide on.

Mango Room
10–12 Kentish Town Rd, NW1. Tel: 7482 5065. Open: L and D Tues–Sun, D only Mon. £££
A menu headed 'traditional and modern Caribbean cuisine' sets the scene for this deeply fashionable eatery. The number one dish on a mainly fish-oriented menu is 'Camden's famous goat curry'. A cool interior and even cooler staff.

Manna
Erskine Rd, NW3. Tel: 7722 8028. Open: D only Mon–Sat, L and D Sun. ££ www.manna-veg.com
A pine interior for the virtuous vegetarian venue – but don't be put off by the 1970s throwback decor, as the salads, curries and pastas are exceedingly moreish. Organic and vegan dishes are highlighted for the committed.

Marine Ices
8 Haverstock Hill, NW3. Tel: 7482 9000. Open: L and D daily. ££

Apart from the unbeatable ice creams this family-run gelateria has been scooping out for 50 years, authentic pizzas and pastas are served in the restaurant by all Italian staff in a cheerful and family friendly environment. Leave room for the wonderful ice-cream desserts.

Singapore Sling
16 Inverness St, NW1. Tel: 7424 9527. Open: L and D daily. ££
An extensive range of Malaysian dishes served in atmospheric surroundings. Friendly service and delicious flavours combine to create a quality venue in one of Camden's trendiest streets. Try a cocktail first in the cosy upper level bar.

The Wells
30 Well Walk, NW3 Tel: 7794 3785. Open: L and D daily. £££ www.thewellshampstead.co.uk
Well-heeled Hampstead villagers have welcomed this charming new gastropub with open arms. The dining area, spread across three rooms, is spacious with pretty views over the green surroundings. Dishes like grilled plaice with garlic crust, braised endive and red wine lentils are executed with flair. Work up an appetite or walk off the feast with a stroll on nearby Hampstead Heath. Booking advisable.

ISLINGTON

North of Clerkenwell and the City, Islington has a lively restaurant scene. It is dissected by Upper Street, a mile-long thoroughfare connecting the Angel tube station and Highbury Corner, packed with more than 90 restaurants, cafés and bars. On summer evenings and weekends the street takes on a Continental atmosphere as it becomes the strolling ground for a youthful crowd out on the town. Chain restaurants prevail (Ask, Belgo, Brown's, Café Flo, Café Med, Carluccio's, Nando's, Pizza Express, Thai Square, Wagamama, Yo Sushi, Miso et al). More interesting, independent restaurants tend to be found in the side streets.

Afghan Kitchen

35 Islington Green, N1. Tel: 7359 8019. Open L and D Tues–Sat. £
Specialising in Afghan home cooking, this tiny restaurant offers a small choice of delicately spiced, melt-in-the-mouth dishes such as chicken in yogurt, fish stew with potatoes, and lamb with spinach. The light, minimalist decor creates a calm, Eastern ambience that somehow makes sharing the single large table a pleasure (there are a few more tables upstairs). Wine and beer available. Cash only.

The Almeida

30 Almeida St, N1. Tel: 7354 4777. Open L and D daily. £££ www.almeida-restaurant.co.uk
This Conran-owned restaurant, directly opposite the Almeida Theatre, specialises in regional French cuisine such as frogs' legs, lapin de moutarde, coquille St Jacques, pot au feu de foie gras, and cassoulet, most of which haven't been seen in faddish Islington for decades. In summer a tapas menu, chalked up on a blackboard outside, is available to a small number of pavement tables.

Casale Franco

Rear of 134–137 Upper St, N1. Tel: 7226 8994. Open L and D daily. £££
This stylish Italian tucked up an alleyway off Upper Street is a favourite with locals, who like its mellow buzz, straightforward food and slick service. The menu includes plenty of fish (halibut, sea bream, swordfish and cuttlefish), succulent lamb and steak, as well as pasta and wheel-sized pizzas. On summer evenings it utilises the yard of the neighbouring garage – an outdoor space made surprisingly pleasant by candlelight and strewn rose petals. Children welcome.

The Draper's Arms

44 Barnsbury St, N1. Tel: 7619 0348. Open L and D Mon–Sat, D only Sun. £££
Tucked into a line of early Victorian terraces off Liverpool Road, this once-seedy pub has metamorphosed into one of the top gastropubs in the area. The menu is packed with robust flavours, such as lamb shank with butter

TIP

Islington has a history of entertainment. The most high profile among its many performance arenas are **Sadler's Wells** (Rosebery Ave), the city's main dance venue, and the **Almeida** (Almeida St), where Nicole Kidman, Kevin Spacey and Juliette Binoche have trodden the boards.

The Almeida, for regional French cuisine

beans and chorizo, and pancetta-wrapped monk fish with a stew of peas and grilled lemon polenta. For pudding, expect to find sticky toffee and crumble, but also one or two more intriguing choices such as Sauterne custard with vanilla roast winter fruit.

The Fish Shop on St John Street

360–362 St John St, EC1. Tel: 7837 1199. Open L and D Tues–Sat. £££

Handy for visitors to Sadler's Wells, this modern fish restaurant is partly owned by Alan and Olga Conway, who for many years ran the much-loved Upper Street Fish Shop. Here a more upmarket menu includes char-grilled whole sea bass, fish stew with sorrel, and lobster, though simple plaice or cod are available, either fried in batter or a traditional Jewish coating of egg and matzo meal. Either way, the quality of all the fish is superb. Child portions available.

Lola's

Upper Street – Islington's restaurant parade

The Mall, 359 Upper St, N1. Tel: 7359 1932. Open L and D daily. ££ (set menus) £££ www.lolas.co.uk

Situated above the Islington Antiques Mall, Lola's is a light and airy eyrie serving seriously haute cuisine. Typical main courses are pigeon and foie gras ballotine, and stuffed saddle of rabbit with mushroom lasagna and carrot purée, while desserts might include strawberry soup infused with lavender or tortellini of greengages with Sauternes. Small but good-value lunch and pre-theatre menus are also available. Not for those in a hurry, as waits between courses can be long.

Patisserie Bliss

428 St John's St, N1. Tel: 7837 3720. Open: 8am–7pm (9am–6pm weekends). £

Bliss does a brisk, mainly takeaway trade in tasty snacks. Top treats include warm and gooey almond croissants, tangy lemon tarts, rich savoury tarts (onion and walnut/stilton and spinach), and toasted French bread topped with roasted vegetable and tapenade. It also supplies pastries to The Crypt, a fair-trade café (Thursday and Saturday only) at St Mary's Church halfway down Upper Street. Cash only.

HOXTON AND SHOREDITCH

Over the past 10 years, Shoreditch has experienced something of a renaissance. A once shabby area best known for its strip clubs, sex saunas and prostitutes, it is now one of London's trendiest hotspots, home to Jay Joplin's White Cube2 art gallery on Hoxton Square, style bible ID magazine, and an increasing number of very fashionable bars, clubs and restaurants, many of which have pioneered a local style, combining a laid-back front bar with a quality rear or upstairs restaurant. The area's eclectic mix of people and venues lies in and around the 'Shoreditch triangle' – bordered by Curtain Road, Old Street and Great Eastern Street.

Cantaloupe Bar & Restaurant

35 Charlotte Rd, EC2. Tel: 7613 4411. Open: daily – bar all day; restaurant, L and D. ££ (bar), £££ (restaurant)
www.cantaloupe.co.uk

The 'oldest' new-style bar and restaurant in Shoreditch, Cantaloupe is still one of the best. The tapas bar menu is always a good bet, serving up roast chicken, fat fries, houmous platters and an interesting vegetarian selection. Good-size wooden tables can sit a group of friends, though on a busy evening eating can be a trial. The formal restaurant at the back is a relatively small space but offers polished service and predictable but well-executed dishes. Be careful where you sit, however, as in certain spots the noise from the bar can spoil your meal, and be warned that two-hour fixed booking periods are strictly adhered to.

Breakfast at Macondo

Cru Restaurant, Bar & Deli

2–4 Rufus St, N1. Tel: 7729 5252. Open: L and D Mon–Sat, D only Sun. ££ (bar), £££ (restaurant)
www.cru.uk.com

Just off Hoxton Square, this is an inviting restaurant with a deli shop front feel – open windows, bottles of olives, and hanging chillies. Up front you'll find an informal sitting area where you can grab a cup of coffee, platters or open steak sandwiches from an all-day bar. To the

rear, separated by a vast wine rack, the main restaurant dishes up gastropub-like mains including fish and chips. Unfortunately, the decor is not wearing as well as one might expect of such a new venue.

Eyre Brothers Restaurant Ltd

70 Leonard St, EC2. Tel: 7613 5346. Open: L and D Mon–Fri, D only Sat. £££ (set menu), ££££ www.eyrebrothers.co.uk

This is arguably the best restaurant in Shoreditch, with an adventurous and original fusion of European-influenced meat and vegetable dishes. Their Catalan 'escalivada', a roasted vegetable salad with anchovies and toast, is typical of the simple distinct flavours you'll find here. The minimal interior is typical Shoreditch – walnut wood, retro leather banquettes and comfortable chairs arranged into four

TIP

For a delicious Latino breakfast of pancakes and pastries *(pictured above left)* head for **Macondo** *(Unit b2 Hoxton Square, N1; tel: 7729 1119; £)*. This laid-back café is open all day every day until midnight for the sampling of Latin American snacks and drinks.

The Real Greek &
Mezedopolio

large dining areas – and the atmosphere airy, with a lively Cuban soundtrack. A real find.

Furnace

1 Rufus St, N1. Tel: 7613 0598. Open: L and D Mon–Fri, D only Sat. ££

Bypass Pizza Express and venture off the beaten track to seek out this quality pizza joint. The beech wood venue is nothing out of the ordinary, but the pizzas are crisp, with inventive toppings such as tender suckling pig with salsa verde, gorgonzola with rocket and cherry tomatoes and sour cream with mozzarella, asparagus and sorrel. The staff are friendly and efficient.

Great Eastern Dining Room

54 Great Eastern St, EC2. Tel: 7613 4545. Open: L and D Mon–Fri, D only Sat. £££ www.greateasterndining.co.uk

Well-executed, contemporary pan Asian food, from dim sum to prawn pad thai, and a wide-ranging wine list is all on offer. However, the space is cramped and can become incredibly hot in summer. It's a noisy, fun eating experience, suited to a young crowd.

The Real Greek & Mezedopolio

14–15 Hoxton Market, N1. Tel: 7739 8212. Open: L and D Mon–Sat. ££ (set menu), £££ www.therealgreek.co.uk

The Real Greek lives proudly up to its name. With its mezze regulars, mousakas, tiny shellfish and tomato cutlets, it's one of London's most authentic tavernas. From intense, stocky lamb or beef pasta dishes to distinctive cheeses and pastries, the key here is to experiment using the knowledgeable waiters as your guides. The Real Greek has won a host of restaurant awards and has opened another branch in Clerkenwell (see page 135).

Les Trois Garçons

1 Club Row, E1. Tel: 7613 1924. Open: D only Mon–Sat. ££££ www.lestroisgarcons.com

One of the most romantic eating experiences to be had in London. Owners Hassan, Michel and Stefan (who also run an interiors shop in Notting Hill, and the nearby Loungelover bar on Whitby Street), have transformed a Victorian pub into a magical world full of stuffed tigers, baroque mirrors, and glittering chandeliers, some of which are for sale. Food is French and elegantly presented. Wine is expensive, but the experience is so expansive and rich that you can forgive the bill – just about.

Did you know?

The transformation of Hoxton began when dynamic young artists such as Damien Hirst and Tracy Emin moved there, many of them creating studios in old warehouses and factories. As they became successful, art dealers and web designers followed, and urban desolation became urban chic.

BATTERSEA AND CLAPHAM

On the opposite bank of the River Thames to Chelsea lie Battersea and Clapham. Battersea's defining landmarks are the decaying power station, its four chimneys visible for miles, and the park with its Japanese Peace Pagoda overlooking the Thames. The green expanse of Clapham Common is less appealing as it is cut through with traffic. Both areas have a good choice of lively bars and restaurants, the main concentrations being on Northcote Road, Battersea Bridge Road and Clapham High Street. Northcote Road also has an excellent produce market, which runs from Monday to Saturday.

Blackpepper

133 Lavender Hill, SW11. Tel: 7978 4863. Open: L and D Tues–Fri, D only Mon, Sat. £££ www.blackpeppersw11.co.uk
This popular Italian restaurant serves delicious, imaginative food in relaxed surroundings. Highly recommended are the scallops on a broad-bean purée with grilled bacon, and its pasta, which is made fresh every day. The staff are friendly and the all Italian wine list has some good choices.

Chez Bruce

2 Bellevue Rd, SW17. Tel: 8672 0114. Open: L and D daily. ££ (set lunch), ££££
French cuisine at its best, cooked by talented, Michelin-starred chef Bruce Poole. Overlooking Wandsworth Common, this is the place to go on a romantic date; the restaurant is snug, the decor smart, and the waiting staff charming and efficient. But such is its popularity that you will have at least a six-week wait to get a table for a Saturday night. The lunchtime set menu is good value.

Dexter's Grill

20 Bellevue Rd, SW17. Tel: 8767 1858. Open: L and D daily. ££ www.tootsies.co.uk
This American-style eatery is both popular and low key. The decor is cool and modern, and its decked outside area at the front is perfect for people-watching. The food is all you would expect from a grill: big servings of steak, barbecued chicken, juicy burgers and racks of ribs, with excellent fries and salads, and creamy milkshakes for the kids.

The Duke of Cambridge

228 Battersea Bridge Rd, SW11. Tel: 7223 5662. Open: L and D daily. ££ www.geronimo-inns.co.uk
This lovely neighbourhood pub is the ideal place for a lazy Sunday roast or a relaxed mid-week supper with a bottle of wine. Its huge tables easily accommodate larger parties and you can either dine in the bar area or in the light, airy restaurant to the rear. Booking is essential on Sundays, but during the week it's possible just to turn up.

Eco

162 Clapham High St, SW4. Tel: 7978 1108. Open: L and D daily. ££ www.ecorestaurant.com
Eco serves some of the best pizzas outside Italy. Not only do they come with the thinnest, crispiest crust, but they are absolutely huge with generous toppings. The atmosphere is lively and the noise levels loud. It doesn't take bookings.

The Gourmet Burger

44 Northcote Rd, SW11. Tel: 7228 3309. Open: L and D daily. £ www.gbkinfo.co.uk
Brainchild of New Zealand chef Peter Gordon, this is arguably the

TIP

During the summer months, a pleasant way to pass a Tuesday evening is to take a picnic to Battersea Park, where you can listen to live jazz as you eat and drink.

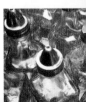

best burger joint in town. You may find it hard to get a seat, as the queue often stretches out the door, but the succulent burgers made with choice ingredients more than make up for the cramped surroundings. There are 23 different varieties to choose from, including chicken and vegetarian options, but despite this, its most popular burger is its cheeseburger. Great milkshakes are an added bonus. No bookings. Branches: 49 Fulham Broadway, SW6, 331 West End Lane NW6, 333 Putney Bridge Rd SW15.

Ransome's Dock
35–37 Parkgate Rd, SW11. Tel: 7223 1611. Open: L and D Mon–Sat, Br and L Sun.
£ (set lunch), £££
www.ransomesdock.co.uk
This relaxed Thames-side restaurant overlooking Battersea Dock has an interesting modern European menu and an excellent and varied award-winning wine list. Chef/owner Martin Lam uses organically reared meat and poultry where possible and quality fresh ingredients. The menu changes monthly, but its popular Morecambe Bay potted shrimps are served all year round. In summer ask for a table on the small terrace.

Thyme
14 Clapham Park Rd, SW4. Tel: 7627 2468. Open: L and D Tues–Sat. ££££
www.thymeandspace.com
This delightful neighbourhood restaurant has won awards for its quirky and creative dishes. Food is served tapas-style, and helpings are small, which means you can sample lots of dishes, from seared swordfish with quail eggs to halibut with chorizo. The staff are efficient and will help guide you through the myriad menu choices, and the wine list offers a complimentary range.

Tsunami
5–7 Voltaire Rd, SW4. Tel: 7978 1610. Open: L and D Mon–Sat. £££
For a truly fabulous, award-winning Japanese experience – albeit in a rather less than salubrious area – visit Tsunami. Sushi and sashimi come beautifully presented, and former Nobu chef Singi Nakamura produces imaginative dishes such as scallops with sweet and sour-marinated seaweed and a lemon sauce and mint tea duck. The wine list is excellent and the service charming. Eat your heart out, Nobu.

Thyme, Clapham's prizewinning venue

The Blue Elephant

FULHAM TO HAMMERSMITH

West of Kensington and Chelsea is Fulham, offical residence of the Bishop of London, whose splendid palace sits in the middle of Bishop's Park at the far end of King's Road. Fulham may not have the lure of the big-name chefs that its neighbouring borough enjoys, but the restaurant scene is far from dull, with a surprising number of quality options.

Heading further west, in the shadow of an unsightly flyover, lies Hammersmith. The oasis in this traffic-choked town is the picturesque riverside walk from Hammersmith Bridge to Chiswick, with a number of good pubs en route. But Hammersmith's main claim to culinary fame is as home to the River Café, one of London's most feted restaurants.

Aziz

30–32 Vanston Place, SW6. Tel: 7386 0086. Open: L and D Mon–Sat, L only Sun.
£ (set lunch), £££

Aziz has a modern feel with its cherry-wood floor, minimalist interior and open kitchen. The menu, created by Michel Giraud, former head chef at Momo *(see page 72)*, has a strong Arab influence, with hot and cold mezze and wonderful tagines. Next door is Del'Aziz, a Mediterranean delicatessen, bakery and café, which serves pastries, breads and seasonal dishes.

The Blue Elephant

4–6 Fulham Broadway, SW6. Tel: 7385 6595. ££ (set lunch), £££ www.blueelephant.com

With an over-the-top interior that boasts babbling brooks, ponds, live koi carp, potted palms and thatched huts, eating at this Thai restaurant can be a surreal experience. However, don't underestimate

the food – its standards are high and the service genteel and efficient. On Sundays it offers an unlimited brunch menu.

The Grove

83 Hammersmith Grove, W6. Tel: 8748 2966. Open: L and D daily. £££ www.groverestaurants.co.uk

This superb neighbourhood gastropub serves health-conscious food with a Mediterranean influence. Organic produce is used where possible and there's always a good choice of organic wines on the list. Much of The Grove's appeal lies in its daily changing menu and generous portions. Sunday nights are always busy, when the pub hosts live jazz.

Jim Thompson's

617 King's Rd, SW6. Tel: 7731 0999. Open: L and D daily. £££ www.jimthompsons.com

Beautiful, brightly-coloured silk drapes hang from the ceiling of this Thai restaurant, along with various

TIP

Fulham has a good choice of gastropubs, including **The White Horse** *(Parsons Green)*, which holds weekend barbecues on its terrace in summer, **The Atlas** *(Seagrave Rd)*, **The Harwood Arms** *(Walham Grove)* and **The Salisbury Tavern** *(Sherbrooke Rd)*.

artefacts, including lanterns, sculptures and wooden puppets, all of which are for sale. Chef Tamas Khan specialises in Southeast Asian cooking and his signature dishes include garlic fish fillet, and five spices chicken and pineapple.

Mao Tai

58 New King's Rd, SW6. Tel: 7731 2520. Open: L and D daily. £££ (set lunch). ££££ www.maotai.co.uk

A top-quality Chinese where the service is impeccable and the food beautifully presented and made from the finest ingredients – the kitchen being a totally MSG-free zone. The menu offers a huge range of appetisers, as well as dumplings and noodles and that perennial favourite, crispy duck. Mao Tai also has a sister restaurant in Chelsea on Draycott Avenue.

Medea

561 King's Rd, SW6. Tel:7736 2333. Open: L and D daily. ££ www.medeabrasserie.co.uk

This tiny bar/restaurant serves delicious North African mezze, tagines and couscous in lively surroundings. The staff are friendly and welcoming, and diners sit on cushions and poufs and eat off low tables. The less supple among you can eat downstairs where there are tables and chairs. The top floor can be hired out for private parties.

Napulé

585 Fulham Broadway, SW6. Tel: 7381 1122. Open: D daily, L only Sat–Sun. ££

This cheerfully chaotic Italian has a great choice of antipasti and pasta dishes, but pizzas are the main draw. Groups can opt for the pizza platter – one long crispy base, sectioned off with different toppings and supported by an oversized board (vegetarians should ask for theirs to be cooked separately).

Olé

Broadway Chambers, Fulham Broadway, SW6. Tel: 7610 2010. Open: L and D Mon–Sat. ££ www.olerestaurants.com

This small, modern Spanish restaurant is so inconspicuous that even locals are unaware of its existence. It serves a fantastic range of tapas, and the generous portions have defeated many a diner.

The River Café

Thames Wharf, Rainville Rd, W6. Tel: 7386 4200. Open: L and D Mon–Sat. ££££ www.rivercafe.co.uk

The River Café's international reputation for fine Italian fare is well deserved (as is its reputation for astronomic prices). The food is simple but faultless, with dishes such as char-grilled scallops with deep-fried artichokes, beef with tomatoes and spinach, and the fresh pasta and risotto combinations always failsafe options. Ingredients are meticulously sourced by the owners, Ruth Rogers and Rose Gray, who once a year visit Italy to pick the best oils from the olive harvest. It may be a trek to get to, but the terrace overlooking the Thames is a great place to dine in summer. Booking essential.

TIP

Heading west towards Richmond and Kew, Hammersmith, Chiswick and Putney may appear to be mainly residential areas but there are many restaurant gems worth making the journey for, including innovative vegetarian restaurant **Blah, Blah Blah** *(Goldhawk Rd)*, **The Brackenbury** *(Brackenbury Village)*, **The Chiswick** *(Chiswick High Rd)* and Italian restaurant **Enoteca Turi** *(Putney High St)*.

The River Café, Hammersmith

Sugar Hut

*374 North End Rd, SW6. Tel:
7386 8950. Open: D only
Tues–Sun. £££
www.sugarhutfulham.com*
You have to ring a bell to gain
entrance to this opulent Thai restaurant, which includes Ruby Wax and
Sacha Baron Cohen among its fans.
The service is efficient, the atmosphere romantic and the food delicious. If there is one complaint it's
the expensive drinks at the bar.

RICHMOND AND KEW

Richmond Park and Kew Gardens lie on a sweep of the Thames that
was for centuries home to the kings and queens of England. Both are
classic days out for Londoners. Richmond Park is grazed by herds of
red and fallow deer that gather under the dappled canopies of huge
oaks. On the north side of Richmond, more manicured Kew is
synonymous with the Royal Botanical Gardens. Both have a village
green, complete with pubs and cricket pitches, which give them a
rural and thoroughly English atmosphere.

Canyon

*The Towpath, Richmond, TW10.
Tel: 8948 2944. Open: L and D
daily. ££ (set lunch) £££
www.canyonfood.co.uk*
On the towpath just west of
Richmond Bridge Canyon is
white, modern and airy. The low
building, with its large river facing
windows, sits in a heated, cactus
filled garden. The food is modern
American, which means that it's
very fresh and healthy with
evocative dishes such as chowder
and Chesapeake Bay soft shell
crab on the menu.

Chez Lindsay

*11 Hill Rise TW10. Tel: 8948
7473. Open: L and D daily. £
(set lunch) £££*
Chez Lindsay feels like it's been
transported staff and all from a
Breton fishing village and is

justifiably popular so booking is
essential. Superb fish and shellfish dishes, gallettes and crepes,
steak-frites and seasonal specials
are on the menu and they offer a
menu prix fixe and *menu du midi*
every day.

Escale

*94 Kew Rd, TW9. Tel: 8940
0033. Open: L and D daily. ££
www.escale-richmond.co.uk*
The Richmond end of the Kew
Road offers an Indian, a Chinese
and a Turkish restaurant. Pretty
standard you may think, but this
being the smart area that it is they
all have a very swish and international air about them and food to
match. Escale's Mixed Meze is
one of the tastiest in London. No
Turkish classics are left out on the
extensive menu and all are very
fresh and well made.

Did you know?
Maids of Honour
Row on Richmond
Green was built in
1723 for Queen
Caroline's maids.
The story goes that
one of them stole
the ancient royal
cheesecake recipe,
and the 'Maids of
Honour' cakes at
Newen's bakery
(*opposite Kew
Gardens*) are still
made to the close-
ly guarded recipe.

Listings

The Glasshouse

14 Station Parade, Kew Gardens Station, TW9. Tel: 8940 6777. Open: L and D Mon–Sat, D only Sun. ££ (set lunch), ££££

The Glasshouse is widely recognised as being the best place in the area and was awarded a Michelin star in 2002. Chef Anthony Boyd was previously at similarly star-encrusted The Square and Chez Bruce, making the set lunch at £17.50 a bargain. There is an enormous wine list and a daily changing menu of French-inspired, modern international cuisine.

The Greyhound

82 Kew Green, Kew, TW9. Tel: 8940 0071. Open: L and D (until 9.30pm) daily. ££

There are three pubs on Kew Green and this is by far the nicest. The staff are friendly and relaxed and the food here is simple and well cooked. Menus change daily and are chalked up on the board and might include such hearty favourites as lamb shanks, Cumberland sausages and mash, or king prawn risotto, with specials at the weekends and great roasts on Sundays. In the summer there are tables on the green and in the garden at the back. Booking advisable especially at weekends.

H20

Floating Restaurant, Richmond Riverside, TW10. Tel: 8948 0220. Open: L and D daily. ££

H20 is an old barge moored next to Richmond Bridge and scores highly for location alone. You can sit on the deck watching people mess about in boats, the wildlife on the river and tipsy locals teetering down the towpath. If you're lucky you may even catch a spectacular sunset reflected on the water. The food is good, unfussy Italian fare, with a range of pizzas and pasta, fish and meat dishes. A memorable place to visit. Booking advisable.

The Richmond Café

58 Hill Rise, TW10. Tel: 8940 9561. Open: L and D daily. £ (set lunch), ££

This inexpensive Thai café is a lovely place to sit in the summer with its outside tables. It's very simple and friendly, offering Thai classics at reasonable prices. They have a spicey Tom Yam soup for £3.65 and offer set lunch for £5.50. It's a great location and away from the crowds, so highly recommended for an authentic and good-quality meal.

The White Swan

25–26 Old Palace Lane, TW9. Tel: 8940 0959. Open: L and D Tues–Sat, L only Sun–Mon. ££

This quaint old pub is in a windy lane that leads from the river to Richmond Green, away from the overcrowded places on the towpath. It has a separate restaurant in a pretty upstairs room, which feels like something out of *The Railway Children*. The menu changes regularly but includes starters like crab cakes, mussels and smoked duck with fillet steak, rack of lamb, chicken and chorizo for main courses.

TIP

Kew Gardens has a number of cafés, but if it's a nice day why not stock up on provisions for an impromptu picnic from the shops clustered around Kew station. **Oliver's** organic supermarket has a mouthwatering selection of cheeses, salamis, olives and bread, and **Oddbins** in the station yard keeps a good selection of chilled white wines in its fridge.

Richmond river front

BLACKHEATH AND GREENWICH

Blackheath is a highly desirable area in southeast London made up of grand Georgian and Victorian houses encircling a well-trimmed expanse of flat grass, known as the Heath. Nestling in a dip at one end is Blackheath Village, which has a number of small shops, wine bars and restaurants. On its northern flank is Greenwich Park, cut through by a road that leads downhill into the heart of Maritime Greenwich. The historic landmarks and weekend craft market make this a popular tourist destination, with no shortage of eating and drinking opportunities.

Chapter Two

43–45 Montpelier Vale, SE3. Tel: 8333 2666. Open: L and D daily, ££ (set menu), £££
www.chaptersrestaurant.co.uk
Like so many of London's villagey suburbs, Blackheath has fallen prey to the chains that monopolise its pretty streets. This restaurant stands out in the crowd, with an eclectic menu (pan-fried nuggets of foie gras and caramelised endives; ham hock boudin and creamed turnips; artichoke and mushroom ragout with leeks and parmesan salad) that rarely fails. Desserts are divine.

Davy's Wine Vaults

159–161 Greenwich High Rd, SE10. Tel: 8858 7204. Open: L and D Mon–Sat, L only Sun ££
ww.davy.co.uk
Back in the days when cargo ships plied the river, Greenwich was a thriving dock. Boats carrying wine from mainland Europe would unload their barrels and roll them

down into these wine cellars – hence the sloping floors. As you would expect, the wine list is informed, with plenty of good options between the £10 and £20 bracket. The star of the mains menu is the char-grilled ribeye steak with warm Bearnaise sauce. The Sunday lunch two-course special for £7.95 is served until 5pm.

Laicram

1 Blackheath Grove, SE3. Tel: 8852 4710. Open: L and D Tues–Sun. ££
This friendly, low-key Thai restaurant, offering the standard satay, pad thai and green curry formula, is popular with locals. Not every dish makes the grade, but the cosy decor and friendly staff make up for any shortcomings.

Spread Eagle

1 & 2 Stockwell St, SE10. Tel: 8853 2333. Open L and D Tues–Sat, L only Sun, D only Mon. ££ (set menu), £££

TIP

Greenwich Park has a café at the top of the hill as well as some lovely spots for picnics with a view down to the Naval College, the Queen's House, the *Cutty Sark* tea clipper, the Thames and the London skyline beyond. At the bottom of the hill, the National Maritime Museum's **Regatta Café** *(Park Row, daily 10am– 4.30pm)* has a terrace overlooking the park.

Occupying a 17th-century coaching inn, the Spread Eagle has been under the same family management for years. However, on our visit it was about to change hands. The food to date has been of the old-fashioned French variety – onion soup, snails and frogs' legs – with a choice of table d'hôte and à la carte menus. The cosy wooden boothed interior will remain, but the menu, while retaining its French bias, will be modernised and the heavier dishes lightened up.

Trafalgar Tavern

Park Row, SE10. Tel: 8858 2909. Open: L and D (until 9pm) Mon-Sat, L only Sun. ££
Visitors to historic Greenwich should at least have a drink in this old Thames-side tavern, best reached via the scenic riverside walk that takes you along the back of the Naval College. Every inch of wall space is taken up with etchings, paintings and memorabilia connected to Nelson and Greenwich's maritime history. If you're planning your Sunday lunch here, best to come early and get your name down on the waiting list. Ask for a window seat if you can. The menu is varied, with the focus on old-fashioned British staples (whitebait, roast lamb, beef and ale pie, fish and chips). Culinary sparks don't fly, but service is keen (if not polished) and the location unbeatable. No bookings Saturday or Sunday lunch.

Electric Avenue, the hub of Brixton Market

BRIXTON AND DULWICH

With leafy streets, stately houses, a spacious park, an important gallery and one of England's most famous public schools, Dulwich Village is an oasis of rural calm, with a luxury chocolate shop, upmarket deli and 18th-century mansion restaurant that serve its genteel residents.

If Dulwich is the Hampstead of south London, Brixton is its Notting Hill. Throbbing with raw energy, generated by a multi-cultural community, it has a thriving club and music scene and plenty of opportunities to sample exotic cuisines from Eritrean to Jamaican. In the crescent of Electric Avenue is the outdoor market, a vibrant hub that sells an impressive variety of Caribbean, African, Asian and European food.

Asmara

386 Coldharbour Lane, SW9. Tel: 7737 4144. Open: D daily, to midnight. ££
www.asmararestaurant.co.uk
Come to this quirky little Eritrean restaurant for a unique, hands-on (quite literally) dining experience. The traditional Messob dinner, 'a royal feast' of pancakes topped with various stews and vegetable concoctions, is placed in the centre of the wicker table and everyone joins in tearing, dipping and generally tucking in. Strong coffee and bowls of popcorn round off the ritualistic dinner. Vegetarian and vegan menus also available.

Belair House

Gallery Rd, SE21. Tel: 8299 9788. Open: L and D Mon-Sat, L only Sun. £££ *(set menus),* ££££ www.belairhouse.co.uk
Set in the grounds of Belair Park this grand Georgian mansion feels more like a rural stately home than a London restaurant. The menu is a combination of British, French and French Caribbean influences. Despite the overly fussy presenta-

tion, flavours are uncomplicated, with offerings such as asparagus soup, spinach and parmesan soufflé, but the chef doesn't shy away from strong meaty mains like braised rabbit. At these prices, though, dishes shouldn't be as hit and miss as they are. Ask to be seated in the conservatory, or on the terrace in summer.

Franklins
157 Lordship Lane, SE22. Tel: 8299 9598. Open: L and D Tues–Sun, D only Mon. £££
A little off the beaten track, this excellent neighbourhood eatery, is worth seeking out. The front end is a shabbily elegant wine bar, while the back is given over to a smart brick, wood and white linen dining room, matched with equally unfussy but sophisticated 'modern British' dishes prepared in the open kitchen. Book ahead for weekends.

The Gallery
256a Brixton Hill, SW2. Tel: 8671 8311. Open: D Tues–Sat, L and D Sun. £
Up the hill, away from the Brixton maelstrom, this no-frills Portuguese restaurant is concealed behind a chicken and chips takeaway. The decor is cheerfully kitsch with tacky tiles and painted friezes of seaside scenes. The menu offers baby spatchcock chicken, four types of bacalhao and the signature pork and clams alentejana, along with a number of unsophisticated but hearty fish and meat options. Portions are generous to say the least.

Neon
71 Atlantic Rd, SW9. Tel: 7738 6576. Open L and D Tues–Sun, L only Mon. ££
www.neonbrixton.co.uk
The poppy red walls cast a warm glow on the spacious interior. At weekends trendy Brixtonian faithfuls and girls on nights out gather noisily round the communal tables to share generous wood-fired pizzas and bowls of creamy Italian ice cream. The pizza list is supplemented by fresh pasta and a variety of Italianate starters. The staff are friendly and the fish tank behind the bar is mesmerising.

The Satay Bar
447–455 Coldharbour Lane, SW9. Tel: 7326 5001. Open: L and D daily (until 2am Fri–Sat). £ www.sataybar.co.uk
Just round the corner from the Ritzy cinema, this noisy noodle bar and watering hole is a good place to fill up on cheap Indonesian rice and noodle dishes before or after the film. The food is efficiently served and satisfying.

TIP

For afternoon tea in a pastoral setting, visit England's oldest public art gallery. Since the **Dulwich Gallery Café** *(College Rd, SE21; tel: 8693 5244; open: 10am–5pm daily, £)* is set in the picturesque grounds, alfresco dining is very much on the menu, helped by a new parasol-shaded patio.

Belair House, the Conservatory.

ey marmue peanul

MUFFINS

FISH

CHIPS

D

ESH

NGE

UICE

WATER SCA

OMELE

LE

VEGETAR

ESSENTIAL INFORMATION

Opening Hours

Last orders for dinner are usually around 10pm, earlier on Sundays. Most restaurants serve lunch between noon and 2.30–3pm. These are just guidelines and opening times vary widely, so it's always best to call first.

Prices

Most Londoners would consider restaurants which charge over £70 for two as expensive, but the £100-plus meal has become increasingly common. The prices given here *(see page 3 for details)* are intended as guidelines only. Note that the best value at quality restaurants is often provided by a set lunch.

Reservations

To avoid disappointment, it's always a good idea to ring first and reserve a table, especially for weekends. The most fashionable places can be booked up for weeks in advance.

Service charge and tipping

At most restaurants, service is discretionary. If service is satisfactory it's usual to tip between 10 and 15%. Some restaurants add a service charge, typically around 12.5%, to your bill, which should be clearly shown on the menu. Sometimes, when service has been added, the final total on a credit card slip will still be left blank, the implication being that a further tip is expected; do not pay it. If you do want to further reward good service, leave cash, as there's no guarantee the tips given on a credit card will be passed on to the staff member who served you. VAT of 17.5% is included in the menu prices.

Credit Cards

Some of the smaller cafés do not take credit cards, so check first.

Public Transport

Train stations are clearly marked on the individual maps. With the help of the tube map at the back of the book you can work out your route. London Underground trains run from 5.30am (Sunday 7.30am) to about midnight. Prices vary according to a zone system. Singles, returns and multiple-ticket carnets are available, as are travel cards, which are valid on the underground, bus and train network and should save money if you're making more than a couple of journeys in a day. London's buses run from 6.30am to around 11pm, with a minimal all-night service. Ask at bus or underground stations for details, or call 020-7222 1234; www.tfl.gov.uk.

Taxis

You can hail a licensed black cab if its 'For Hire' sign is lit. You can also call for a black cab on 020-7272 0272.

What to Eat Where

The main concentration of London's restaurants are to be found in the West End, with **Soho** providing the widest, most eclectic choice, while **Covent Garden** offers good-value pre- and post-theatre suppers. The districts of **Mayfair**, **Knightsbridge**, **Kensington** and **Chelsea** have a high concentration of upmarket restaurants. While still central, **Bloomsbury**, **Fitzrovia** and **Marylebone** have a more neighbourhood feel. The **City**'s surfeit of wine bars and olde-worlde taverns do a roaring trade with business lunchers, but by night it's a ghost town. Just east of the square mile, however, **Clerkenwell**'s bars and trendy restaurants buzz at night with young movers and shakers. Over in the west, **Notting Hill** has a fast turnover of exotic restaurants that bow to the whims of its hip residents. Most neighbourhoods have a good Indian restaurant, but for a full-on Indian experience head for **Brick Lane** in the east. For Chinese food, **Chinatown** in Soho is the obvious destination, but **Bayswater** also has a good selection. The **South Bank** and **Borough** offer a curious mix of exclusive dining rooms with stunning views over the Thames, and workman-like cafés down Dickensian backstreets.

African/Caribbean

The Africa Centre (Covent Garden) 42
Asmara (Brixton) 167
Calabash (Covent Garden) 30, 42
The Mandola (Notting Hill) . 119
Mango Room (Camden) 156
Yum Yum's (Notting Hill) . . . 119

American

Ashbell's (Notting Hill) 119
The Big Easy (Chelsea) 92
Canyon (Richmond) 165
Christopher's (Covent Garden) 30
Dexter's Grill (Wandsworth) . 161
Ed's Diner (Chelsea) 92
Ed's Easy Diner (Soho) 16
The Gourmet Burger (Clapham) 161
Hard Rock Café (Mayfair) 64, 75
Joe Allen (Covent Garden) . . . 30
Lucky Seven (Notting Hill) . . 119
Navajo Joe (Covent Garden) . . 30
PJ's Bar and Grill (Chelsea) . . 92
Rainforest Café (Soho) 75
Smollensky's Balloon (Strand) 42, 75
Sticky Fingers (Kensington) . . 75
Texas Embassy Cantina (St James's) 75

Australian

Osia (Piccadilly) 64

Austrian

Tiroler Hut (Bayswater) 119

Belgian

Belgo (chain) 74
Belgo Noord (Camden) 155

Brazilian

Rodizio Rico (Notting Hill) . . 120

British

Boisdale (Belgravia) 106
Boot and Flogger (Borough) . 146
Brian Turner Mayfair (Mayfair) 64, 89
Brinkley's Wine Gallery (Kensington) 92
Butler's Wharf Chop House (Bermondsey) 146
Chelsea Bun (Chelsea) 92
Chelsea Kitchen (Chelsea) . . . 92
Clark & Sons (Clerkenwell) . 132
Clerkenwell Dining Room (Clerkenwell) 132
Cockney's Pie and Mash (Notting Hill) 120

Court Restaurant (Bloomsbury). 48, 127
Davy's Wine Vaults (Greenwich) 167
Dust (Clerkenwell). 132
Ffiona's (Kensington) 93
Foxtrot Oscar (Kensington) . . 93
Golborne House (Kensal Town) 120
The Guinea Grill (Mayfair) . . 64
Langan's Bistro (Marylebone) 79
Lindsay House (Soho) 16
Maggie Jones's (Kensington) . 93
Manze's (Bermondsey) 146
Notting Grill (Notting Hill) 89, 120
Oscar (Fitzrovia) 48
Pelican (Notting Hill) 120
The Quality Chop House (Clerkenwell) 132
Rules (Covent Garden) 30
St John (Clerkenwell) 132
St John Bread and Wine (Clerkenwell) 133
Sausage and Mash Café (Notting Hill) 120
Simpson's (Covent Garden) . . 31
Smiths of Smithfield (Clerkenwell) 133
Sophie's Steakhouse (Kensington) 93
Stanley's (Fitzrovia) 48
Tate Britain Restaurant (Westminster) 106
Trafalgar Tavern (Greenwich) 140, 168
El Vino (Holborn) 31
Ye Olde Cheshire Cheese (Holborn) 31, 39

Chilean

El Vergel (Borough) 146

Chinese

Aaura (Chinatown) 16
Four Seasons (Bayswater). . . 121
Hakkasan (Fitzrovia) 48
Harbour City (Chinatown) . . . 16
Hunan (Belgravia). 106
Imperial China (Chinatown). . 16
Jenny Lo's Teahouse (Belgravia) 106
Joy King Lau (Chinatown) . . . 17
Kai (Mayfair) 64
Ken Lo's Memories of China (Belgravia) 106
Mandarin Kitchen (Bayswater) 121
Mao Tai (Fulham) 164
Mr Kong (Chinatown). 17
Mr Wing (Kensington) 94

New Diamond (Chinatown). . . 17
New Mayflower (Chinatown) . 17
The Oriental Restaurant (Mayfair) 65
Poons (Bloomsbury) 48
Poons & Co (Chinatown) 18
Royal China (Bayswater) . . . 121
Royal China (Marylebone) . . . 79
Royal Dragon (Chinatown). . . 18
Sheng's Tea House (Bloomsbury) 48
Wong Kei (Chinatown) 18

Cuban

Cubana (Bayswater) 42

Fish

Aquarium (City) 133
Back to Basics (Fitzrovia) 49
Brady's (Wandsworth) 85
Costa's (Notting Hill) 85
fish! (Borough) 146
Fish Central (City) 85
Fishmarket (City) 132
The Fish Shop on St John Street (Islington) 158
Fryer's Delight (Holborn) 85
Geales (Notting Hill) 85
Golden Hind (Marylebone) 79, 85
Green's Restaurant & Oyster Bar (St James's) 65
Livebait (Waterloo) 147
Lobster Pot (Kennington) . . . 147
Masters Superfish (Waterloo) 85, 147
Nautilus (Hampstead) 85
North Sea Fish Restaurant (Bloomsbury) 49, 85
Olley's (Herne Hill) 85
Le Palais du Jardin (Covent Garden) 32
Poissonerie de L'Avenue (Chelsea) 94
Randall & Aubin (Soho). 18
Rock & Sole Plaice (Covent Garden) 85
Rudland Stubbs Fish Restaurant (Clerkenwell) 134
Scotts (Mayfair). 65
Seafresh (Westminster) 85
Sea Shell (Marleybone) 85
J Sheekey (Covent Garden). . . 32
Toff's (Muswell Hill). 85
Two Brothers Fish (Finchley). 85
Wheeler's of St James's (St James's) 65
Zilli Fish (Soho) 18
Zilli Fish Too (Covent Garden) 32, 75

MISCELLANEOUS